# EMPATH AND PSYCHIC ABILITIES

## 3 BOOKS IN 1

The Complete Guide For Highly Sensitive People To Thrive And Develop Inner Powers Such As Intuition, Clairvoyance, And Telepathy | Includes: Shadow Work Journal Book

© Copyright 2022 by Jason Art - All rights reserved.

The following Book is reproduced below with the goal of providing information that is as accurate and reliable as possible. Regardless, purchasing this Book can be seen as consent to the fact that both the publisher and the author of this book are in no way experts on the topics discussed within and that any recommendations or suggestions that are made herein are for entertainment purposes only. Professionals should be consulted as needed prior to undertaking any of the action endorsed herein.

This declaration is deemed fair and valid by both the American Bar Association and the Committee of Publishers Association and is legally binding throughout the United States.

Furthermore, the transmission, duplication, or reproduction of any of the following work including specific information will be considered an illegal act irrespective of if it is done electronically or in print. This extends to creating a secondary or tertiary copy of the work or a recorded copy and is only allowed with the express written consent from the Publisher. All additional right reserved.

The information in the following pages is broadly considered a truthful and accurate account of facts and as such, any inattention, use, or misuse of the information in question by the reader will render any resulting actions solely under their purview. There are no scenarios in which the publisher or the original author of this work can be in any fashion deemed liable for any hardship or damages that may befall them after undertaking information described herein.

Additionally, the information in the following pages is intended only for informational purposes and should thus be thought of as universal. As befitting its nature, it is presented without assurance regarding its prolonged validity or interim quality. Trademarks that are mentioned are done without written consent and can in no way be considered an endorsement from the trademark holder.

# Table of Contents

PREFACE ........................................................................................................................... 5
PART 01 MENTAL ABILITIES ........................................................................................ 7
CHAPTER 01 A BRIEF HISTORY OF THEORY AND TESTING OF GENERAL AND SPECIFIC MENTAL ABILITIES ........................................................................................ 8
CHAPTER 02 WHAT ARE MENTAL ABILITIES (PRIMARY & SECONDARY MENTAL ABILITIES) .................. 16
CHAPTER 03 SPIRITUAL HEALING: WHAT IS IT? DOES IT WORK AND DOES IT HAVE A PLACE IN MODERN HEALTHCARE? ........................................................................................ 20
CHAPTER 04 WHAT IS TELEPATHY AND HOW TO PRACTISE TELEPATHY ................. 28
CHAPTER 05 AURA AND AURA READING WHAT THEY ARE & WHAT TO EXPECT DURING A READING 33
CHAPTER 06 PSYCHIC DEVELOPMENT COURSE ........................................................ 38
CHAPTER 07 ASTRAL PROJECTION/OUT-OF-BODY EXPERIENCE ............................ 47
CHAPTER 08 HOW TO RECOGNIZE AND DEVELOP YOUR PSYCHIC ABILITIES ....... 54
DOWNLOAD YOUR BONUS ............................................................................................ 58
PART 02 EMPATHY ......................................................................................................... 59
CHAPTER 01 ................................................................................................................... 60
INTRODUCTION .............................................................................................................. 60
CHAPTER 02 ................................................................................................................... 61
WHAT IS EMPATHY ........................................................................................................ 61
CHAPTER 03 CLASSIFICATIONS OF EMPATHY ........................................................... 65
CHAPTER 04 THE DEVELOPMENT OF EMPATHY THROUGHOUT HISTORY .............. 71
CHAPTER 05 EMPATHY IN HUMAN DEVELOPMENT .................................................. 75
CHAPTER 06 INDIVIDUAL DIFFERENCES IN EMPATHY .............................................. 78
CHAPTER 07 DISORDERS IMPACTING EMPATHY ....................................................... 82
CHAPTER 08 THE ECONOMICS OF EMPATHY ............................................................. 88
CHAPTER 09 EMPATHY IN SOCIAL SETTINGS ............................................................ 92
CHAPTER 10 EMPATHY IN INTERCULTURAL CONTEXT ............................................. 96
CHAPTER 11 ETHICAL & PHILOSOPHICAL DILEMMAS SURROUNDING EMPATHY .. 100
CONCLUSION ................................................................................................................ 104
PART 03 SHADOW WORK JOURNAL .......................................................................... 105
INTRODUCTION ............................................................................................................ 106
CHAPTER 01 WHAT IS THE HUMAN OR PSYCHOLOGICAL SHADOW ..................... 107
CONCLUSION ................................................................................................................ 111
CHAPTER 02 WHAT IS SHADOW WORK? ................................................................... 112
CONCLUSION ................................................................................................................ 115
CHAPTER 03 SHADOW SELF: OWNING OUR DARK SIDES ....................................... 116

CHAPTER 04 WHAT ARE THE BEST PRACTICES FOR DOING SHADOW WORK ................................................ 119
CHAPTER 05 THE BENEFITS OF SHADOW WORK (PLUS, ARE THERE ANY DANGER) .............................. 122
CHAPTER 06 SHADOW WORK: MEET YOUR SHADOW ARCHETYPES: 13 DARK ARCHETYPES ................ 126
CHAPTER 07 WHAT IS GOLDEN SHADOW? ................................................................................................ 129
CHAPTER 08 THE SHADOW WORK JOURNEY: HOW TO HEAL YOUR INNER CHILD: THE SPACE BETWEEN HURT & HEALED ........................................................................................................................................ 134
CHAPTER 09 WHAT ARE 'SHADOW VALUES'? AND CAN WE DO ABOUT THEM? ..................................... 138
CHAPTER 10 7 SHADOW WORK EXERCISES TO EMBRACE YOUR SHADOW & HEAL YOUR SOUL ............ 142
CHAPTER 11 JUNGIAN SHADOW WORK: BENEFITS OF JUNGIAN SHADOW WORK .................................. 147
CONCLUSION ............................................................................................................................................. 150

# PREFACE

PART 1 Mental Abilities: Psychometrics and neuropsychology are opposing methodologies used to measure mental capacities throughout history. These two traditions have different beliefs and procedures, but their tests are very similar.

In the past, neuropsychology has emphasized specific, clearly different talents over the predominance of a generic component in psychometrics. This topic has recently piqued the interest of various academic departments.

This book contains the insights of experts from various fields, including psychometrics, neuropsychology, speech, language, hearing, and applied psychology. Experts have different perspectives on how vital general and specialized skills are to one another.

Despite more than a century of research, the nature of human mental abilities is still a matter of debate. However, there are a lot of practical considerations that make this topic necessary. If there is a single dominant feature, issues like gender, ethnicity, and age-related disparities in mental ability are relatively straightforward to solve.

Any collection of challenging cognitive tests should be able to measure such a trait. There are numerous distinct mental abilities, so it will be difficult to quantify and address the ensuing social problems.

Education policies may be affected by the relative weight of general and specialized skills. For instance, may specific learning problems be remedied, and do certain teaching methods assist some pupils more than others?

I initially thought about using "universal and specific cognitive abilities" as the title for this book. Instead, I went with cerebral prowess. I believe the term "cognitive" is used far too loosely.

Cognitive processes include, for instance, perceptual and motor functions. When I once questioned a renowned authority in cognitive psychology about where cognition started, he responded, "at the retina." This implies to me that all mental processes are cognitive.

However, a phrase loses significance if it describes every area of mental life. Processes that are particular to a sensory modality should be considered perceptual phenomena. Similar to cognitive activities, motor processes ought to involve particular output modalities, the term "cognitive" should only be used to describe "thinking" processes, not "automatic" ones.

The authors in this book offer a variety of perspectives on several topics, including the relative value of broad and specialized mental ability. For example, are skills developed or discovered? In other words, do our constructs represent real things, or are they just handy models? My perspective on these issues is still developing.

PART 2 Empathy: It's common to think of empathy as a straightforward matter: Either I can or cannot feel what another person is going through, and that's where empathy ends. But empathy is a highly complex concept that encompasses a variety of emotional states as well as several physiological and psychological conditions.

It influences how we perceive and interact with the world, encouraging us to take on helpful behaviors but sometimes giving rise to "amoral" or surprising viewpoints. Many of our actions have an unacknowledged underlying explanation; for instance, our strong convictions or feelings of hatred may result from solid sympathetic impulses.

The separation of empathy into its two main classifications—affective empathy and cognitive empathy—shows the intricacy of this phenomenon. Affective empathy is the capacity to respond to the mental states of others around us appropriately. It enables us to comprehend a person's feelings differently from ourselves and, in a sense, be impacted by their "emotional contagion" (Shamay-Tsoory et al., 2009).

The ability to conceptually comprehend another person's state of mind despite not experiencing the same emotional state and understanding the logical justifications is known as cognitive empathy (Gerace et al., 2013). Both affective and cognitive empathy play a role in how we react to, experience, and learn from the world around us.

We will thoroughly investigate empathetic rage and distress to show how much empathy affects our lives. According to Hoffman (1990), empathetic fury is an emotional state that is felt when another person is harmed and causes one to act on their desire to either aid or punish. The person's level and experience with empathy play a crucial role in predicting how they would react.

A person's receptivity to new ideas is correlated with how furious they become in response to hostility and provocation (Hoffman, 1990).

For clarification, sympathetic anger is a sort of empathic pain that manifests when an individual's response to another person's suffering is fundamentally self-centered and does not result in compassion or just sharing feelings (Dowling, 2018).

The overpowering negative feelings can prevent people from offering assistance or might encourage them to flee the situation for their protection. Feelings of unfairness or guilt are two more distressing emotions. A new philosophical debate is necessary to determine whether or not these feelings are considered pro-social or moral.

We will investigate the idea of empathy from various angles and fields, and it plays a significant role in understanding how humans comprehend various aspects of the world, from philosophical conundrums to scientific phenomena.

PART 3 Shadow Work Journal: Would you like to feel good about yourself, at peace with others, and in connection with the whole universe? Would you like to know how to improve your life and your relationships with others once and for all? Have you always sought an 'external' answer to your desire for well-being but never managed to feel complete?

It is normal... We all feel incomplete, but now I will give you positive news: the answer to every question is within us.

Remember how good it was as a child? No worries, every day was a discovery; everything was new and wonderful. Unfortunately, the daily hustle and bustle cancel out our spiritual well-being. The need for material goods, temporary gratification, and gratification from other people completely removes us from our inner child.

In Jungian psychology, this unconscious aspect of the personality that the conscious ego does not identify is called the Shadow. It is your unknown ego, which can include everything outside the light of consciousness and can be positive or negative. It is often rooted in your past experiences and upbringing, including past trauma and difficult people. Since you tend to reject or ignore the less desirable aspects of your personality, the Shadow is usually largely negative. However, this side of you can become a source of emotional wealth, and recognizing it is an essential step in your path of personal growth.

In this part, you will learn:

- What Is A Shadow And How To Accept It
- How To Recognize The Shadow Within Yourself
- The 7 Easy Ways To Work With Your Shadow
- How To Acknowledge Your Emotions Self
- Discovery And Self-Acceptance Techniques
- What An Inner Child Is And If Your Inner Child Is Wounded
- 3 Techniques To Heal Your Inner Child
- How To Embrace Your Shadow And Reach Self-Love

Even if you're new to the idea of this approach, the Shadow Work Journal provides tried-and-tested techniques that will put you on the path to confidence, wealth, and inner balance by learning to accept and embrace your Shadow.

# PART 01
# MENTAL ABILITIES

# CHAPTER 01
# A BRIEF HISTORY OF THEORY AND TESTING OF GENERAL AND SPECIFIC MENTAL ABILITIES

This study highlights concerns about general and specific abilities while summarizing the early development of theories and testing mental abilities. A significant amount of information is always left out of such reviews. Although certain people's contributions are discussed, it's important to remember that they should be seen from the perspective of their contemporaries.

The reader may want to consult some sources to obtain a sense of each period's vocabulary and way of thought. This review has been primarily arranged by chronology rather than topic to maintain the order in which events occurred.

There is a lengthy history of conjecture regarding the nature of human mental abilities. Aristotle, for instance, distinguished between analytical, practical, and creative types of intelligence (Tigner & Tigner, 2000). Ancient Chinese and Greek cultures tested people's mental ability (Bowman, 1989). (Doyle, 1974). The Chinese tests were a component of a complex hiring system that developed over time.

According to Bowman (1989), debates about testing procedures in ancient China foreshadowed many present problems with mental ability testing. These included the balance between memory and subject-matter expertise, the impact of social status on test performance, and the application of geographic quotas.

## THE PSYCHOMETRIC STRATEGY

Most tales of attempts to assess human intelligence date back to the turn of the 20th century. This endeavor was a part of the experimental psychology movement, a new field that had only recently emerged because of Wundt's work (Mackintosh, 2011). Wundt's pupil J. McKeen Cattell created an association test in which subjects had to write down as many words as they could in 20 seconds in response to a single audible phrase (Cattell & Bryant, 1889).

Modern word fluency tests have a lot in common with this approach. A series of tests that gauge elementary perceptual skills, response speed, and a letter span task were suggested by Cattell and Galton (1890) to evaluate mental ability.

They asserted that data gathering using these activities on a broad population of people would reveal information regarding the consistency and interdependence of mental processes. In the years that followed, Columbia University students' observations of these examinations were documented by Cattell and Farrand (1896).

Wissler (1901) used Pearson's freshly created correlation method to analyze Cattell and Farrand's tests. "If a test is universal, then its findings should correlate with many other special tests," claimed Wissler (1901, page 1). "And, in turn, if there is an intrinsic relation between general and specialized ability, then the latter's results should correlate with the former."

He claimed that there was no "significant" link between the scores, but the definition of "significant" he employed was not based on probability but on how the word is used in everyday speech. His results indicate a connection of 0.21 between letter cancellation speed and color naming speed with an n of 159, resulting in a probability of p 0.01 according to my calculation.

Similarly, Wissler characterized a correlation between the auditory and visual digit span of 0.39 as substantial but modest. The highest correlation between a student's academic ranking and their performance on mental tests was logical memory, with an r= 0.19.

On the other hand, correlations between students' relative ranking in various classes were substantially more significant, ranging from 0.60 to 0.75. The results of Wissler's analysis indicated that the Cattell & Farrand (1896) mental tests had little interdependence and were not helpful in real-world situations.

This study significantly argued against the usefulness of speeded response and perception tests as intelligence indicators. But Wissler's assessment of the strength of correlations was far different from what is done today.

Mental exams should be subjected to "correlational psychology," according to Spearman (1904). In contrast to Pearson's correlation, Spearman's correlation involved rank sorting of the data. He used this approach on "chosen laboratory psychics," or young students, who underwent three-sensory discrimination tests and three teacher-assessed intellect assessments. All nine correlations between these measurements that Spearman (1903) discovered were positive, concluding that they all indicated a single factor.

He proposed a hierarchy of the different bits of intelligence. He put forth a hypothesis of "intellective oneness." he arranged this hierarchy according to how "saturated" each object was with general intelligence. Each measure was thus seen as consisting of general intelligence and a particular factor unrelated to other particular variables.

According to Spearman (1903):

*All branches of intellectual activity share a single fundamental function (or set of functions). Still, the activity's remaining, more specialized aspects appear to vary significantly from one branch to the next.*

According to Jensen (2000), Spearman's concerns mainly were in theory and the makeup of cognition. Later, Spearman (1914) provided a better approach for testing his two-factor theory, which applied to a more extensive collection of Thorndike's mental exams. The tetrad discrepancies between the ratios of pairs of correlations among the four mental tests were computed using Spearman's method. The difference between these ratios should fall within the bounds of sampling error if a single shared component causes correlations.

According to Spearman (1914):

*Success is determined by two independent factors: first, the development and organization of the particular group of neurons, and second, the overall state of the cortex. The former could be referred to as the "specific" element because it is unique to that specific performance. The latter makes up the "general" element because it is necessary for every performance.*

To explain how his two components were dependent on the physiology of the brain, Spearman provided an elementary theory. Spearman has developed several methods for obtaining test score loadings on a single element (Vincent, 1953). As a result, Spearman might be regarded as the inventor of single-factor analysis.

Spearman's claim was disputed by Thompson (1916) with a dice-throwing experiment that demonstrated that it could form the hierarchy of intelligence without the need for a general factor (g). Then, using playing cards, Thompson (1919) conducted more simulations. These simulations involved giving values from dice or cards to made-up variables to produce simulated test results.

The earliest Monte Carlo simulations of the performance on mental tests were likely performed in Thompson's experiments. In Thompson's opinion, Spearman's support for a general component was not at all essential and could be explained by several different independent factors. This study first offers evidence that Spearman's g might be a statistical artifact.

It's interesting to see how Thompson and Spearman's perspectives changed as they continued to argue about a general component. In a series of meetings outlined by Deary et al. (2008), Spearman seems to have agreed that in addition to general and specific variables, there may also be group-level factors (i.e., factors shared by a subset of tests).

Similar to Thompson, who is said to like Spearman's g, it is reported that he once said, "Surely the real defense of g is that it has been beneficial" (Deary et al.). Although historical narratives may portray researchers' opinions as being fixed, these two people's perspectives, like many other scientists, evolved throughout time.

To decide whether to send a young child to a "special class" or keep them in a regular classroom, Binet & Simon (1916) developed a method. They did not intend to make any assumptions about the etiology or prognosis; instead, they wanted to characterize the child's current situation. Their methodology was distinct from that of earlier researchers like Cattell & Galton (1890) in that Binet and Simon used more challenging tasks involving judgment and reasoning than straightforward laboratory exercises.

The scale that we'll explain, according to Binet & Simon (1916), "is not a theoretical work; it is the outcome of long investigations," All the tests we provide have been tried numerous times, and those that didn't hold up to testing were kept.

Thus, an empirical inquiry led to the development of Binet & Simon's scale. Boake (2002) established the scale's validity because scores rose with age and could detect children with mental impairments. Indeed, Binet & Simon (1916) studied the nature of the traits that set "mental defectives" apart from other kids.

They believed that good judgment, comprehension, and thinking were essential. However, they disagreed with the idea that memory was essential. As an example of how memory is comparably insignificant, they used the instance of a "backward" girl with excellent memory—what we would now refer to as a savant.

According to Boake (2002), Binet stressed that a specific test taken in isolation is of limited significance and that the crucial data is included in the subject's average performance across several tests. On the other hand, Binet & Simon (1916) noted that they "found it difficult to specify which mental functions are being exercised because they are quite numerous" when discussing their tests measured.

Terman (1916) later translated and altered the Binet & Simon scale, adding new items and standardizing the test on a sizable group of kids. The Stanford-Binet scale became the name for this scale. Terman included questions that distinguished between kids of various ages and were relevant to the overall scale.

Including elements that correlate with the overall score gives the Stanford-Binet scale the appearance of measuring a single talent. Still, Terman claimed that a single test was insufficient because intelligence has multiple facets.

Terman (1916) proposed several uses for IQ testing beyond spotting mental impairments. According to Terman (1918, page 165), his approach "probes beneath the facade of schooling and provides an index of basic brain ability." Terman (1924) also emphasized the use of mental tests as a methodology that is equally suitable for experimental psychology as the use of controlled trials for a significant amount of time. Many of the experimental psychologists working now, he observed, agreed with this viewpoint.

Based on variations from his "point scale," Yerkes (1917) critiqued both the Binet and Stamford-Binet scales. According to Yerkes, they should choose tests to measure fundamental psychological processes rather than differences across age groups. The psychological function tests developed by Yerkes can be used individually or in combination. Furthermore, according to Yerkes, a test item should be relevant to all age groups and result in a continuous score. The Yerkes point scale, however, eventually fell short of Binet and Terman's scales in terms of popularity.

Terman (1918) contributed to the development of tests that the US army utilized in the First World War. A group of well-known experimental psychologists of the time, led by Yerkes, created these scales (Kevles, 1968). This group developed two tests: the Alpha, which was designed for those who could read and write English, and the Beta, which was designed for those who couldn't. There were multiple choice questions in the army's Alpha and Beta tests.

The ability to be a good soldier, according to Spring (1972), was the criterion utilized to validate these exams. Evaluated this skill by comparing test results to officers' assessments of the worth of their soldiers as practical soldiers. As a result, Spring hypothesized that this process of validation was comparable to Binet's attempt to assess whether or not youngsters were suitable for receiving regular school instruction.

According to Spring, the army testing project and Binet and Simon's study assessed how well people could operate under a highly structured institutional structure. According to Kevles (1968), this effort helped intelligence testing obtain a large following after not receiving much regard previous to the war.

According to Thorndike (1918), psychologists frequently boil down an infinite number of inclinations to think, feel, and act in particular ways in response to various situations to a small number of inclinations known as traits, abilities, and interests.

> "If the scale by which individuals are measured is very roughly divided, their differences may be masked," wrote Thorndike in 1918. Thorndike (1918) added that depending on whether one desired to emphasize similarities or variations between individuals, there can be "one single type or as many kinds as there are individuals."

According to Thorndike (1921), intelligence is the capacity for wise decisions. Spending too much time attempting to separate intelligence from emotional and vocational aptitudes, in his opinion, would not be prudent. Thorndike also believed that a person's aptitude changed depending on the work. He thought test results were valuable more for their potential to forecast future performance than for their ability to reveal some general strength in the individual.

In Thorndike's opinion, the more the test's content deviated from the expected skills, the less accurate the prediction. In his time, exams "preferred words, numbers, space-forms, and photographs, disregarding three-dimensional things, and scenarios involving other human beings," as noted by Thorndike. He suggested that convenience might play a role in this. Thorndike created several assessments of specific skills and accomplishments for subjects, including reading (Thorndike, 1914a) and mathematics (Thorndike, 1914b).

Spearman's approach to tetrad differences, according to Thurstone (1934), frequently fails to demonstrate that only one factor can explain the correlations between tests in a battery. Thurstone (1934) stated that the proponent of g would view the tests as insufficient and disregard them, whereas the opponent of g would view Spearman's theory as insufficient.

Thurstone thought both conclusions were false and that more than one general component was required to explain the relationships seen. Before we can advance toward the isolation and description of specific skills, Thurstone (1934) remarked, "The multi-dimensionality of mind must be recognized." To extract these numerous elements, Thurstone used the centroid approach (Vincent, 1953).

Thurstone (1935) pointed out that this issue involves at least two components when discussing techniques for extracting many elements. The first focuses on the minimum variables required to explain observed test score intercorrelations.

The second concerns the bare minimum of factors for each attribute necessary to explain correlations between test results (the smallest possible number of factors can describe, i.e., each trait). The rotation of components is involved in the second problem.

According to Thurstone (1935), one can find the answer to the issue of an endless number of potential factor rotations in basic structure when numerous factor loadings are vanishingly small, simple structure results (i.e., a sparse matrix of factor loadings). Thurstone created techniques for higher-order factor analysis as well.

Multiple component analysis required a lot of manual labor at the time, and Thurstone & Thurstone (1941) recognized the contributions of several assistants in carrying out the computations. Using these techniques, Thurstone & Thurstone (1941) identified verbal comprehension, word fluency, space, number, memorization, and inductive reasoning as the six main mental capacities they deemed indicated. Additionally, they pointed out that perceptual speed and deductive reasoning were two additional mental skills that did not as clearly characterize.

Thurstone & Thurstone, however, noted that:

*Nobody is sure of the exact number of main mental faculties. Although there is now just one memory factor known, there may be many more.*

In 1943, Raymond Cattell noted many definitions of intelligence in the literature of the day. He proposed that the adult brain could be considered a collection of malleable and solid skills. The ability to distinguish between different things and recognize relationships was part of Cattell's fluid intelligence.

The patterns established earlier with the aid of fluid intelligence included crystallized intelligence. The fluid intelligence was no longer necessary after having created the crystallized intellect. Later, added nine additional components to this hypothesis to account for both cerebral prowess and general personality traits (Horn & Cattell, 1966).

These nine characteristics were fluid intelligence, crystallized intelligence, imagery, speed, usage of concept labels, and carefulness, all related to academic performance. Horn & Cattell's solution's nine elements were associated, which these authors regarded as the result of interactions during the person's growth.

The findings of a committee of the American Psychological Association on the subject of test validation were summarized by Cronbach & Meehl in 1955. As previously mentioned, test developers employed various methods to choose test items and justify their use.

The following criteria were used: *content validity,* which is the degree to which test items are a sample of the trait or ability the investigator is interested in, as determined deductively; *predictive validity,* which is the ability of a test or battery to predict (i.e., correlate with) some future performance of interest; *concurrent validity,* which is the correlation of a test with similar measures taken at the same time; and *construct validity,* which includes many different types of the evidence that supports i. The validation procedure' emphasis on theory was an essential aspect of construct validity.

According to Cronbach and Meehl (1955), construct validation is a continuous process in which tests are not validated but instead supported by evidence of their validity. The inclusion of experimental research in the construct validation process was also recommended by Cronbach (1957). He noted that investigators using experimental methods had become entirely separate from those using correlational methods. The time when experimentalists like Terman first developed mental tests was significantly different from the current scenario.

According to Cronbach (1957), collaborating between the two fields could benefit both. It does not appear that this exchange occurred then, though.

The Illinois Test of Psycholinguistic Abilities (ITPA), created by Kirk & McCarthy in 1961, is a tool for evaluating kids with particular difficulties in areas like language, perception, or behavior. It was long thought that children with learning difficulties had vast skills disparities, leading to poor academic performance. Kirk (1968) believed that the Stanford-Binet and other diagnostic instruments were insufficient for this task.

The ITPA has nine subtests that assess three functions—decoding, association, and encoding—in each of the two organizational levels' auditory, vocal, and visual channels (symbolic and non-symbolic). Thus, the ITPA constituted a first attempt to evaluate specific skills in kids with particular learning issues. Elwood covered the prospect of automating psychological assessment in 1969.

He pointed out that automation might potentially standardize test item presentation, boost the reliability and validity of test results, and improve the accuracy of recording and scoring replies, in addition to saving time.

He provided details of a machine that could administer most WAIS subscales. Results from this automated system were comparable to those from manual testing. Elwood's device was built on antiquated technology by today's standards. However, despite the enormous technological advancements, computerized mental ability testing is still uncommon.

Carroll (1993) re-factored correlation matrices from a massive body of earlier research. Carroll's method involves obliquely rotating the initial correlation matrices, higher-order factoring the correlation matrices for the first-order factors, and occasionally the third step. Carroll (1993) created a three-stratum theory based on these findings, including narrow, broad, and general variables. Carroll considered his interpretation of the components at each level to be the creation of a theory. The third and highest strata level is considered general intellect (i.e. g).

The abilities of the second stratum were defined as fluid intelligence, crystallized intelligence, memory, visual perception, auditory perception, retrieval ability, and cognitive speediness. Carroll added that it's possible to find more second-order factors.

Carroll (1993) states the following:

*It is evident that all of the top names in psychometrics—Binet, Spearman, Thurstone, and Guilford, to mention a few—have had a deep interest in intelligence. They have also all acknowledged that developing a theory of intelligence entails developing a theory of cognition.*

Carroll also stated that these pioneering theorists relied more on common sense explanations of features than sophisticated cognitive theories to explain behavior. Several conversations Carroll had with his contemporaries shed light on his beliefs regarding mental faculties.

One of these debated whether g was unitary with Kranzer & Jensen (1991). Four principal components obtained from a battery of "elementary cognitive activities" were independently shown to contribute to the prediction of an estimate of g by Kranzer & Jensen (1991).

They concluded that because these components were orthogonal, g had to have at least four different parts. Kranzer & Jensen concluded that their findings supported Detterman's (1982) theory that intelligence is the sum of several orthogonal variables.

Kranzer & Jensen (1991), according to Carroll (1991), only had an estimate for g. He suggested that it was more economical to assume a unitary g and provided hypothetical example factor matrices to demonstrate how they may achieve their conclusions given this assumption. Humphries (1994), who proposed a behaviorist perspective of intelligence akin to Thorndike's, engaged in discussion with Carroll (1994).

According to Humphries, intelligence is the acquired collection of all intellectual abilities and knowledge that a person has access to at any one time. Additionally, Humphries claimed that intellect was not always more than a mathematical dimension. Carroll (1994) disagreed, arguing that cognitive traits like intelligence are inherently present in every person as opposed to learned skills.

## THE NEUROPSYCHOLOGICAL APPROACH

Finger (1994), Democritus (c. 460–370 B.C.), who believed that the head governed logical functions, and Galen (A.D. 130–200), who connected intellect with the brain, are the origins of the field of neuropsychology. According to an ancient Egyptian papyrus, a head injury and speech loss were related (Sondhaus & Finger, 1988).

However, Broca's description of a patient who had lost their ability to speak owing to a lesion in the left inferior frontal cortex was a particularly significant event in thinking about localization of function that predicted the origins of contemporary neuropsychology (Finger, 1994).

Teuber (1955) suggested using double dissociation to pinpoint the location of a function. This technique involves using two behavioral tests to demonstrate the functional separation of two brain regions, with each test being impacted by a lesion in one region but not the other. Following that, many neuropsychological studies employed this technique to describe the types of deficits that people with brain damage experience.

Shallice (1988) reviews the literature and suggests that double dissociations demonstrate functional specializations for sub-processes in the perception, memory, speech, and output systems. However, double dissociation is a technique that is not without its detractors. For instance, Plaut (1995) "lesioned" a synthetic connectionist network that lacked a modular framework to create a twofold dissociation. These results, according to Plaut, call into question the theoretical ramifications of relying solely on single-case investigations.

Scoville and Milner (1957) presented examples of severe memory loss that occurred after the hippocampus was removed to cure uncontrollable epilepsy. Both used causal explanations for the patient's behavior and clear distinctions between the Wechsler intelligence and memory scales to describe this memory loss. Toal (1957) and others' subsequent research (Erickson & Scott, 1977) questioned the Wechsler memory scale's suitability for describing organic memory issues.

The Wechsler memory scale, according to Toal, is based on an unclear "common-sense" concept of memory that leaves no clear indication of what is being measured. Numerous studies have been conducted to describe the characteristics of amnesic impairments and pinpoint dissociable memory disorders due to Scoville and Milner's report (Butters et al., 1995). As a result of this research created, specialized memory test batteries (e.g., Delis et al., 1991) and the Wechsler memory scale were revised (Kent, 2017).

Chase et al. (1984) investigated the association between WAIS scores and cerebral glucose metabolism in Alzheimer's patients and healthy individuals. According to their findings, performance on the verbal subtest was linked to activity in the left perisylvian areas. In contrast, performance on the performance subtest was linked to activity in the right posterior parietal areas. This study was a pioneer in mapping brain regions linked to individual differences in mental skills using contemporary neuroimaging techniques.

Additionally, correlations between cognitive task performance and neuroimaging have led to innovative theories, such as the idea that higher performance is related to more significant mental efficiency (Deary & Caryl, 1997).

Evidence for independent processing of form, color, movement, and depth in the monkey visual system was provided by Livingstone & Hubel (1987a). They demonstrated that the concept of distinct processing channels for these identical visual elements was also supported by human psychophysical evidence (Livingstone & Hubel, 1987b). Individual variations were not a focus of their investigation.

However, the hypothesis of distinct processing streams turned out to be quite helpful in directing later neuroscience research to focus on how information is processed in specialized networks. This caused a shift away from the rigid localizationist viewpoint that had been the primary concern of researchers like Reitan. The argument between localization of function and equipotentiality may be resolved by the idea of "selectively distributed processing" (Mesulam, 1998).

Trends And Issues

The history of ability testing has been interpreted in various ways over time. Early mental tests have widely varying definitions of intelligence, according to Tyler (1965). This includes concepts of judgment, abstract thought, learning capacity, etc.

According to Tyler (1965), "the predominantly practical focus of mental testers protected psychology from bogging down in a swamp of semantic complexity." This point of view matched the time's pragmatic orientation, which emphasized performance prediction across various disciplines.

According to Carroll & Maxwell (1979):

*There has long been a conflict between those who think that can neatly sum up human cognitive abilities in a single. All-encompassing definition of intelligence and those who prefer to stress the idea's multidimensionality. The majority of current research is based on a multifactorial view...*

More recently, the progressive character of theory development in this field has been highlighted in various studies of the history of research on human mental talents (e.g., Flanagan et al., 2014; Schneider & Flanagan, 2015). This point of view aligns with the growing interest in using individual characteristics to construct theories. Currently, the Cattell-Horn-Carroll (CHC) model is well-liked.

According to Schneider & Flanagan (2015):

*The CHC hypothesis is not so much a novel theory as it is an expansion of some substantial discoveries made by Spearman, Thurstone, and numerous other pioneering scholars.*

According to Geisinger (2000), psychological testing is still developing quickly. Similarly, Riley et al. (2017) claim:

*Every new iteration of the Wechsler Adult Intelligence Scale (WAIS) or Wechsler Intelligence Scale for Children (WISC) includes adjustments based on new information on the nature of cognitive functions published in both primary and applied literature.*

Contrarily, Boake (2002) claims that this most popular IQ test has undergone numerous changes and remained essentially intact. He points out several WAIS sub-scales existed before the Wechsler-Bellevue was put together.

All Wechsler-Bellevue subtests, except Block Design, were derived from Army tests, claims Boake (2002). Since then, the substance hasn't changed all that much. For instance, the third revision's Symbol Search supplemental sub-test was the only content change (Tulsky et al.,2003b). Most modifications concerned new methods for computing index scores and revising norms.

Boake (2002) states:

The Wechsler-Bellevue Intelligence Scale, created between the 1880s and World War I, is a collection of intelligence tests. The Wechsler subtests originated from the main pre-World War I methods of cognitive evaluation.

Therefore, the WAIS scales have undergone significant interpretational alterations rather than substance. Since the invention of these tests, there has been "waxed and waned" public debate regarding testing mental talents (Cronbach, 1975). These debates touch on racial, socioeconomic, and immigrant variations in test results for intelligence.

According to Cronbach (1975), these are due to journalists, who often only cover the contrary side of an argument when reporting on scholarly articles, altering the original to make it more intriguing.

However, it is also evident that psychologists have independently made controversial public statements, such as the book by Hernstein & Murray (1994) that covered, among other topics, disparities in intelligence between races and social classes.

Galton, Jackson, Maudsley, and Spearman each cited science to support upholding the status quo in society, according to Walsh et al. (2014). Jensen (2000) asserts that Spearman believed that one could assess a person's eligibility to vote or have children based on the measurement of g.

Thurstone acknowledged that people have a wide range of skills, but he also said:

If the data support the genetic explanation, the biologists cannot be accused of being undemocratic. Mother Nature must be undemocratic in this matter if anyone is (Thurstone, 1946).

According to Neisser et al. (1996), generalizations concerning these topics are problematic since there is uncertainty regarding the nature, sources, and measurement of intelligence.

According to Neisser et al. (1996),

*In a field with so many open issues and unanswered questions, the confident tone that has characterized most discussions on these topics is unacceptable.*

# CHAPTER 02
# WHAT ARE MENTAL ABILITIES
# (PRIMARY & SECONDARY MENTAL ABILITIES)

## DEFINITION OF MENTAL ABILITY:
The ability to learn or remember information, comprehend the context and implications of your actions, and possess the attributes (capacity, ability, and power) necessary to complete a task are just a few examples of the many varied definitions of mental ability.

## GENERAL MENTAL ABILITY
The phrase "general mental ability" (GMA) characterizes how well a person learns, comprehends directions, and solves problems. Scales that evaluate particular constructs like verbal, mechanical, numerical, social, and spatial aptitude are included in tests of general mental capacity.

The total score is the most important factor since it accounts for more significant performance variation than specific abilities.

## GENERAL MENTAL ABILITY TESTS
General mental capacity tests assess various characteristics and general cognitive ability.

Longer tests usually gauge the following characteristics:

- General knowledge: The extent to which a person has learned information on various subjects. Long-term memory.
- Social intelligence: Both verbally and visually able to use norms for moral and ethical judgment to assess social behavior and anticipated outcomes.
- Arithmetic: Problem-solving and mathematical thinking skills.
- Verbal ideas: The capacity to classify, understand similarities and contrasts, and draw nuances in comparisons.
- Vocabulary: Extent of acquired linguistic notions. Demonstrates effective information utilization, receptivity to information, and communication abilities.
- Coding: Flexibility and quick learning.
- Orienting details: The capacity to recognize critical facts through perceptual and analytical abilities.
- Spatial rotation: Being able to envision things from many angles and dimensions.
- Spatial reasoning: The capacity to comprehend an object's various components and how they work together.

## Shorter Tests
Although many shorter tests can assess general mental capacity, the Wonderlic Personnel Test, which lasts 12 minutes, is the most reliable and famous today. Conceptual comparisons, word and sentence meanings, deductive logic, sequential reasoning, detail matching, analysis of geometric figures, and story issues demanding mathematical solutions are just a few of the problem kinds it includes.

In contrast to the typical multi-choice style, test takers must enter their responses so that a wealth of data is available for examination. Can compare the test result of the candidate to the minimum standards advised for various occupational categories.

The Wonderlic Personnel Test offers numerical insight into how well people can adapt and solve difficulties while working, how readily they can be trained, and how likely they will be content with the job's demands.

Higher scores will benefit more from formal training and are more likely to learn from on-the-job training efficiently. On the other hand, those who scored lower will need more in-depth explanations, hands-on practice, more time and repetition, and constant supervision.

## Tests of Critical Thinking

Managers must objectively assess staff members' opinions and business offers. The most widespread critical thinking test is the Watson Glaser. It evaluates one's capacity for several forms of critical thought. To evaluate given a conclusion and a set of data;

- What unstated presumptions exist?
- What can be inferred about the conclusion's relative truth or falsity?
- Does the evidence support the conclusion logically?
- The relative merits or deficiencies of a claim and its conclusion

Can compare scores to those at comparable management and occupational levels.

## TYPES OF MENTAL ABILITIES

Basic Mental Capabilities

- Memory association: a person's capacity for memory and recall.
- Numerical Ability: the capacity for mathematical problem-solving.
- Perceptual speed: the capacity to spot contrasts and resemblances between objects
- Reasoning: the ability for rule discovery
- Spatial visualization: The capacity to visualize relationships spatially.

## IMPORTANCE OF MENTAL ABILITIES:

Mental ability is one of the essential aspects of functional capacity for a worker, especially a mental worker, to carry out job obligations since it represents a child's "brain power" in many competency areas, including verbal, arithmetic, spatial, and logical thinking.

Mental skills, often known as psychological skills, are used by the mind. It includes, among many other abilities, the ability to use constructive self-talk, build confidence, set goals, and adopt the most productive mentality. Your overall well-being and academic achievement can both be improved by developing your psychological abilities.

## CATEGORIES FOR MENTAL ABILITIES

There are two categories of mental abilities: primary and secondary.

## Intelligence

When you look into it, intelligence is a surprising thing to quantify. When working with a county program, I can still clearly recall measuring this man's I.Q. He appeared to be relatively normal and could carry on a conversation. Once his I.Q. was tested, he was classified as borderline, between far below average and barely above mentally handicapped.

A broad definition of intelligence is the intrinsic capacity to absorb knowledge and apply it to solve problems or navigate through challenging circumstances. Due to two factors, I say loosely. The first, the more general explanation, is that it is not a physical structure or anything that can be taken out of the skull and measured. Because it is a theoretical construct, we have learned about it through psychological research, testing, and the development of hypotheses about how we process information. While we are measuring it as a real object, it isn't exactly as simple to do so as measuring your spleen's output or your skull's volume.

There is a disagreement between primary and secondary mental abilities, which is the second reason we are using a broad definition of intelligence. Both will require some explanation, so let's give them each their part.

## Primary Mental Abilities

L.L. was the first to talk about primary mental capacities. Thurstone in 1935 might be characterized as latent core constructs that can account for almost all cognitive differences. When intelligence tests were first introduced and disagreements between the two main camps, Thurstone conducted research. One group claimed that all intellect

reflected a single, general intelligence. Others held that intellect is multidimensional and can have higher and lower features.

Numerous psychological tests were conducted by Thurstone, who discovered that we exhibit our intelligence in a limited number of ways even if he could not determine whether intelligence is derived from a single source or is multiple. That's a little perplexing since it seems I'm expressing the opposite of two things. Thurstone discovered that only a few factors are genuinely relevant when evaluating I.Q. He discovered, for instance, the following aspects:

- Verbal understanding.
- Spatial orientation
- Using inductive logic
- Quantity facility
- Word fluidity
- Relational memory
- Perceptual speed

The problem is that these are challenging to learn on your own. Imagine attempting to research associative memory without also incorporating language. Alternatively, how can one use numbers without also requiring language? Or, additional factors can affect or support these fundamental mental faculties.

We must examine secondary mental talents to completely understand the fundamental ones.

*Function Of Primary Mental Abilities:*
Primary mental abilities are essentially like Legos or parts of an erector set. However, you can't do much with just one Lego or erector set component, even though they are each distinct and exclusive ways to gauge intellect.

## Secondary Mental Abilities

The prevailing opinion is that secondary abilities are derived from core talents and their overall clusters and constantly interact with these broad underlying themes.

Most of the study on mental capacity and intelligence demonstrates that, while "intelligence" is hard to define and quantify, specific mental capacities can offer a profile of an individual's strengths and shortcomings.

Knowing what each cognitive test is assessing when thinking about secondary mental talents will help you better grasp what the person is being asked to do and will show you which skills and abilities are being used.

The two essential secondary mental capacities that are frequently cited in the literature are:

- Crystallized intelligence.
- Fluid intelligence.

## Crystallized Intelligence:

Our ability to demonstrate comprehension, expressive thought, and understanding, or crystallized intelligence, is usually assessed using linguistic techniques like vocabulary, analogies, and comprehension questions.

A person is more likely to be able to integrate knowledge in an exceedingly sophisticated way if they receive a better score on this test.

Crystallized intelligence is usually said to be significantly influenced by somebody's education level, experiences and exposures in life, and culture.

## Fluid Intelligence:

In contrast to crystallized intelligence, fluid intelligence is a smaller amount structured and knowledge-based. It's the capacity to acknowledge linkages, comprehend patterns, and predict the consequences of these relationships and patterns.

These skills include reasoning, the flexibility to infer, problem-solving, and intellectual flexibility. Fluid reasoning and fluid intelligence are helpful when presented with novel settings and scenarios.

Human fluid reasoning is believed to develop through trial and error and is comparatively independent of those constructions.

Primary mental abilities are the most guiding principles for grouping secondary mental abilities. Many of those talents are evaluated using either implicitly or explicitly standardized IQ tests. Like IQ tests and results, it is essential to consider how education, culture, age, and other variables may affect somebody's ability. In keeping with research, secondary mental abilities are particularly liable to the lifespan developmental process.

These skills are more amenable to repetition and reinforcement; it's widely believed that many of those skills must be utilized and exercised continuously throughout one's life to avoid losing them.

## CONCLUSION:

Our emotional, psychological, and social well-being are all parts of our mental state. It influences our thoughts, emotions, and behaviors. Additionally, it influences how we reply to stress, interact with others, and keep decisions. Every period of life, from childhood and adolescence to maturity, is essential for mental state.

# CHAPTER 03
# SPIRITUAL HEALING: WHAT IS IT? DOES IT WORK AND DOES IT HAVE A PLACE IN MODERN HEALTHCARE?

This chapter will cover the following points:

- Self-healing visualization
- My introduction to the healing
- The healing session
- Possible mechanisms of effect
- Research evidence of effectiveness
- Its place in modern healthcare

## SELF-HEALING VISUALIZATION

To express my understanding of spiritual healing—which is best experienced rather than described—I thought I'd start by leading us through a self-healing visualization. It will give us a taste of the process and boost our energy levels.

Since it is excellent practice to encourage individuals to help themselves as necessary, we frequently provide this transcript to people who come for healing to use on their own as a self-care tool.

## THE INTRODUCTION OF MY HEALING

I figured you might be interested to hear how I overcame my complete doubt and started to heal. My mild-mannered businessman uncle first revealed his intention to become a healer around Christmas about fifteen years ago. All of us felt startled.

Although I thought that this was most definitely biased reporting, he told me about his experiences with how healing has helped individuals. I was sufficiently intrigued to want to try to learn more. I called the healing tutor in Leeds, where I lived, after my uncle had given me her phone number.

She started talking to me about a healing introduction course that she was offering, but I cut her off to emphasize that I wasn't interested in becoming a healer; I was curious to learn more. She advised that I enroll in this introductory course in three months. In the interim, though, I might practice by sending healing, benevolent energy via me to animals, plants, or my children. I can't believe I'm doing this; I thought as I held my hands in front of a cactus plant in the kitchen, feeling foolish.

Anyway, I had forgotten about healing until about two weeks before the course was scheduled to begin. Around three in the morning, I was gasping in bed due to a cold and worried that I would have to get out of bed to retrieve my inhaler for the third night.

I decided to try this healing lark because I was so exhausted that I couldn't be bothered. (Exact words I used; I wasn't precisely persuaded; I was just worn out and ill.) I just requested healing while lying in bed with my hands lifted over my chest because I wasn't sure what to do.

I was astonished by what followed: I felt a band of heat around my chest, my fingers began to tingle, and I saw a blue light in my head. My gasping abruptly ceased. As you might imagine, I was somewhat alarmed by what had transpired and told my husband the following day that he would never guess what had happened the previous evening.

I listened, though, because I knew there was something in it, and I wanted to learn more when I went to the healing course instead of sitting in the back and rolling my eyes to the ceiling while questioning everything.

I presently do healing in three very diverse locations:

First, let's talk about the Leeds Healing Centre, a drop-in location where individuals go particularly for healing.

Second, there is the Positive Care Programme, a recognized charity that provides 24-week individual and group complementary therapies and motivational workshops. For those with long-term illnesses and their caregivers (referrals are mainly by the Primary Care Mental Health Team, local charities, healthcare day centers, etc.). Around 80% of individuals experience level 1 and level 2 mental health issues.

The third is the York Association for the Care and Resettlement of Offenders, where we work to influence the staff and ex-offender energy in a more constructive direction.

## A DEFINITION OF HEALING

*A method of healing that includes sending energy from the healer to the patient. It encourages self-healing by relieving physical tension, calming the body, and boosting the immune system. Healing is organic and non-intrusive, intending to restore equilibrium and overall wellbeing to the recipient (NFSH Healing Trust).*

A confident faith is not connected to spiritual healing. It can heal even highly skeptical individuals. Thus, it is not faith healing.

The Latin word "spiritus," which means "breath of life," is where the term "spiritual" comes from. The spiritual element alludes to spiritual energy acting profoundly on our spiritual selves. In other terms, the healer connects with "Universal" or Divine energy to channel healing for the mind, body, and soul. Energy is transferred during the healing process.

## COMPONENTS OF HEALING:

- With the right intention, one can guide the universal energy or spirit (in a non-religious sense).
- The human body's "spiritual vibrations" are raised when attention is directed to it through the aura (human energy field).
- One's highest nature can then fully develop, and one's health is improved.
- Multiple treatments are required to overcome the body's inertia and achieve maximum healing.
- It's usual for people to complain about having "poor energy" when they're ill; nevertheless, when someone is healthy, we say they have "bursting energy."

Improvement frequently requires 6–8 sessions, especially for people with chronic diseases.

## WHAT HAPPEN IN THE THERAPY SESSION?

- Recipient seated on a couch or chair.
- Healers tune into the energy of healing.
- Energy is channeled on and around the body to promote healing (typically with the healer's hands).

It must guarantee no particular result. Since it only serves as a conduit for the healing energy, healers cannot genuinely claim to be able to do this. When the healer is not physically present with the patient, they can also provide healing remotely. In this case, the healer uses attunement and visualization to encourage the patient's health and self-healing.

## WHO CAN BE HELPED?

- Anyone. Healing helps lessen many individuals' unwanted energetic weights (such as anger or fear).
- Typically, those who are "short on energy" or generally feel "out of sorts," such as those with long-term mental and physical health disorders like depression, anxiety, bipolar disorder, backache, arthritis, cancer, and ME.

## WHAT HAPPENS TO PEOPLE DURING THE HEALING PROCESS?

Several feelings, best characterized as a "flow of energy":

- Warmth (from the healer's hands or a reassuring sort in general)
- Cold
- Tingling

- Other sensations (such as a sense of movement, touch, or surfacing pain)

## EFFECTS OF HEALING:
Although frequently very significant to the patient's life, not always specific. e.g.

- Pain reduction
- A more profound sense of calm and a lighter load
- Relief of bodily symptoms
- A feeling of connectedness with the cosmos
- An increase in vitality

## CASE STUDY:
- David, a customer of the Leeds Healing Center (His MIND support worker had suggested him to us; he arrived looking quite untidy)
- Ten years of depression and worry, lack of sleep
- Taking an antidepressant
- Took a course in CBT
- Near the end of his rope
- The First session was relaxing; the following week, the client reported having slept soundly for the first time in a very long time
- Attended regularly for four months, then roughly every two weeks for the following two months
- Felt 'lighter,' more at ease, and content
- Anxiety attacks ceased
- Stopping the use of antidepressants (with the agreement of his GP)
- Currently adjusting to volunteering at a nearby charity shop

## WHAT IS THE HEALING PROCESS' MECHANISM?
The biggest obstacle to its acceptability in healthcare is the unclear healing mechanism. Healing will continue to be dismissed as merely a placebo effect until a robust mechanism is uncovered, which I don't believe is the case. I'll explain why.

When I channel healing, I visualize the energies. A black cloud of "bad" energy surrounding the woman as she received healing at the Leeds Healing Centre was seen to escape from the top of her head on the right side.

When I asked the woman how she thought the healing had gone, she replied that she felt good and had felt "something" pass through her skull during the healing, pointing to the precise location where I had witnessed this happen. While watching, another healer overheard what the woman was saying to me and then revealed to us that she, too, had witnessed the black cloud emerge from the woman at that location on her head. So, it appears that all three of them independently felt the same vibe.

The mechanism of healing has been studied in laboratory tests. These results lend credence to the idea that the healer is a conduit for energy. Electromagnetic experiments reveal "extraordinarily massive"

Low-frequency magnetic fields will be recorded from healers' hands and are not just the results of their internal body currents. They need low frequencies, like those employed in various electrotherapy forms, to hurry up tissue mending.

It has been discovered that in a healing session, the patient's brain waves shift to synchronize with the healer. Electroencephalograms have shown enhanced alpha brain waves within the healer. Numerous investigations have demonstrated remote EEG connectivity between two people. Regardless of what the healer does, the patient appears to receive it.

The Distant Intentional Connection experiment, which made use of functional resonance imaging (fMRI), seems to be in favor of distant healing:

- "Sending thoughts at a distance" is the definition of distant intention
- Unknown to the recipient, distant intention healing was transmitted every which way at intervals of two minutes (in sensory isolation from the healer)
- Extremely statistically significant variations between send and control (no send) within the recipient's activation of specific brain functions

Therefore, there's proof of a lively link between people (healer and recipient). And the way it operates?

Oschman is thinking of a possible mechanism. Consistent with his "model of the intelligent body," the animal tissue of the body extends into the cell plasma, forming a continuum that connects all cells and vibrates with electromagnetic energy. The body works because each component communicates with the others instantly and continuously (20 times faster than the central nervous system). (The theory of chemical transmission through synapses is too sluggish).

He contends that a coherent environment and a healthy body are necessary for optimal magnetic flow. This electromagnetic energy flow extends to the body's world, referred to as the aura. Where there's interaction with the surface world, this makes it possible for people to receive intents or healing vibrations.

Undoubtedly, many folks can "know" when there has been a fight in a room after we get in. Through our aura, we will feel bad energy. No matter what someone says or does to us, we will always tell if they're acting with good or evil intentions.

Perhaps to know to heal, we want to require a new examine reality, which is now over ever thought to be of a quantum nature within which everything is interconnected. Thus, long after their first interaction—possibly at the instant of the "Big Bang"—two objects remain connected via time and space without exchanging conventional communication. This connection was dubbed "spooky action at a distance" by Einstein.

According to Einstein's Special Theory of Relativity, matter (atoms) and energy (photons) are two sides of an identical coin. Consistent with Dean Radin, the bioelectromagnetic fields surrounding our bodies are entangled with electromagnetic fields within the immediate environment and with photons (energy) from the remainder of the universe. He has proposed that there's an entangled fabric of reality in which everything is connected.

Another possibility could be a holographic world, within which the universe could be a 3-D image projected from a tier of reality that exists independently of your time and space despite appearing to be fabricated from material objects.

David Bohm, a physicist, and Karl Pribram, a neurophysiologist, separately developed this idea. A renowned quantum physicist and Einstein's protege, Bohm was. Bohm and Pribram independently came up with their theories to clarify not just all the phenomena seen in natural philosophy and other neurophysiological problems but also eerie and mystical experiences. Scientists who study the universe mathematically utilize this paradigm.

Michael Talbot questions if the mystics' assertion that reality is a complete, resonant symphony of wave patterns instead of an illusion referred to as "Maya" is accurate. A "frequency domain" that transforms into the globe as we all know it only after it enters our senses?

John von Neuman and Henry Stapp both concur. They contend that the conscious mind directs a dynamic dispersion of concurrent virtual states into one focused awareness state. This raises the likelihood that one person's thoughts or brain can affect another person, an item, or other human organs.

Probabilistic brain states preferentially collapse into specific states. This might be how a healing intention has an impression. It's challenging to elucidate the mechanics of something as ethereal as healing because we don't fully understand the essential workings of reality.

But I prefer this declaration by English biologist T. H. Huxley:

*The adage "Sit before fact sort of a little child, and be prepared to convey up every preconceived thought, follow humbly wherever and to whatever abyss Nature leads, otherwise you shall learn nothing" describes a way to approach facts.*

He adds that I'm too skeptical about dismissing the likelihood of anything. Regarding the method of healing, Jack Angelo states the following:

*The basic idea of spiritual healing is that everybody is interconnected on an "energetic" level, which is now confirmed by natural philosophy. It's believed that healing can affect the equilibrium of the mind, body, and spirit by influencing thought at a lively level.*

The legitimacy of healing depends on the NHS accepting it. Thus, knowledge of the healing process is crucial. From the patient's perspective, the positive outcomes—not the method of achieving them—are essential. Similarly, I can confer with my friend while calling from abroad on my movable as if she were nearby.

## RESEARCH EVIDENCE OF EFFECTIVENESS OF SPIRITUAL HEALING

At least 2,200 published studies on spiritual healing, prayer, energy medicine, the benefits of mental intention, and intentionality in distant healing are described by Jonas and Crawford. However, many use subpar techniques. According to anecdotal evidence from healers, it is uncommon for people to experience no benefits to their minds, body, or spirit after receiving multiple healing sessions. It is unusual for healing to not be beneficial in some way, according to the NFSH Healing Trust.

A few people notice the effect right away. After the initial healing session, several clients reported feeling their despair lift or their chronic pain vanish. A small percentage, nevertheless, don't seem to benefit from mending. Perhaps some of these individuals are reluctant to give up the sick person role because they have a stake in continuing to be ill.

A survey of those who support complementary therapies but aren't necessarily in favor of healing has revealed:

- 87% (92/106) of those who said healing had benefited them agreed or strongly agreed.
- 12% (13/106) said they were "unsure." (Of them, most had only attended one or two sessions.)
- One individual voiced their disagreement.

The first person to take healing seriously as a scientific topic was Dan Benor. He examined 155 controlled experiments with various experimental individuals (enzymes, micro-organisms, cells, plants, animals, and humans). Moreover, half generated statistically significant data that backed up the healing effect. He found that there isn't much rigorous, controlled research on human sickness.

There have been two reviews of human healing randomized controlled trials (RCTs). Approximately half of the trials in each showed statistically significant differences from controls:

- 10 out of the 22 publications reviewed by Neil Abbott showed a substantial impact on healing.
- The review by Astin, Harkness and Ernst covered 23 trials involving 2,774 patients. Thirteen trials (57%) produced statistically significant treatment effects; nine showed no difference from controls, and one revealed a detrimental difference.

However, many trials had poor methodology or trial design, with biased reporting and tiny sample sizes.

There was no statistically significant pain decrease in an RCT looking at the impact of spiritual healing on chronic pain (which was the primary endpoint). It did demonstrate significant differences from the controls in terms of both large, non-specific effects and psychological benefits.

However, the trial received criticism on various fronts, but mainly for its design, which was criticized for assuming an impact size deemed unsuitable for chronic pain. There were "changes" in discomfort and "strange" feelings (such as seeing colors or light) among the non-specific symptoms that were recorded. These complicated results were written off as "part of the healing folklore."

Research methodologies must consider the goal of healing – not just to relieve symptoms and restore wellbeing but to assist people in the process of self-healing within a holistic view of health – to prevent erroneous evaluation in the

investigation of spiritual healing. Typically, reductionist research methodologies do not look into this. When the healer (X) placed her hand on the woman's back, for instance, the woman said:

*When X (the healer) put her hand on my back, I thought about something awful that had happened to me in the past." I just realized that this wasn't a part of me anymore and that I could let it go (I hadn't been thinking about it, and it startled me that I suddenly thought about it). I have to go now.*

She had come for healing to alleviate her back discomfort. In a trial looking at pain relief, I would not have noticed her "non-specific impact" from the healing. Randomized controlled trials must overcome several methodological challenges to assess the effectiveness of spiritual healing.

First, there are issues with the sampling that include:

- Generalizability: Patients selected for a trial may differ from usual patients who visit for healing, for example, in their belief systems or coping methods, and this could alter treatment outcomes because traditional medical care is typically distinct from the administration of healing.
- Therapeutic Expectation: Results in non-blinded trials may be skewed if there is an expectation of therapeutic benefit due to faith in the benefits of healing.
- Wide range of symptoms: People who come for healing may do so for other reasons, such as the fact that they "feel fatigued" or "low energy," rather than because they have a particular condition. Therefore, a study on the efficacy of healing based on a particular ailment may not be applicable.

Second, the trial treatment may encounter issues:

- Standardization: The practitioner is frequently explicitly acknowledged as a component of the treatment, making treatment standardization within trials a potential issue. It necessitates, for example, stratification by individual healers in the randomization process.
- Practitioner and user influence: The healing act strives to enhance the patient's whole healing process and goes beyond a simple collection of skills. Keeping the human experience at the heart of reductionist scientific analysis could be challenging.
- Controls: Sham controls are made-up situations that skew practice. Blinding is frequently not an option; instead, pragmatic trials using standard medical care as the control are required.
- Recognizing the healing process: What component helps in healing? Is it the intention to heal, the energy channeling, the users' expectations, the relationship with the healer, or the supportive, empathetic listening that goes along with it? Or are they all crucial?

Third, outcome measurements may have issues.

- Suitable outcome measurements: Significant changes like spiritual transformation or personal development might not be quantifiable after healing. The choice of RCT end measures may significantly alter efficacy assessments.
- Illness role: Some ideologies say that disease highlights a balancing issue in the body, mind, or spirit. (For instance, we all know folks who, when worried, develop a cold or a backache.) The way people live their lives after receiving treatment and any resulting gains in health need to be captured in research.
- Chronic illness: People with long-term diseases require long-term follow-up since the disease frequently has a relapsing and remitting pattern, and change is typically gradual and inconspicuous. The reported effects may eventually be caused by elements other than the trial treatments.
- Variations in experience: For one person, treatment may be beneficial immediately while taking a few weeks. Must consider these variables in trial design. The tricky part of using evidence-based decision-making and practice is fusing complementary therapists' philosophical concerns with rigorous methodological requirements.

# HEALING'S ROLE IN MODERN HEALTHCARE

The House of Lords Select Committee on Science and Technology researched complementary and alternative medicine and its usage in healthcare by speaking with numerous industry experts.

They classified healing as a "Group 2" therapy in their report on complementary and alternative medicine since it is a supplement to traditional medicine and makes no claims to be able to diagnose disease.

Increasingly common alternative therapy is spiritual healing:

- The primary healing organizations have registered over 14,000 healers.
- Physicians recommend healers to their patients.
- The NHS (GP offices, oncology units, hospices, and mental health hospitals) use it.
- The UK is home to NFSH Healing Trust Healing Centers.
- Healers work for the NHS as volunteers and, on occasion, as employees (although this is rare at the moment).

We require more excellent research, adequate training for healers, high professional standards, and clinical governance if healing is firmly established within contemporary healthcare.

For the following reasons, you may want to get in touch with the NFSH Healing Trust (Charity No. 1094702) if you want to refer patients for healing:

- In the UK, it is the biggest and most established membership organization for spiritual healers.
- It is trained to national standards by certified instructors.
- The minimum training time is two years, with the final examination meeting national requirements and emphasizing the healer's personal growth and professional standards.
- It is covered by professional insurance, a disciplinary process, and a code of conduct for professionals.
- In the UK, more than 50 Healing Centers are run by volunteers.

Due to my talk, the NFSH Healing Trust now offers a new healer membership course for nurses and medical workers. Due to significant prior learning, this course is shorter (four days of theory). The following step is mentoring a seasoned healer member for at least 12 months.

# VISUALIZATION TO RAISE ENERGETIC VIBRATIONS

You can do this either standing or sitting

You can ground yourself by concentrating on where your feet' soles contact the Earth. At that precise moment, notice the energy transfer between your feet and the ground below. Feel the support of the Earth.

Now turn your attention inward to the energy or lightbulb that makes up your true self, your Soul, or life force. If you cannot "see" this, do not be concerned; all you need to do is sense or know that this energy is present in your body.

Now turn your focus upward into the cosmos until you see or sense a far-off point of Light, which is the Divine Light, the source of all joy, serenity, and love. Keep focusing on fusing that Light with your life force. Allow this connection to occur as the Divine Light descends to surround you. Feel, see, sense, or "know" that this potent Divine force is entering your Soul, fortifying it, and giving you a sense of wholeness.

Allow this Light to spread outward, filling each cell in your body and nurturing and healing it.

Imagine the Light enlarging even more, outstretched about an arm's length from your body on all sides, above your head, at your feet, and especially behind you. Imagine that this empowering Light is filling you up until it forms a protective sphere around you. It is vital, serene, loving, and energizing.

Return your focus to the bottoms of your feet and experience that connection to the Earth. Feel anchored and like your energies have now returned to a level appropriate for going about your daily business. Then open your eyes.

*This visualization elevates your energetic frequencies with Divine Light from within, making it an extremely potent, healing visual. Continually practice this throughout the day, as often as is beneficial.*

# CHAPTER 04
# WHAT IS TELEPATHY AND HOW TO PRACTISE TELEPATHY

Have you ever thought of somebody and some seconds later you got a text from them? The reality is that it could result from your telepathy instead of a hilarious coincidence.

*The term "telepathy" was initially employed by psychologist Frederic W. H. Myers in 1882. Although it's still thought to be pseudoscience by many since it's hard to verify, research has suggested that it will be effective.*

But what precisely is telepathy? To seek out more about this and to understand the way to practice and apply telepathy to your lifestyle, we got in touch with telepathy experts.

## TELEPATHY IS ALSO CALLED:
- Mental Surfing
- Mind Induction
- Telepath Physiology
- Telepathic Abilities/Powers
- Thought-Casting

## WHAT IS TELEPATHY?

According to the dictionary, "telepathy is the capacity to communicate ideas and/or thoughts through means other than the five senses children learn about in school—seeing, hearing, smelling, tasting, and touching". According to psychic and clairvoyant Davida Rappaport, telepathy might be a type of nonverbal communication.

"One person is also thinking or feeling like transmitting a concept to a different person, so the other person may develop or experience that very same thought," the author claims.

This explains why she texted you the following day when you thought of your college supporter at random. Or perhaps your cousin contacted you and said, "OMG, I was just thinking about you!"

## CAPABILITIES

Information is often transmitted between users by way of mental channels. However, because these skills coincide with the basic idea of telepathy, many other mind-based talents are classified as telepathy. Common telepathic skills include the flexibility to read others' thoughts at command and sense the presence of other minds through E.S.P.

## WHY USE TELEPATHY?

Telepathy can be helpful when you're at a loss for words or don't know how to say something. Perhaps you worry about being ignored or rejected. You may not feel comfortable calling your ex, yet you still feel the need to express your feelings.

According to aura reader and podcast presenter Mystic Michaela, "it's not always possible to say the things we need to say or want to say to someone in our corporeal world. By taking the time to accomplish this telepathically, the higher selves and soul identities can participate in bringing these messages. In a telepathic conversation, things that can't always be realistically accomplished in face-to-face ones, like deep connections, forgiveness, and even closure, can be resolved."

Follow the advice of celestial mentor and energy healer Andrea Donnelly and see telepathy as a natural extension of your human talents if you're feeling anxious, stupid, or like you're going to get it wrong.

My family used to refer to it as our "small voice," she explains. For those just getting started, I find it helpful to think of it as a sixth sense or another language you were born with and only need to remember. Through it, you can communicate with anyone or anything, including other people, plants, animals, and the stars. It works like a psychic telephone network."

*According to Donnelly*, you will notice telepathy more and more as you become more accepting of its existence "the signs and messages coming from your ancestors and spirit guides, as well as the coincidences or synchronicities that have always run through your life. Your life and relationships may significantly change if you learn to use this form of communication."

## HOW TO PRACTICE TELEPATHY:

*Telepathy is a beautiful skill that anyone can use (or practice). According to Rappaport, everyone can communicate thoughts and ideas to other individuals, but few are aware of this capacity or actively using it. Just like with any gift or skill, you must practice.*

The experts we spoke to advise testing your telepathy on a friend or member of your family first. Why? You're more likely to be telepathically conversing with someone on some level already (even if you aren't aware of it!). Mystic Michaela asserts that telepathy functions best when you already have a connection or bond with someone, such as family, friends, and love relationships. It's important to first pay attention to the telepathy between the individuals you are surrounded by.

1. Begin In A Meditative State.

She advises that you imagine [the person you want to connect with] sitting or standing in front of you as you sit in a meditative state. "Consider sending them feelings of love, gratitude, or urgency. Consider that emotion is an energy condition that can send to them."

2. Communicate With Someone You Care About Informally.

Before you move to sleep, Mystic Michaela advises, ask your higher self to "visit" their awareness and deliver a message to strengthen a dream telepathic connection. "Start communicating with someone through your thoughts and emotional states. during this situation, ask them to verify to you that they received the message you sent," she claims.

3. Be Prepared For Feedback From People.

According to mystic Michaela, you will be astonished by what percentage of calls or texts you receive the following day. "They might express what quantity they need been puzzling over you or why they felt prompted to contact you today. They could question you at any time whether you would like anything or if everything is well," she claims. Contacting someone no longer part of your way of life can be more passive. She continues, they could suddenly DM you a fast hello or a social media post.

4. Be Patient.

Rappaport emphasizes the requirement of patience when it involves telepathy. "Getting good at it'll take time, like mastering a new skill. Repetition is helpful because thoughts are strong," she argues. While some people can be better at sending than receiving, others could be better at receiving than sending, et al. may be equally adept at both.

5. Seek A Psychic Mentor.

Last but not least, Donnelly advises that you maintain good spiritual hygiene. Implying that you are taking care of yourself while your psychological development proceeds. In step with Donnelly, this is often a part of why enrolling in programs and employing coaches and advisors are crucial.

*"With love, of course, you want to be ready to release things that aren't your own, like ideas, worries, thoughts, and more from the collective. which will require practice, so finding a mentor will be beneficial."*

## TELEPATHY EXERCISES:

Ask That Your Partner Brings An Item From The Shop.

For the next time your companion makes a late-night trip to the grocery store, Rappaport suggests another simple experiment. "Even if you do not meditate or find it difficult to unwind, just clear your head and say aloud, 'Can you bring this specific item from the store?' You'll even picture them doing it. Next, let it go," she claims. If it worked, you'd soon learn that your partner bought your preferred snack without asking. Try again if not.

## Send A impression To A dearest.

Donnelly proposes performing the identical activity with a buddy or a partner instead of separately. She first advises you to sit quietly, consider this individual, and act as if you're communicating with them. Then, "Try seeing a selected image, like a teddy, but wait to inform them until after." Then, request that your buddy or spouse receive what you're sending.

Perhaps they will not see a teddy, but Donnelly predicts that folks will detect qualities like "softness," "childhood comfort," or "plush." It'd not be literal and understanding how you see or experience telepathy involves doing this.

## DETERMINE THE CALLER'S NAME.

She advises trying to tap into the one that is asking you as another simple practice exercise. "We all have displayed, but when the phone rings, feel into it to work out if you already know who it's before you look. The more you are trying things out and practice, the more you'll realize you're usually right".

Mystic Michaela advises constantly inquiring for a "confirmation" from the recipient to affirm verification more quickly. She claims it'll be simpler for them to call you out on your telepathy the more in tune they are with their higher selves.

## BENEFITS OF TELEPATHY:

Donnelly says that you notice more significant patterns in your life after you start using telepathy. in keeping with Donnelly, "you start to appreciate that things happen with and for you, not to you." Even the disturbing things start to weave together into a beautiful tapestry.

"You start to take other people's actions less personally and realize that we are truly acquiring harmony with one another, the Earth, and therefore the stars," she continues. "Instead of interpreting life as a stream of random occurrences that happen inadvertently." As we proceed in these externally turbulent times, "It may be a gift and a way of communication that may facilitate your keep calm and focused."

Mystic Michaela believes that telepathy may be a valuable tool for couples and friends. As an illustration, suppose you haven't heard from a disciple for a while. Instead of assuming she's upset with you, you send her a message to let her know you're thinking of her and ask if she'd wish to connect with you when she's ready.

It's beneficial to attach to someone who can sense your emotion and why you may not be replying to texts at the instant. Or what's happening without you ever having to mention one word. Soon, while someone is in your area; you'll be able to sense them.

## NEGATIVE EFFECTS OF TELEPATHY:

Donnelly and Mystic Michaela agree that receiving and imparting such much information is stressful. Donnelly advises that you just should be tuned in to both your own and other people's boundaries. "As tempting because it is also, invading another person's right to privacy is rarely appropriate, and prying is equally unethical. to not say you will not receive information you were not trying to find, but it's more important to navigate the psychic realm with honor."

Conversely, Mystic Michaela asserts that there are often instances within which you do not want to receive psychic signals from others. "Unfortunately, toxic people are pretty good at grabbing onto our energy and tricking our psychic connections into communicating with us adversely."

According to Mystic Michaela, if you're in an exceedingly foul mood, you'll become perplexed or feel guilty and think about a reason to urge to bear with them another time. To manage the relationships and bonds between us, she continues, it is essential to be aware of telepathy in ourselves and others.

*While learning telepathy may take your time, persevere, and maybe at some point, your lover will bring home your preferred snack without you having to offer them a touch.*

## TELEPATHY IN PSYCHOLOGY

In general, psycho telepathy may be a sort of energy transmission. If you like science, you want to remember the energies and frequencies in our surroundings. Similarly, the material body is capable of exchanging a range of frequencies. Telepathic contact is feasible when these frequencies match another person's vibrational range. One can communicate with divine energies because of their psychic talents. Although pseudoscience, telepathy could be a feature of parapsychology (ESP) shared by psychic systems.

I hope I've changed your opinion on telepathy at this time. Let's continue and learn more about the assorted styles of telepathy and their definitions.

## TYPES OF TELEPATHIC POWERS

There are primarily six forms of telepathy within the psychic space:

1. Latent Telepathy:

It postpones telepathy and is the capacity to receive information with a time delay. There's a slight lag between information delivered and received during this good telepathy.

2. Retrocognitive Telepathy:

This psychic ability allows one to inquire about a person's past. This is incredibly helpful for psychics who want to know why certain things are happening in a person's life right now.

3. Precognitive Telepathy:

A person who possesses this kind of psychic ability can learn about the future.

4. Instinctual Telepathy:

One can learn about current situations by using the way of gut feelings.

5. Emotive Telepathy:

Information or words are the focus of the telepathic abilities stated above. But this psychic ability is concerned with emotions. With the use of their emotions, psychics can exert influence or control.

6. Superconscious Telepathy:

Even insights that do not exist in a person's head can be attained by using the power of the subconscious.

## ARE TELEPATHY SUPERPOWERS REAL?

Since this kind of psychic skill cannot be observed or quantified, many people view it as a fictitious kind of communication. But telepathy is real, like electricity or the force of gravity, according to believers. Telepathy and mind-to-mind communication phenomena are not new to the planet. You'll be amazed to learn that everyone has the capacity for telepathy within them; it has existed for eons.

It can create a psychic link with someone far away without bodily senses. One can perform several tasks with psychic abilities, such as:

- Reading: One can hear or feel the thoughts of another person's intellect through telepathy.
- Communication: Interact with others without using words or actions.

- Impression: The other person's mind can be planted with an image, concept, or message thanks to psychic telepathy.
- Control: The actions or thoughts of another individual may be influenced or directed by telepathic communication.

Furthermore, it won't be very objective to think of telepathy as a spiritual occurrence. In actuality, there is a strong link between science and psychology and the development of telepathy.

## FINAL THOUGHTS

Here is everything you need to know about telepathy in general and spiritual telepathy in particular. Do you want to know if you have any psychic abilities, such as telepathy? Anytime Astro's knowledgeable astrologers can provide you with psychic readings to alleviate any of your uncertainties. Additionally, they can help you find a fulfilling life.

# CHAPTER 05
# AURA AND AURA READING
# WHAT THEY ARE & WHAT TO EXPECT DURING A READING

Are you fascinated by the vibrant, mysterious realm of aura readings? Here's a detailed explanation of auras, their appeal to spiritual communities, and how to interpret what your aura could be trying to tell people about you.

## WHAT IS AN AURA?

A person's aura is an electromagnetic field that surrounds their body and is connected to their energy; while some individuals can actually *see* an aura, everyone can *feel* it. The original form of a vibe check is having your aura read.) Auras may spread, which explains why being around a happy, upbeat person makes you feel happier than usual and why being around a miserable person makes you incredibly exhausted.

The aura is described in the dictionary as "an invisible emanation or energy field that surrounds all living things." But there is also an energy field surrounding inanimate objects and those manufactured by humans. In contrast to the aura, which serves as a blueprint for the physical body and is nourished by the heart (the body's chief electrical generator), these energy fields are supposed to originate from the object. Our personalities, lifestyles, thoughts, and emotions are reflected in the energies that flow through our aura.

## FUNCTION OF THE AURA

The aura shields you from the negative energies in your environment, shielding you from its physical, emotional, and psychic forces (it acts as a lightning rod). Your aura links to the energies around you (it acts as an antenna or bridge).

The chakras and other energy centers are then connected through the aura to these energies (which further process them, often resulting in nerve, hormonal, vascular, and other activity in the physical body).

Your aura emits signals that convey information about you and draw specific energies to you. The blueprints for your physical body, emotions, consciousness, relationships and personal development are stored in the aura, which comprises several interconnected areas.

## WHAT ARE THE AURA'S SEVEN LAYERS?

The seven primary chakras originate in the physical body, but they are also present in every layer of the aura. The energy moves faster and vibrates higher with each level. Each layer is connected to the chakra denoted by the same number

Your aura, according to Grace, is made up of seven auric layers, also known as bodies or planes, each of which stands for a distinct concept. Imagine them as the layers of an onion, with your physical body in the middle.

1. Physical Aura Plane:

The physical aura level, as its name implies, is the layer that symbolizes our bodily well-being. It is the skin's outermost layer. Additionally known as the ethereal plane.

2. Emotional Aura Plane:

The emotional aura is the plane to which your feelings correspond. This plane will display your emotional state if it is high. It changes hue based on how you're feeling and will look dull or smear if you're upset.

3. Mental Aura Plane:

This plane is about logic, cognition, and reasoning. It is your body's third layer to the outside.

4. Astral Body Aura Plane:

This plane is concerned with your spiritual well-being as it moves outward. You store your potential for love there as well.

### 5. Etheric Aura Plane:

Your psychic powers are found on this plane. Your ability to connect with others on your wavelength and tap into their energy is much easier by having a transparent etheric plane.

### 6. Celestial Aura Plane

Your dreams and intuition are kept on this plane. Additionally, it is the level of enlightenment; those with a solid heavenly aura are frequently very creative.

### 7. Causal Aura Plane:

The last aura plane is this one. It balances out all the other layers and effectively acts as a road map for your life.

## WHAT DO THEIR COLORS MEAN?

One of the seven major chakras—the root, sacral, solar plexus, heart, throat, third eye, and crown—represents your aura's hues. These chakras are connected to your aura, which comprises the aforementioned auric layers.

Understanding which colors represent particular chakras will aid in deciphering what your aura is trying to tell you.

### Red:

The color red causes your root chakra to vibrate. According to Grace, it is located at the base of the spinal column. It houses your fundamental concerns, including who you are, your house, your job, your manifesting abilities, your sexual energy, and your values. When you have read in your aura, you essentially operate from a stable foundation.

### Orange:

Your sacral chakra, found in your lower abdomen, is connected to the color orange. It has the initial emotional body energy, creativity, the capacity to connect with people in relationships, and sexual energy, according to Grace.

Orange indicates that you're the emotional equivalent of curling up under a weighted blanket if it appears in your aura. You're also self-sufficient and realistic.

### Yellow:

Yellow corresponds to the chakra in your solar plexus. You'll find this chakra a few inches above your belly button.

It "holds your emotions, identity, personal strength, and personality," according to Grace. It expresses your identity to the outside world and yourself." A yellow aura indicates that you are imaginative, curious, and upbeat.

### Green:

The heart's center is represented by the color green, representing the energy of transformation, recovery, compassion, and expansion. Parents, teachers, healers, and nurses frequently have green auras.

### Pink:

Pink auras are uncommon, but they share much in common with the general green vibe of being kind, compassionate, and genuinely loving. A pink aura indicates a lot of love and compassion to share.

### Blue:

The light hue blue stands in for the throat chakra, which is all about expressiveness, self-expression, and speaking one's truth. The third eye chakra, associated with intuition, mental clarity, and inward focus, is represented by the color dark blue.

### Purple:

This color represents the crown chakra. A purple aura holds compassion, empathy, and the power to manifest, denoting magical and uncommon energy. Purple, however, can signify the need for rest or recovery in an aura.

Violet:
You are a creative, innovative, and spiritual person! You likely attended a liberal arts college. You often get caught in daydreams or fantasies; you live in the sky. You have a great sense of intuition; you may be incredibly spiritual or have good instincts; trust them! Even though they don't always "understand" you, your family and friends admire your empathy and insight.

Brown:
The aura's color range is grounded by the tans and browns (which makes sense). They are also driven by their careers and enjoy manual labor. Unlike purples, you're pretty sensible and practical; you're the friend with a strict budget and a thorough 10-year plan. You are aware that perseverance and planning can help you achieve your goals.

Magenta:
You are very independent if your aura is more magenta. You're the kind of person with some million TikTok fans because you're witty and creative. You create trends rather than following them. Although some people may find you odd, they secretly respect your uniqueness. You are exceptional.

White:
White auras are pretty uncommon. This color resonates with your crown chakra, which is above your head. Grace claims that it instills a sense of Oneness, All That Is, and the understanding of our interconnection.

Black:
If your aura is dark, you may harbor unfavorable emotions and thoughts impeding the passage of energy through your chakras.

## THE BEST PLACES TO GET AN AURA READING

There may be local aura readers that can read your energy in person and provide you with a summary if you live in a large city. Another well-liked way of viewing your aura in a photograph is aura photography, which is frequently inexpensive.

While they could be less precise, apps like AURLA and Aura & Energy will provide free virtual readings if there isn't an aura studio nearby.

## HOW TO LEARN TO READ YOUR AURA.
According to Grace, you can also learn to visualize your aura "by focusing on body parts (like your hands), in meditation, or visualization," she says.

You can also check if any colors start to form as you move your hands slowly and purposefully apart and back together by rubbing them together to produce friction.

You might try to read the auras of your friends and family once you have the hang of it.

## HOW TO READ AN AURA PHOTO
Christina Lonsdale, a visual artist and the author of Radiant Human, uses Polaroid film to capture the radiant energy of others and herself. She soon realized that each image component represented a distinct aspect of the subject's personality.

The basics are as follows:

- Photo Top: The space above your head represents your mental state and what is happening to you right now.
- Photo Left: The color in the lower left corner represents your internal state, persona, and the part of yourself that you only reveal to your closest friends and family.
- Photo Right: This demonstrates your public identity or who you appear to be.
- The Arch: This represents your aspirations or your ideals.

According to Lonsdale, *"We're dealing with layers of self here – the intricacies of self – and that's what I find so rewarding."*

## WHAT TO EXPECT FROM AN AURA READING.
With "tremendous insight and clarity to grasp themselves and their present position, including life lessons or obstacles," Grace has witnessed customers leave readings. I've personally had my aura captured on camera before. Photographed my aura on a Polaroid after I had been motionless for around 20 seconds.

It mainly was crimson with a hint of pink, which my reader saw as self-assured, passionate, and unrestrained. This all felt entirely accurate because I had recently ended a long-term relationship that wasn't healthy for me and had rediscovered myself.

## THE DIFFERENCE BETWEEN AURA PHOTOGRAPHY AND AURA READINGS
Most spiritual practices aim to improve self-awareness, and an aura reading or photograph shares this goal. However, they are distinct experiences.

When Mystic Michaela, an aura reader and the author of The Angel Numbers Book, does a reading, she notices patterns, feels the energy, and pinpoints potential growth areas for those being read. "For me, reading an aura is a journey where I take someone by the hand and show them all the parts of themselves that deserve more love, that need to develop, and that are waiting for the right circumstances to heal," the author claims.

On the other hand, Lonsdale claims that having a tangible item to refer back to is a benefit of capturing aura images. She adds that you may think about and discuss it with others.

## WHEN SHOULD YOU CHECK YOUR AURA?
How frequently should your aura be captured on camera? Lonsdale says, *"It depends on your original curiosity and what is happening for you."* "Given the people I've previously photographed, I know many advise having a predetermined period, but I believe it is more organic than that.

However, if someone wants an annual birthday review, that has some significance attached to it. If people do some deep personal work, it would be more frequent whenever they notice a shift."

Aura readings show the same thing. It all comes down to what, in Michaela's opinion, feels right intuitively. The author warns that any reading provides an opportunity for self-reflection, but excessive reading might distance you from your true self. "All the solutions are already inside you; you already know them."

## CAN THE COLORS OF YOUR AURA CHANGE OVER TIME?
The hues of a person's aura can undoubtedly alter with time. Your aura's colors change throughout your life because they represent changes in your energy. If one aura color dominates you repeatedly, you can learn more about that color's meaning and how to counteract its vital energy by reading about it.

For instance, since folks with purple auras tend to be highly sensitive, intuitive, and more introverted, they would want to work on creating stronger boundaries so they don't pick up on the negative energy of others, says aura reader Rachelle Terry. By doing this, they can observe that their aura gradually loses its propensity for the color purple over time.

## DON'T LIKE WHAT YOU SEE? HERE'S HOW TO CLEANSE YOUR AURA.
There are several things you may do to change your energy if you're not satisfied with it. Grace suggests that anyone may take care of their aura by bathing in the sun or swimming (especially if it's chilly). Smudging or sagging herself, performing chakra-balancing meditations, engaging in sound therapy, clothing for the aura you want, or seeking the advice of an energy healer.

For further individualized guidance, you can also request, after receiving a personalized reading, some tips on how to balance, clear, and develop your chakras and energy.

# THE BOTTOM LINE.

All living beings have invisible energy fields around them called auras. They can use their hues to interpret your personality, biases, and patterns. You can learn to read auras on your own or have your aura read in person or electronically.

You can change the colors of your aura over time if you're unsatisfied with them through energy cleansing practices like chakra work, sound therapy, and meditation.

# CHAPTER 06
# PSYCHIC DEVELOPMENT COURSE

## INTRODUCTION
You'll undoubtedly come across people with rather obvious psychic skills if you spend time in metaphysical or Pagan societies. However, many individuals think everyone possesses some latent psychic ability. Some people's abilities tend to show themselves more overtly, whereas others quietly lurk beneath the surface, ready to be used.

You probably have your own intuitive, psychic-leaning skills, regardless of your opinion on psychics and their abilities (you might have yours on the fast dial, never seek a reading from one, or fall somewhere in the center). One expert even asserted that we all had that sense of the supernatural; all we need is guidance on cultivating our psychic powers.

This is because "psychic," according to psychic medium Laura Lynne Jackson, author of Signs: The Secret Language of the Universe can frequently be used interchangeably with "intuitive." Using your powers represents your capacity to perceive information outside of the cognitive domain, which, according to the speaker, frequently occurs both consciously and unconsciously.

Need persuasion? Have you ever sensed someone staring at you and turning around? Or perhaps you had a fleeting idea about someone, then you ran into them later that day. Or perhaps you had a horrible feeling as you entered the place. These are all instances of intuitive psychic ability in use.

## WHAT DOES PSYCHIC EVEN MEAN?
The definition of "psychic" in Webster's New World Dictionary is:

- about or involving the psyche or mind
- outside of known or natural physical processes
- appearing sensitive to forces beyond the physical world

Anything that requires sensitivity to non-physical or supernatural nature is considered psychic labor. We must first comprehend what psychic work is not before we can comprehend what it is.

Our five senses—sight, taste, hearing, touch, and smell—and our logical/linear brain—represent the typical methods for acquiring and processing information. The practice of gathering information without using these strategies is known as psychic work. Extrasensory (beyond the senses) techniques are employed in psychic work to understand individuals, events, or situations that would otherwise not be accessible to the usual range of senses. An illustration of this would be reading a person's personality before meeting them, which eliminates the possibility of logically evaluating them using the five senses.

Those who claim to be psychic describe their work in terms of the extrasensory means through which they acquire knowledge. A few are clairvoyance (the ability to see without using physical eyes). Clairaudience (the ability to hear without using physical ears), and clairsentience (feeling without the physical body itself). It could be challenging to understand, but consider this:

You can only express the spiritual senses physically or materially through the physical senses. Like electricity comes before the toaster, energetic or spiritual sense comes before the physical. It implies that there are spiritual eyes hidden beneath the physical eyes. Spiritual ears are located behind the physical ears, and so on. Psychics can focus on the incredibly subtle operations of these spiritual senses and translate the data they acquire.

In the same way, we regularly see the road in front of us, a discussion with a buddy, or the flavor of a fresh strawberry; a psychic can pick up on those subtleties. All humans possess the gift of communicating on a spiritual or psychic level; a psychic is just someone who has mastered the skill of noticing incoming information that is typically ignored.

Some psychic powers have names that start with the French word "Clair," which means clear. Many psychics combine many of these abilities. There are four central claims:

- Clairvoyance – clear seeing
- Clairaudience – clear hearing
- Clairsentience – precise feeling/sensing
- Claircognizance – clear knowing

The less common claims are:

- Clairtangency – explicit touching (also called psychometry)
- Clairgustance – clear tasting
- Clairalience – clear smelling

## THE DIFFERENCE BETWEEN A PSYCHIC AND A MEDIUM

The emphasis is on communicating with spirits in the afterlife or another dimension, regardless of whether a person calls themselves a psychic medium, spiritual medium, intuitive medium, or any other title in a similar vein.

Even though some persons are called "psychic mediums," there is a big difference between a psychic and a medium. A medium is a psychic, although not every psychic is one. This is a crucial distinction because many people conflate the two, so it's an excellent place to start.

By detecting or feeling aspects of someone or something's past, present, or future, psychics can tune into that person or thing's energy. Defined, to acquire information for the individual being read, psychics rely on their fundamental intuition and psychic ability. More is done in the case of mediums.

Medium taps into the spirit energy surrounding a person to use their psychic or intuitive ability to view the individual's past, present, and future happenings. It suggests that the existence of non-physical energy external to oneself is necessary for the information meaningful to the medium.

Another significant contrast is that while mediums focus on past and present difficulties, psychic readings frequently focus on forecasting future events. While forecasting the future can be helpful at times, it also reduces people's agency. Never forget that you do have control over how your future plays out.

Despite what any psychic or medium may "see" for you in the future, it's crucial to remember that you were endowed with free will when you entered this planet, and you may at any time change your course and lead the life you desire by altering your thoughts and deeds.

Psychic knowledge frequently provides insight into what might occur based on the path you are currently taking, and it should only be used as a guide to assist you in making the best decisions for yourself.

## TYPES OF PSYCHIC ABILITIES

Psychic skills come in a variety of forms. Certain people can predict the future. Others receive communications from the afterlife. Some people may be able to read others' thoughts or detect "auras" that reveal how they are feeling.

- Precognition: Precognition is the capacity to foresee events. Some people receive clear instructions, such as "You're going to board a bus and meet a dark-haired man." Others may receive vaguer messages, such as, "Someone close to you is going to experience some significant changes in their family."
- Intuition: The capacity to intuitively *know* things without being instructed is known as intuitiveness. Since this talent offers them an advantage when reading cards for clients, many intuitive make outstanding Tarot card readers. Some people refer to this as clairsentience.
- Clairvoyance: The clairvoyant can perceive things that are concealed. The use of divination in distant viewing has occasionally been attributed to helping people discover missing children and lost items.
- Empathy: Understanding another person's thoughts, feelings, and emotions is known as empathy. Empaths frequently need to learn how to protect themselves from other people's energies to avoid becoming depleted and worn out.

- Medium: A medium is a person who receives communications from the afterlife. This can appear in various ways: some mediums receive messages from actual spirits by sight and sound, while others do so through dreams or visions. Some people can "channel" the spirit, allowing them to write or speak through them.

## 7 WAYS TO DEVELOPING YOUR PSYCHIC SKILLS

Developing your psychic abilities can be a practice in many different kinds of self-awareness if everyone has some latent psychic ability. Meditation is one of the best techniques to develop psychic skills since it enables us to access our subconscious and everything that resides there.

1. **Achieve Deliberate Clarity.**

While it may seem complicated, this is not. You must learn to be constantly aware of your surroundings to reach purposeful clarity. Keep an eye out for changes in the wind, changes in the light and shadows, and people coming and going from a space. Take mental notes on everything; this will aid you in determining which messages are genuine and which are the product of your wishful thinking or imagination in the future.

2. **Pay Attention To What Is Said And What Is Not.**

People frequently say one thing while meaning something completely different. When your friend replies, "I'm fine," when you ask how she is, "Fine. They are good kids," but her marriage is not mentioned, so possibly there is a reason. Recognize that communication can still occur through omission.

3. **Regularly meditate.**

Meditating is one of the best strategies to grow your intuition. You open a channel for messages to pass through, allowing your mind to stray into the depths of the subconscious.

4. **Learn To Trust Your Gut.**

Have you ever had the feeling that something is off? Have you ever been forced to turn left when you usually would have turned right at a stop sign? Be mindful of things like these. Frequently, those intuitive messages have a purpose.

5. **Take Notes On Everything.**

Have you ever dreamed about a specific person or circumstance? Have you had a feeling that something significant is about to occur? Keep a journal so you can track these sensory messages. You can revisit them later to determine whether there was any truth. Keep in mind that occasionally we receive messages but cannot verify their integrity.

Remember that occasionally we receive communications and are unable to determine whether they were accurate or not since there is simply no way to do so.

6. **Test Yourself.**

Try to verify your suspicions if you have any. Try to figure out, for instance, what music your best friend was listening to in the car when she was on her way to meet you for coffee. Then inquire of her when she shows up. How well did you do? Try to imagine who might be calling before you pick up the phone, and check the Caller ID if your phone rings. When you pick up the phone, check to see if you were right. You can enhance your natural abilities by engaging in easy workouts like these.

7. **Practice Makes Perfect.**

Okay, so it won't make you flawless, but it will help you learn new abilities. Learn about many types of divination, then practice using the one that speaks to you until you are confident in the integrity of the signals you receive.

## WHAT IS INTUITION?

Your intuition, also known as your inner direction, is a form of instinctual understanding that does not depend on or use rational mental processes. As some have described, it is a different level of awareness, an alternative source of knowledge, or an inner voice. To varying degrees, we all have this mechanism and the ability to improve it further.

Why is it vital to cultivate your intuition? From Immanuel Kant to Carl Jung, renowned thinkers have underlined the value of intuition and its significant influence on their personal and professional lives. They described it as "a priori" knowledge, which refers to the justification that is made without consideration of prior knowledge, and as a crucial tool for us as humans.

Jung listed the four primary mental processes as intuition, sensation, thought, and feeling. We can reach our full potential by striking a balance among these internal processes. Intuition, according to him, is another way to express one's creativity, particularly in literature, music, and the visual arts. However, it is not just used in those fields.

Many people have amassed enormous wealth and reputations due to their ability to make crucial decisions by trusting their intuition or gut instincts in science, business, and entrepreneurship.

Your connection to your subconscious mind eventually comes through intuition. It is the method by which the unconscious speaks to the conscious mind. It is such a fantastic source of ingenuity, knowledge, and understanding because of this. It goes beyond the limits of logic.

## HOW TO DEVELOP YOUR INTUITION SKILLS

Stop thinking and pay attention. Spend some time in stillness each day. Use any breathing or meditation technique you like to practice to calm your mind. Let go of the desire to think, analyze, and attempt to understand everything. Listen and remain open. Allow your thoughts to wander, and be receptive to the suggestions and answers that come to you. You are connected to deeper information when you pay attention to your intuition. Typically, it uses symbols, feelings, and emotions to communicate.

Learn to believe in your gut instincts and intuition. Likely, something isn't correct if it doesn't feel right. What is correct for one individual could be entirely incorrect for you. How often have you experienced that unsettling sensation in your gut that compels you to act in a certain way or not?

You possibly avoided a car accident due to listening to it, or you were in the right location at the right time to land that fantastic job or meet that special someone. Learn to trust your intuition because it is your inner guide. Trusting it could initially feel a little terrifying, but give it time to grow.

Remain alert and pay attention. To hone your intuitive abilities, you must be aware of your environment. Your subconscious mind has more information to work with when you need to make a big decision the more data and information you take in from your environment.

The more information you have available, the better the solution will be since your intuition utilizes the data obtained by your conscious mind. Similar to how experience-based wisdom and understanding improve the caliber of information offered by your intuition. Remember that your intuition is how the subconscious mind conveys information to the conscious mind.

Other varieties of intuition manifest as inspiration or fleeting thoughts. The secret is to pay attention. You will encounter more of them if you pay more attention. You know how it feels if you've ever disregarded your gut feeling and then dealt with adverse outcomes. Pay attention to the minute tips and clues you receive to avoid similar errors. While you're sleeping, use your subconscious.

Think about the problems and questions you couldn't resolve during the day before you go to bed. Consider and investigate several options. This will spark your creativity and encourage your subconscious to develop ideas as you sleep.

If you wake up in the middle of the night with a beautiful idea, make sure you have a pen and paper handy to write it down. You can gain access to emotions, thoughts, and ideas that you might not usually be aware of through journaling or keeping a journal. This technique is fantastic for revealing inner messages, insights, or untapped information regarding a circumstance or issue that must resolve.

## THE BENEFITS OF DEVELOPING INTUITION
- Reduces stress by assisting with better problem-solving and identification.
- Release your imagination and creativity.
- Connects you to your subconscious, which enables you to find hidden.
- Realities about you and your life's circumstances.

- Being in tune with your intuition helps you avoid accumulating unfavorable feelings and thoughts.
- Integrates left and suitable brain activities, providing a more thorough understanding of problems.
- Aids in improving and integrating your decision-making enhances emotional, mental, and physical wellbeing.

The process of developing intuition is similar to learning a new skill. The more you practice something, the better you become at it. Start cautiously and build up your intuitive muscles over time, similar to how you would with any new exercise or routine to which you are not accustomed.

Awareness of subtle energy that goes beyond the senses and expands your perception beyond the boundaries of physical time and space is what it means to develop intuition. As your intuition grows, you combine all of your senses with your conscious and subconscious minds to gain a well-rounded understanding of the universe. So, you may consider uniting your body, mind, and soul when developing your intuition.

## HOW TO DISTINGUISH INTUITION FROM IMAGINATION

If there were a method for determining your intuition and imagination, that would be terrific, but I don't believe there is. There are a few considerations to bear when attempting to discern between intuition and other things.

1. Practice and Feedback

Because they receive more input than anyone else, practicing psychics find it simpler to discriminate between intuition and fantasy. They receive confirmation of, or denial of, their psychic perceptions. Do what practicing psychics do to feel confident in their abilities: (1) practice as often as you can, and (2) seek feedback on your intuitive insights. This practice will help you build confidence and clearly distinguish between your intuition and your imagination.

To gain feedback on your intuitive insights, you don't need to provide professional readings for others; you only need to put them into practice in your own life and observe the effects. For instance, if a voice inside prompts you to act, pay attention to how that voice sounds and feels before observing the outcomes. The hitch is that you must learn to be detached to perceive the outcomes of using your intuition.

Many people act on their intuitive ideas, but if they aren't immediately validated, they become disappointed. Avoid approaching the growth of your intuition in that way. Don't worry if the information is not instantly proven to be accurate. Even when you're wrong, you learn something because every time you use your intuition and observe the outcomes, you get closer to understanding how your particular intuitive voice or nudge feels. However, to advance in your psychological growth, you must be prepared to acknowledge your errors. Even practicing psychics occasionally make mistakes, as do all emerging psychics.

2. Pay Attention To The Feeling That Comes With Your Intuition.

After some practice, you may identify every intuitive information's distinctive energy signature. You can recognize the sensation that comes with genuine intuition more readily as you practice receiving it. The next time you receive intuitive guidance, consider how it makes you feel.

You may also receive feedback on how accurate your intuition is through your emotions and obtaining gut sensations about things. You will know if the information is incorrect or if it "feels" wrong or off to you (and it's not a good feeling). You feel good and inspired when I deliver facts you know are true. If any information is inaccurate, it might make you feel uncomfortable.

3. While Intuition Is Passive, Imagination Is Active.

The fact that imagination is an active process, whereas intuition is a passive one, is another significant distinction between the two. When you imagine anything, your imagination is actively working. At the same time, intuition comes when you make yourself a conduit and quiet your thoughts (through meditation). You stop being active. Work on controlling your thoughts if you're concerned that they're giving you information when you'd want your intuition to have more of a say.

Stop what you're doing and calm your thoughts if you have insight but are unsure if it came from your intuition or your mind being overly active. To do this, focus on your breath for a minute or two. This is a great way to distract your mind so you can listen to your intuition. It would help if you made larger spaces between your conscious ideas to hear your actual intuitive voice since intuition emerges there.

When it's not your intuition:

- You feel awful, discouraged, or denigrated by the voice speaking to you.
- When the speaker conveys information to you that sounds hazy or perplexing. Intuitive information should fit easily into your conceptual framework and be brief and straightforward. It's probably preferable to throw something away if it asks you to put faith in its correctness yet makes no sense to you.
- Obey the voice when it commands you to. Usually, intuition is free of agendas. It will provide insight from your Higher Self and Guides, but since you have free will, you are not obligated to follow it or consider the advice.

If in doubt, don't worry; if you don't understand an intuitive message the first time, it typically repeats itself.

As you can see, the human brain has so many different components that it can get confusing: intuition, ego, subconscious, guides, higher self, etc. A couple of these topics have already been covered in introductory courses. In the following section, we'll discuss your higher self, from whence some of your counsel and communications come. In the following section, we'll discuss your higher self, from whence some of your counsel and communications come.

## THE DIFFERENCE BETWEEN PSYCHIC ABILITY AND INTUITION

Although "intuition" and "psychic" are sometimes used interchangeably, there is a distinction between them, despite how close they are related. So, what exactly is intuition? How does it differ from psychic ability, and how?

A more generalized feeling or a hunch, intuition is a tug in a specific direction that is frequently impossible to explain rationally. This is referred to as "gut instinct," "simply a feeling," or "just a hunch." Consider your initial reaction when meeting someone new and if you should believe it or not.

Intuition can also be thought of as your inner voice, higher self, or just the part of you that is connected to something more than yourself. Its voice is audible when you're still and quiet enough.

Psychic knowledge is more in-depth intuitive knowledge. It strengthens your intuition and offers more insight and clarity, typically with more (detailed) information. Someone might communicate this knowledge with clairvoyance, clairaudience, clairsentience, claircognizance, or clairgustance.

For instance, when you meet someone new and "see" a picture or "know" a particular piece about their life, this information is more psychic than intuitive.

## ARE YOU PSYCHIC OR INTUITIVE?

Yes! Everyone has intuition and the potential to enhance their psychic skill. By doing this, you may live the life put you on this earth to live and navigate life much more quickly. Opening Pandora's box to begin this trip can be intimidating, but the payoff is well worth it. Although it's unnecessary, modern mainstream society perceives the issues as frightening or "out there."

You must not only learn to recognize your intuition but also come to trust it if you want to use it successfully in daily life. It's rare for intuitive or even psychic knowledge to make sense immediately. Sometimes it takes a few days, weeks, or months for the knowledge to click or to come together. Although it can be pretty annoying, the wait is always worthwhile. Focus first on your intuition, those hunches or guesses you have about your life, and then begin to use your psychic talent to gather more specific information.

## EXERCISES FOR CALMING AND QUIETING THE MIND

Practice is essential to master the ability to silence the constant chatter in the brain. Learning to be proficient in getting knowledgeable about the internal process. You will get so used to how to silence the noise that you won't even need to perform the exercise. You will be able to do it on command.

1. Walking on Rocks

Ancient indigenous practice is among the quickest ways to calm the mind. However, because it calls for some agility, it might be risky. On top of a field of huge rocks, in this exercise, you progress from walking at a steady pace to a gradual run (when you're ready).

As you move forward on the rocks, you'll see that your mind will compel you to put each step individually. Until it gets sick of telling you, your mind will keep doing this for a while. You will realize that taking the right moves doesn't require your mind to mentally direct you after you reach a particular stage of mental exhaustion. When you reach this stage, the mind begins to give up trying to direct every action you do.

The mental merry-go-round finally comes to an end at this point. Please spend some time staying here and getting comfortable with it. Repeat this procedure frequently to become comfortable with the breaking point. You will get accustomed to the space inside of yourself where you can live without the mental merry-go-round as you get more comfortable with this state. Try this on a series of little rocks on the beach instead of high rocks so you won't damage yourself.

2. Meditation

Your ability to meditate will improve after you learn to stop the mental merry-go-round. There are many meditation techniques, and you must follow their specific rules to get the best effects. Your ability to contact the heart becomes easier when you calm your thoughts and emotions during meditation. You will enter the higher frequencies more deeply as a result. Communication with the higher self becomes most straightforward in this location.

The messages that suddenly settle into your awareness that inspire, heal, inform, or lovingly warn you are typically coming from the higher self or your higher intelligence as you reach this open and vulnerable condition (when everything else is still and quiet inside of you).

## ADDITIONAL MEDITATION TECHNIQUES

### Meditative Journeys

While visualization has no precise goal, meditative journeys sometimes have one. You can conjure up a specific sequence of images to connect with your higher self, visit an island where you'll meet your animal or spirit guide, or go to your spiritual haven to review documents in your Akashic records. Only your imagination's limits can limit the seemingly limitless possibilities.

### Visualization CDs

If visualizing is difficult, look for CDs that will walk you through the process. These are fantastic techniques to teach you how to relax or utilize them for things like letting go, curing physical ills, communicating with your guides, etc.

Remembering that what works for one person may not work for another is the most crucial aspect of meditation. Since everyone is unique, many approaches can help people discover the one that suits them the best.

## 4 GUIDELINES FOR MAKING MEDITATION EASY

1. Put Your Expectations Aside.

When you meditate, let go of whatever expectations you may have and sincerely accept whatever transpires. Whatever may appear to be happening, if you are adhering to the fundamentals of your practice, something beneficial happens every time you meditate.

Even if it doesn't appear to be, meditation is causing beneficial changes in your innermost being. Soon, you will notice these inner changes coming to pass in your outer existence.

2. Thoughts Are Not Your Enemy.

How can inner peace exist if you are constantly at war with your thoughts? One of the ways that tension is released during meditation is through thoughts, which are a natural byproduct of the mind. Occasionally, the thoughts will stop on their own. The outcome of just following your method's instructions in their entirety. But as you continue to meditate, you'll learn that you may feel profound relaxation and inner calm even when your mind is racing.

3. Make A Calm Attempt To Meditate.

Trying your brains out and drifting off are two extremes of relaxed effort, also known as "medium effort," which is in the middle of the two.

4. **Meditating Becomes Easier And More Joyful The Less Worried You Are About What You Experience.**

Overvaluing something usually makes it more challenging to achieve.

## PSYCHIC DEVELOPMENT

Our hearts typically get complex when we dwell apart from nature. Disregarding for evolving living things quickly turns into disdain for other animals and people. Our typical perceptions and perceived capacities are not sufficiently exercised and developed for those who live in huge communities, big towns, and cities nowadays since we are not as near to the natural environment. This indicates that we only utilize a tiny portion of our sensory apparatus. An increase in awareness happens as you hone your ordinary senses.

We must first awaken the five senses of touch, taste, smell, sight, and hearing to activate the sixth or psychic sense. The first step to activating the inner psychic senses is improving the use of the ordinary senses. And we can all put this into practice.

### EXERCISE: Awakening Your Senses

1. Find a quiet spot in nature, preferably among the trees. This might be close to a river or stream or on a hillside. There should be a park where you may be surrounded by beautiful nature, even in our modern cities.
2. Locate a tree with room around it and a substantial trunk. The tree trunk should support your back as you sit comfortably upright and face the sun.
3. Now, focus on each of your senses for a few minutes in turn:

*Sight:* Observe how the sun moves as it catches the tree leaves, and take note of the vibrant variations of color. Investigate the hues of the plants' blooms and bushes and their crinkly leaves. Feel the tree trunks' texture and the arms and fingers of the branches during the winter. Keep an eye on the clouds as they pass through the sky.

Think about how the grass is wavy where your feet are. Keep an eye out for nearby animals, birds, or insects as they move. Just focus solely on gazing and observing.

*Hearing:* Now, turn all of your focus to listening. Pay attention to the noises of nature. Listen for the wind's rustling in the trees, the birds' melodies, the rustling of the small moving creatures, and the hum of the insects.

*Touch:* Pay attention to your sense of touch. Feel the sun's warmth on your face; the wind's caressing your hair, or the rain's kiss on your lips. Remove your shoes and allow the bouncy, soft ground to embrace your feet. Feel yourself to be a part of nature.

*Smell:* Smell the earthiness of the soil beneath your feet, the flowers' lovely aroma, and the grass's scent. Focus entirely on your sense of smell and take in the natural fragrances.

*Taste:* Taste and smell are related senses. Open your mouth and let your tongue experience the flavor of each aroma in the air. Your taste buds may begin to respond with saliva due to the freshness. You will likely never have experienced such a close connection with nature if you spend at least five minutes using all of your senses in this manner.

Even if you spend 30 minutes a week in this peace, you will soon notice your senses opening, your creativity and intuition becoming more acute, and your knowledge of the spirit of things growing. You will eventually learn to hear nature's sounds concealed from view as you do this technique.

## THE BENEFITS OF DEVELOPING PSYCHIC ABILITIES

If you have psychic talents, you can:

- Spend less money, time, and effort on the little things.
- Avoid taking routes that will lead to nowhere for you.

- Understand the "why" behind the occurrences, people, and circumstances in your life by looking beyond your rationality.
- Make decisions without second-guessing yourself.
- Before you try something, you should know what will make you happy and fulfilled and what won't.
- You want to understand how to read auras and discover the true nature of others.

Most people aren't accustomed to following their intuition or paying attention to their spirit. Western culture does not encourage or promote listening to something so ethereal, especially something that comes from within, due to its emphasis on science. Instead, our logical, scientific culture encourages us to obtain information and direction from various outside sources before weighing it. That strategy is logical.

Conversely, intuitive guidance is frequently seen as an unreliable source of knowledge because it is illogical and does not compile data from numerous sources. As a result, we frequently question or doubt our intuitive direction and fail to share it with others. After all, when people ask us to defend our opinions or provide evidence for our assertions, all we have to say is that we "just know it" or that our gut is telling us. Most people prefer to hear specific facts that are supported by proof. Thus, we frequently learn to refrain from speaking when we believe we are in the know (without knowing how we know).

By developing your psychic awareness and intuition, you can become more spirit-driven rather than being controlled by ego or fear. This fosters fortitude, development, and confidence in the cosmos. Because of this, psychedelic, personal, and spiritual development are inextricably linked. As your psychic powers advance, so do you personally and spiritually. However, I assume you already know those facts.

## WORK THAT A PSYCHIC CAN DO:
- Tarot and oracle readings
- Psychic consultations (phone or in person, or by email)
- Other divination techniques include reading tea leaves, crystals for lithomancy, etc.
- Using your abilities to help you identify any potential trouble spots on your client (human or animal)
- Telepathic communication with animals
- Helping people make decisions about their present and future through psychic counseling

## CONCLUSION
As you can see, psychic abilities and intuition developing psychic talents require hard work and effort on your behalf. Recall that while it is not your obligation to assess your development, you are the only one who can determine how far you have come.

# CHAPTER 07
# ASTRAL PROJECTION/OUT-OF-BODY EXPERIENCE

## INTRODUCTION

After all, astral travel is like vacationing without ever leaving your house. Simply leaving your body is all that's required. Astral projection could be a conscious experience, contrary to the experience some people describe once they are near death.

According to Jane Aspell, a cognitive researcher at Anglia Ruskin University in England, "an experience (OBE) could be a transient experience some people have. While conscious, they seem to become separated from their body, float above the body, and appear back at that body from an elevated location. Astral projection (AP) may be a purposeful OBE that typically involves the perception of the self appearing to go away from the body and travel, sometimes to distant lands or maybe other planets."

Western esotericism uses astral projection to seek advice from an intentional OBE. in a very nutshell; it refers to the temporary separation of the human consciousness or soul, often called the "astral body," from the build. The astral body is claimed to be capable of various miraculous feats because it's not tied to human flesh and blood.

Robert Rubin, a card expert at Mysterium Philippines, writes: "Astral projection is when a human's consciousness is projected outside his body into what we call the astral world. When consciousness is transported to the heavenly variety of this realm, astral projection occurs (i.e., the heavenly representation of Katipunan, Manila, point of entry, etc.).

Most of the time, it resembles its real-world equivalents somehow." In other words, you may be ready to travel anywhere you prefer if you'll harness the ability of this event. It'd help within the middle of one more order for a stay-at-home parent.

## WHAT IS ASTRAL PROJECTION/OBE?

The definition of "out-of-body experience" is somewhat imprecise. It does not describe any situation where one feels divorced from the experiential nature of the body. Astral projection and the out-of-body experience (OBE for short) are similar events.

The terms "astral projection" or "astral travel" deal with the feeling of escaping the boundaries of body consciousness, allowing one to travel inter-dimensionally. However, they're less frequently employed when the phenomenon is researched from a physics standpoint. Variable levels of awareness may be present during both astral projection and out-of-body experiences.

Every time we sleep, our consciousness is projected while our bodies are in states aside from the regular waking ones. This happens spontaneously and typically without our awareness. To be explicit, "OBE" will subsequently be used interchangeably with "astral projection."

Although "OBE" is also easier to mention and undoubtedly less contentious, it appears that "astral projection" is the most accurate term to use when about the intentional projection of consciousness, with "OBE" tending to be related to skepticism among people who practice the phenomenon for private purposes.

## HISTORY OF ASTRAL PROJECTION

The practice of astral projection isn't new. It's existed for an extended time and is present in various cultures and religions. However, the 1800s saw the major recent comeback of it within the West.

Dr. Susan Blackmore, a writer, psychologist, and professor at the University of Plymouth in England, writes: "The theory stems from a 19th-century mystical doctrine called theosophy which states that humans have seven bodies, from very cheap physical to the best spiritual and mental bodies. "The astral body is claimed to be ready to roam within the astral worlds and break away the physical."

Helena Blavatsky, a Russian immigrant who helped start the Theosophical Society in New York in 1875, is credited with popularizing theosophy within us. She was raised in a wealthy household and traveled much, absorbing many spiritual views as she went and eventually transforming them through theosophy. Blavatsky's theories concerned the celestial body's capacity to travel beyond the boundaries of physicality and roam unrestrainedly to other locations.

Laura Brown, the creator of Intuitive Alchemy and a self-described "spiritual life stylist," writes in an email, "I have found that almost all people explore astral projection as a component of their spiritual development." Astral projection further solidifies the concept that we are over just our physical Earthly bodies as we delve deeper into our spiritual investigation. Not to add, that feeling like you've left your body and are weightless is quite bizarre.

According to Rubin, people typically engage during this activity "to comprehend the more profound importance of what exists beyond this domain or to jaunt locations their bodies cannot reach. To communicate with, engage with, and occasionally even talk with non-physical beings, including gods, spirits, and the recently deceased."

## HOW DOES IT WORK?
Understanding OBE in terms of dimensions and how it functions requires a solid understanding of some topics.

**Physical Plane:** The physical plane is the dimension—the terms "plane" and "dimension" are interchangeable—in which you're located while you read this. It's tight and restrictive in terms of energy, and when one is constrained by it, they're compelled to interact with their environment solely through their five physical senses.

**The Real-Time Zone:** The real-time zone is the next dimension closest to the physical. This possesses the characteristics of dimensions outside physical reality (a direct and accurate reflection of physical reality) and specific characteristics (fluid, nonphysical realities). Most projectors start within the real-time zone when commencing to project for the primary time.

**Mental Plane:** The mental plane, which is directly above or above this level in terms of the same old progression, is where dreaming, both lucid and non-lucid, takes place. Compared to the physical plane or real-time zone, this environment is significantly more pliable and at risk of the influence of the perceiver.

**Astral Plane:** Although there are variations, the mental plane is usually seen as a component of the astral plane, a more comprehensive dimensional description. Because there seem to be many astral planes, they're frequently defined in higher and lower vibrations.

Therefore, the full order of vibration or frequency is as follows:

4+) Astral Plane(s)

3) Mental Plane

2) Real-Time Zone

1) Physical Plane
   - These are the foremost critical dimensions to remember, while there are numerous tales of realms of experience above or aside from the broad category of "astral planes." Before having practical experience with the planes, this is often still useful for understanding how everything functions.

All of this may be extremely helpful, but the sole reason to truly understand what it means on an expert level is to interact in astral projection and see the planes yourself. Though they're only worlds of perception across which awareness can move without being restricted to the physique, they're likely to think about them as rigid physical structures. Since each of those dimensions has distinct qualities, I can say more about them.

The flesh is consistently fused with a nonphysical element, or energy body, while the person is awake. A component of the energy during this energy body separates from the shape during the projection phase. This procedure takes place while we sleep and is unnoticed by us. One can effectively steer their awareness through the dimensional planes without being constrained by physical ways of perception if they learn to transfer their consciousness into that external energy duplicate.

The environment changes during an astral projection from being viewed and processed for knowledge to being perceived as a direct understanding; it also becomes less spatial, fluid, objective, and subjective. Working toward releasing the constraints of physical experience united is at home with it while awake, traveling, speaking, and commencing to think about conscious interactions in terms of telepathic, telekinetic, and teleportation-oriented experience, is advantageous.

These are essential things to consider beforehand. Still, the experience will probably remove all the barriers without you putting in much additional effort. But at absolutely the least, it is usually a simple idea to acknowledge that anything is conceivable so that when something unexpected happens, it won't come as a complete surprise and may be examined to one's benefit.

## HOW TO PERFORM ASTRAL PROJECTION

## Part 1: Preparing

*1. Learn About Astral Projection.*
Before you get ready for it and have a clearer idea of what to expect, it's best to have a fundamental understanding of astral projection. Consider reading about or viewing astral projection experiences from others.

*2. Start In The Morning.*
Start your astral projection exercises in the early morning while you're still sleepy rather than right before you go to bed at night. Some claim that daybreak is the best time to achieve the required level of relaxation and increased awareness. However, astral travel is possible at any time. Thus, there are no strict limitations. When we feel empowered to accomplish it, we simply astral travel according to our unique preferences.

*3. Create The Right Atmosphere.*
It would help if you practiced astral projection in an area of your home where you feel entirely at ease because it involves a state of deep relaxation. Relax your mind and body by lying on your couch or bed.

- Astral projection is more straightforward to accomplish on oneself than with a partner present. A room other than your bedroom should be your choice if you typically share a bed with a spouse. You should do it while no one else is there and ensure that nobody will enter the room while you are on a heavenly flight.
- Eliminate distracting noises by drawing the blinds or drapes. The level of relaxation you need to reach could be disturbed by any interruption.

*4. Lay Down And Relax.*
In the room of your choice, lie on your back. Try to block out any distracting ideas by closing your eyes. Pay attention to how your body feels. The aim is to reach a state of total relaxation of the body and mind.

- Your muscles should be flexed and then relaxed. Work your way up your body, starting at your toes and moving toward your head. When you're through, make sure every muscle is relaxed.
- Please take a few long breaths and let them all out. Relax; don't keep tension in your shoulders and chest.
- Pay attention to your breathing. Don't let your mind wander to worries of the outer world or become fixated on the notion that your soul might leave your body just yet. Let yourself relax.

- A quartz crystal can help you prepare by raising and accelerating your vibrations. Close your eyes, take a deep breath, and gently place the crystal on your third eye, just above the middle of your brows. Feel the vibrations and your mind clearing; if you choose, picture a golden, white, purple, or another color of light. When meditating and astral traveling, you can hold the crystal in your hand or place it on your chest or abdomen. Due to the crystal's strong vibrations—negative energies have lower vibrations—which will strengthen and shield you.

## Part 2: Soul Extraction from the Body

*1. Reach A Hypnotic State.*

The hypnagogic state is the usual name for this hypnotic state. Allow your body and mind to go close to falling asleep, but avoid falling asleep altogether. Astral projection can only occur while a person is in a hypnotic state, which is the border between awake and asleep. Use the following strategy to get to this state:

- Try focusing on a body part, such as your hand, foot, or a single toe, while keeping your eyes closed.
- It would help if you concentrated on the body part until you could picture it while your eyes were closed. Focus on your goal until all other thoughts go.
- Your body part can be flexed mentally, but not physically. Imagine your fingers or toes tightening and loosening, or both, until they appear to be physically moving.
- Increase your awareness of your entire body. You can only move your head, arms, and legs with your mind. Maintain your concentration until you can move your entire body using only your mind.

*2. Enter Into A State Of Vibration.*

Many claim to experience waves of vibrations with various frequencies when the spirit gets ready to exit the body. Instead of being terrified of the vibrations because fear can make you lose your meditative state, give in to the vibrations as your soul gets ready to go from your body.

*3. Use Your Mind To Move Your Soul From Your body.*

Visualize the space where you are lying in your head. Stand up by mentally moving your body. Take a look around you. Get out of bed, move across the room, and then turn to face the body still on the bed.

- If you have the impression that you are looking at your body from another room and that your conscious self is now distinct from your body, your OBE was effective.
- Some people need a lot of work to reach this level, while for others, it comes as naturally as breathing. In either case, anyone can do it if they are motivated and diligent. If you have problems separating your soul from your body, start by simply separating one hand or one leg. Practice more until you can move around the room.

*4. Return To Your Body.*

Your soul will always be joined to your body by unobservable energy known as a "silver cord." which will compel your soul to return to your body.

Reenter your body now. Go back inside your body. Allow yourself to restore consciousness by moving your fingers and toes physically, not just mentally.

## Part 3: Exploring The Astral Plane

*1. Confirm That Your Soul Is Being Projected From Your Body.*

You will want to verify that you were on two different levels once you have mastered the technique of projecting your soul from your body in the same space.

- Don't stare at your body when you turn around the following time you practice astral projection. Instead, step out of the room and into another one of the house's rooms.
- Look at something in the other room that you had never previously noticed in the physical sense. Make a mental note of its color, form, and size, paying attention to as many characteristics as possible.

- Go back to your body. Enter the space you previously imagined yourself in physically. Go to the object you looked at during your astral flight. Can you verify the specifics you took note of when you mentally examined the item?

*2. Explore Further.*

Continue to visit places becoming less and less recognizable to you during consecutive astral projection sessions. Every time, take note of particulars you hadn't noticed previously. Verify the information in person each time after the session. After a few excursions, you will have enough confidence in your ability to make astral projections to venture into wholly uncharted territory.

*3. Return To Your Body.*

Some claim that astral projection is risky, particularly when one gains enough experience to explore strange regions; however, this is not always the case. Because they don't employ enough protection, such individuals don't comprehend or fear it. As long as you request protection in your way, the experience will be positive.

It's helpful to picture yourself submerged in a bright, white light before beginning an astral projection. This will shield you from other thoughts or negative energy forms; visualize it as a cloud around or residing inside you.

- There is a lot to learn, but remember that nothing wrong will ever happen to you unless you let it. Some people spend much time outside their bodies during OBEs, which is supposed to weaken the silver chord. However, it cannot weaken the silver cord. It would help if you weren't concerned about astral travel since it is natural, strong, and healing. It is pure energy and cannot be deleted or removed; it can only shift from one place to another or from one form to another.
- Although the silver link cannot be severed, it is believed that if you spend too much time outside your body, your soul may take longer to return. However, because your spirit and body are so inextricably linked, the soul will return on its own accord when the time is perfect.
- Some contend that devils may enter the body when the soul is being projected. If you are concerned that this might occur, shield your body by praying for the space before you project. Since you already have requested light protection and it is simply a rumor, nothing awful will happen.
- Additionally, your soul can communicate with other astral projections. Try it out with a friend who has had the same amount of practice as you. Some people find astral sex to be mind-blowing. But always remember to come back to your body.
- While astral traveling, it is possible to heal other people; this is a particularly potent type of distance healing. Think about the sick person, perhaps in bed. Time and distance vanish in the astral world, so it doesn't matter if they're not actually in bed when you're doing it. You can ask during astral projection whenever and however you like for protection, healing, and direction from anyone you pray to and envision light.
If you're ready, place one hand on their forehead and the other on their abdomen and pour the light into them while maintaining the whitest, purest light you can manage into your palms. Your motives must be sincere, and you must only feel love for them. Even though you didn't tell them you were the cause of anything fantastic happening to them, people occasionally report back to you that it did. Have fun on your astral travels!

## WHAT IS POSSIBLE ONCE A PROJECTION IS ACHIEVED?

It is feasible to perceive physical, immediate occurrences in real-time if they are projected into that time zone. One can fly across a representation of the physical dimension, pass through walls and doors, soar at incredible speeds, or instantly teleport themselves to another location. With the proper purpose, any time and place can be visited or experienced in the astral since there is an immediate quality to space and time.

While in a condition of conscious projection, one can locate and communicate with other astral creatures and projectors. Just like humans, animals also project. But in addition to people and animals, there are spiritual beings that live in the lower and higher dimensions but not the physical ones. As a result, some of them are only fully exposed to us during altered states of awareness.

Finding one's "spirit guide," a spiritual being that functions to lead and aid a person in their growth and development, is a typical occurrence. A person, animal, plant, or anything else that is thought of as serving in a teaching or supportive capacity can serve as this guide.

It is possible to gain access to what is known as the "Akashic Records." This is like a vast library where you may find any piece of information about human history or a hint about what the future might hold. This supports the idea that can view projection as restoring the link between personal consciousness and the collective unconscious. All of human history—past, present, and future—is preserved in the form of these "records," accessible to everyone.

One's energy body vibrates during astral projection at what many would refer to as a higher frequency. As a result, cerebral energy and development grow, which increases the possibility of many goals. With more energy accessible to move through the energy body as a result of this increase in energy, the chakras are kept more balanced and in tune, and this condition of stability is reflected in and manifests in the person's emotional and physical health. By focusing specific energies in particular ways, healing is made possible thanks to this understanding.

Our humanity depends on a more excellent investigation of the elements of reality. By comprehending these more subtle facets of ourselves, we may put a complete picture together and can make better decisions in all areas of experience.

## Other Things

- The ideal setting for practicing complete relaxation and projection is warm and inviting.
- Darkness is advantageous. A shirt sleeve to cover one's eyes can be helpful when training while lying down during the day.
- During all stages of the projection sequence, breathing through the diaphragm and deep belly breaths are the most beneficial for both creating energy to use while exiting and helping to relax the body.
- When this is not possible, white noise or soft nature sounds can employ streams or rain showers to block out outside distractions. Little to no noise is beneficial for focus. However, one should remember that it is better to avoid relying on these stimuli for adequate focus. Thus, they shouldn't be employed in every situation if a high degree of control is required.
- Many people concur that the widespread sensation of falling into one's bed as one awakes can be explained by a sudden reintegration of the energy body with the physical body. As that happens, a brief moment of awareness in the energy body causes the incredible experience one has right after awakening.
This explanation of the falling sensation seems pretty convincing given that the energy body most frequently reintegrates from above and that the most frequent spontaneous OBE experience occurs when one senses that they are floating above their body while physically asleep.
- To build up energy that can subsequently use to vivify the projection process and facilitate out-of-body travel. It can be beneficial to work on activating the energy body through energy training.
- Fear can manifest enormous power when one eventually experiences the dissolution of awareness from the physical body, or it can play a role early on in the theoretical study of astral projection. This limit can be surpassed with perseverance and effort, but whether or not to do so is undoubtedly a matter of personal preference. In the face of situations like these, fear is quite prevalent.
There is a connection known as the "silver cord" that exists. At the same time, a person is physically alive and causes the anxiety of the connection between consciousness and the body being severed. The idea that astral projection is risky because it causes a detachment from the physical body is refuted by the fact that this is constantly present but rarely observable, even in the astral, unless it is specifically sought out.
Many people also think that just a portion of one's awareness leaves the body with energy. It is common to have brief experiences where one is simultaneously conscious of their physical and energy bodies, collecting information from both points of view. This experience adds weight to the claim that awareness does not seem entirely separate from the physical body while in this state, even if it can be overwhelming and shouldn't be discussed in detail.
- All that is required is a focus on and purpose to reintegrate with the physical body, return/reintegrate with it, and either wake up or enter unconscious slumber.

## BENEFITS OF OBE

By realizing that we are not our "body," the tantric perfected lucid OBE and dream states help people overcome their dread of dying. Additionally, they found that OBEs allowed for profound physical recovery because the mind can be quite demanding on the body. And although the body rested, yogis continued their work throughout the night rather than missing time to meditate.

Athletes who practice lucid dreaming can use it to improve their performance. Working in a dream or out-of-body experience helps people visualize, have a "felt sense" of their practice, and even develop the muscle memory for successful routines. Others gain from the chance to investigate former incarnations and from increased personal growth.

## IS ASTRAL PROJECTION REAL?
Astral projection is a long-established concept. Astral projection is a popular method of self-care and spiritual healing practiced by many people, from New Agers to Shamans. An interview with Dr. Deganit Nuur of Nuurvana Clairvoyant Healing is featured in an article on Elite Daily. She is a well-known clairvoyant, acupuncture specialist, and spiritual instructor. Astral projection should be practiced deliberately and purposefully, according to Nuur. This is due to the possibility that when people experience traumatic events, they may end up astrally projecting and losing control.

Nuur clarifies:

*When we don't feel protected, we may unconsciously act this way... After leaving the body, the spirit projects elsewhere. It can be incredibly disempowering when not done perfectly since you lose a sense of seniority and authority over your body.*

## ASTRAL TRAVEL AND SCIENCE
There is currently no means to scientifically test whether a person's spirit may leave and enter the body during sleep or meditation, even though astral projection may be a philosophical experience. Out-of-body experiences can most simply be attributed to fantasizing or dreaming. Live Science also summarizes it as follows:

People who use LSD or peyote may be convinced that they had interactions with God, the dead, or angels while in their altered state. Despite astral projection practitioners' insistence that their experiences are accurate, all of their proof is anecdotal. The practice of astral projection is a fun and safe hobby that has the potential to seem profound and, in some cases, even life-altering. However, there is no proof that out-of-body sensations originate in the brain rather than the physical body.

## NOW THAT'S INTERESTING
*According to Vice magazine, the U.S. Army tried to learn through investigating psychic tests and phenomena, such as astral projection and out-of-body experiences, in the 1970s and 1980s. Under hypnosis, Project Center Lane officers tried to use their minds to go to the "astral plane." They allegedly employed this enhanced state for time travel, physical wound healing, and "remote viewing," which allowed them to visit other locations, including planets, and report on what they saw.*

## CONCLUSION
In conclusion, astral projection is a remarkably unusual phenomenon. Astral projection is distinct from other kinds of OBEs because it involves a sense of spirituality, yet each person who experiences it does so in a unique way. As in Marco's case, spirituality is sometimes religious, and the phenomena are undoubtedly mentioned in the mythology of many religions, but astral projection can also be a secular event.

My experience and Muldoon's were enlightening, but neither of us cites a religious leader. It's challenging to pin down astral projection in the realm of folklore and stories. It's different from La Llorona, from the hook, and other legends that occur in the actual, physical world.

# CHAPTER 08
# HOW TO RECOGNIZE AND DEVELOP YOUR PSYCHIC ABILITIES

## WAYS TO RECOGNIZE AND DEVELOP YOUR PSYCHIC ABILITIES
Do you have doubts about the reality and existence of psychic abilities? You can even question the reliability of intuition. However, it's likely that you already know, albeit secretly, that those psychic powers are natural and that you've probably even had your own psychic experiences. Let's rejoice in your talents and how you can improve them.

## RECOGNITION TO DEVELOPMENT
The only thing standing between your beliefs and your gifts is frequently your lack of awareness of your psychic powers. Unfortunately, this can occasionally be challenging, particularly if you have a natural skepticism of everything metaphysical. It's frequently even more straightforward than that. The only thing stopping you might be your ignorance that you might already be using your intuition. Knowing that you are experiencing psychic interactions or episodes can inspire you to hone your abilities.

To develop psychic flashes, how do you notice them? Easy! Be mindful. The most straightforward approach to moving forward is to start paying attention to when something piques your intuitive interest. You will typically feel a little different when you have a supernatural encounter. Perhaps you asked yourself, "Hmmm, what was that?"

Additionally, you can feel as though whatever happened didn't quite seem regular to you. The start of your consciousness is right now. The three exercises listed below will assist you in identifying and developing your psychic abilities.

### Clairsentience And Clairempathy: Feel Your Way
Most people get some psychic impression at some point. There are numerous psychic senses, which means numerous ways to identify your psychic abilities. Being intuitive is pretty prevalent. Because of certain metaphysical senses, we can psychically feel things. The French word "Clair" means "clear," and the term "sentient" refers to feeling or awareness. Therefore, the term "clairsentience" means "clear feeling." Another type of clear feeling is called claim empathy, in which you assume another person's emotions or physical sensations.

You might realize that you've previously had this type of psychic perception. Consider a time when you walked into a room and sensed the energy there. You either felt very at ease, or you wanted to leave immediately, without apparent cause. Whether or not you were close friends with the others in the room had nothing to do with how crowded it was.

The presence of humans isn't even necessary; the space may have remained empty. It's the atmosphere in space. Your clairsentience interprets whether the energy feels pure or corrupted based on the energy you can feel with your soul. You are prepared to develop your psychic, clairsentient sense now that you have identified it as such.

*Practice It!*
Use a companion to assist you with this activity. You'll be driven to three separate locations while being blindfolded and wearing earplugs to block out sound. To conceal your actions, feel free to cover the blindfold with sunglasses. They are free to take you anywhere, including the mall, a restaurant, a park, a school, a cemetery, or someone's house. Ask your driver to wait until you are sensory-deprived before taking the wheel. Additionally, request that they take you to three different locations (don't, for instance, visit three parks or businesses).

When you reach your destination, ask your friend to lead you slowly into the center of the area. Take some time to absorb the energy surrounding you. Observe your feelings. Observe how your body is responding. Are you feeling at ease? On guard? Do you have the urge to stay or sense the need to leave? Do you get shivers or excitement? Do other people's energies affect you? Do you enjoy their enthusiasm, if so? Do you find them to be attractive or repulsive? Is there anything new that you can feel in your body? Do you experience extreme weight or a floating sensation? Do you feel comfortable where you are standing right now?

Tell your friend how the energy feels to you after you've answered each of these questions and given yourself enough time to tune in properly. After that, take off your blindfold and ear plugs. Are you aware of your location? Before removing the sensory-deprivation products, did you know? Do your current feelings, based on where you can see and hear yourself, make sense in light of how you felt telepathically? Or was it unexpected? Did you like the vigor? How did you find the exercise in general? Did you find it stressful or enjoyable?

You've just activated your clairsentience and Clair empathy psychic powers.

## Clairempathy: Feeling Your Friends

You can utilize Clair empathy to determine someone's problems. Can even utilize this psychic ability to examine a person's body for signs of illness or damage. When I have people who are experiencing medical problems, I psychically scan their physical bodies. My clairsentience and Clair empathy allow me to sense potential problems. I get an "alarm" when I discover physical suffering in another individual. My root chakra, located in the first chakra, suddenly hurts. This demonstrates that either my client is experiencing discomfort in the area I'm scanning or that they are ill. This demonstrates that my client is experiencing pain in the region I'm scanning or due to a particular ailment.

*Your psychic abilities can develop by becoming more aware of how other people's problems influence you. It does have two edges, though.* To avoid absorbing or acquiring the other person's ailments, you must also take measures to prevent yourself from absorbing their energy. Although it is a straightforward process, it is crucial if you want to advance your psychic talents.

*Practice It!*

Locate a comfortable position and take a few deep breaths. Imagine a vast bubble of brilliant white light forming around you when you're at ease. Imagine inhaling good energy as you continue to breathe, inflating the bubble. Feel any negativity leaving the bubble with each exhalation. Allow any pain, discomfort, and negative energy to be sealed off by this bubble. For the remainder of this exercise, maintain this security bubble around you.

Call a few of your friends and get together. Ailments can be actual conditions they are experiencing or fictitious diseases they claim to have, so have them each list five. Please make sure at least one of them is recorded as being accurate. Inform them to visualize where they would present in their bodies as they write them down. The time to begin is almost here. Consider that bubble enclosing you and protecting you before you start.

Look at the list made by the first person you choose. Read each person's recorded words out loud one by one. Could you close your eyes and say it out loud? Keep track of any changes to your physique. Pay attention to any changes you see; you might experience intense pain or numbness wherever. Decide if you don't feel anything, which is equally crucial. Write "what I experienced" next to that issue on their list.

Examine where, if anywhere, you felt anything in your physical body once you've finished the complete list and noted your feelings. Were you able to identify each condition they listed? Talk to the individual who provided the list about what you observed. Does it align with their actual problems? The validity of the problems you perceived may you infer? Or hypothetical? Did you experience a Clair empathic onset? Exhale any diseases that don't belong to you and release your bubble for rapid cleaning. You shouldn't hang on to anyone else's possessions, whether they be genuine or not!

## Clairvoyance: Did You See That?

We regularly employ our psychic sight. We refer to this as clairvoyance. Even if we use it, we might not be familiar with it. We spend so much time trying to get everything done in a day that we don't always see the unique ways that our intuition is being used. We hardly ever stop to think about what we are experiencing psychically, let alone acknowledge that we are.

We will practice by slowing it down a little. We frequently assume that psychic communication is just in our heads when we receive one. We rarely jump to the correct conclusion—our prophetic skills are at work here! If you see images while you daydream or prefer to see things drawn out to help you comprehend them better, you may be using your psychic vision without even recognizing it.

## Clairaudience: What?

Clairaudience, often known as psychic hearing, is quite common among experts and skeptics. A typical example of psychic hearing hears tunes or phrases in your head when nothing is being played or spoken out. You might also observe that you frequently try to focus by blocking out surrounding noise to listen closely to what is being spoken. This is a clairaudient person's trait, according to this.

Even if it seems like your imagination, psychic hearing also applies when you are thinking about someone, and a song comes to mind that somehow makes you think of them. We can tune in by hearing what isn't being said, whether or not we are aware that we are using our psychic abilities.

## DO WE NEED TO KEEP EVERYTHING SEPARATE?

Can strengthen your connection and psychic powers if you let them work together. Although defining each makes it easier to comprehend how they function, this does not obligate you to keep them separate from one another. Using them together seems to make them more effective.

Consider them all as coworkers who collaborate to complete a task; while each performs a distinct task, the total result is greater than the sum of their parts. Additionally, you might be unable to tune in using your intuition to acquire all the psychic information you require. A combination will provide better details, giving you a clearer picture.

For example, a client once asked me where I saw them living in five years during a reading. I immediately noticed a spiral shape when I tuned into my intuition, but I could not identify it. When I asked them if it meant anything to them, they were also unable to make sense of it. I re-tuned instead of imagining that I was out of place. This time, I used my clairalience—a psychic sense of smell—to detect salt. I re-asked her if that meant anything to her, to which she once more responded,

"No."

I thought, "What the heck?" and switched it back. The seagulls' "caw caw" and the sound of breaking waves were audible this time, so I inquired what they indicated.

"Oh! Whether or not to relocate to the beach has been up for discussion. The spiral you said is made up of shells, and the salt is made up of salt water. Now everything makes sense!"

I believe my client has since moved to a beach house and is happy with her life. I would never have received the whole picture if I had given up after the spiral.

*Practice It!*

It's your turn now! Take a deep breath, close your eyes, and create a bubble around you to shield you from bad energy. Imagine the magnificent white bubble forming as you breathe positive energy and exhale anything that no longer serves you. Do this repeatedly until you reach a state of tranquility and vigor.

Take another deep breath when you are prepared to start. Consider a question you have regarding the future. It might be related to your family, job, or Relationship. Start by visualizing whatever you picked as it is right now. Five years from now, use your clairvoyance to reach out with your psychic mind.

*Relationship As Your Guide:*

Listen in and respond to the questions below, using Relationship as your guide:

- Do you see anything?
- Do you notice anyone else?
- Tall, short, bulky, thin, thin, or chubby?
- Hair color?
- Curly, straight, long, short, bald?
- Glasses or none at all?
- Clothing design?

Now tune in using your clairaudience:

- Do you hear a name?

- Do you hear them talking?
- Do you have any music in mind?
- Are there any other noises?
- Do you notice any evocative words?
- Can you hear a timeframe for when this person or persons will enter your life, or can you already hear them?

Now, use your clairsentience:

- How do these people make you feel?
- Hot or cold?
- Honest or furious?
- Happy, sad, enthusiastic, or satisfied?

Lastly, pay attention to anything else you perceive using your clairaudience, clairgustance, or claircognizance (knowing). You can use this exercise to inquire about your family, work, and other topics.

Put together all of your psychic impressions at this point. What do you suppose? Was one sense preferable to the other? Did using them all feel comfortable? When you integrated them all, did you get additional information? What did you learn?

CONGRATULATION! There are some psychic powers you may not even be aware of that you have! With skills that will benefit you in every aspect of your life, you are now well on your way. Instead of giving them away, use them to better use to guide others and yourself and advance your understanding of the universe's knowledge.

**DOWNLOAD YOUR BONUS**

Hello, dear reader!

## Thank you for purchasing this book.

## <u>Your Bonus Awaits You!</u>

Before, I want to let you know how important your purchase and judgment can be to me.

To give you a brief introduction: I'm a small writer. I write for passion, and I think that the arguments of this book can help people deepen the topic, answer some questions, and get the basis of their knowledge about the ideas inside this book.
Writing a book is a great challenge that keeps you busy for hours on end, trying to create the best you can do.

Like the other independent writers, I don't have the big advertising budget that many other publishers and businesses spend online.

So, you can support my work by leaving me a review of this book.

## *Scan the Qr Code to download your bonus and leave a review.*

*<u>Thank you so much for taking the time to do this.</u>*

# PART 02
# EMPATHY

# CHAPTER 01
# INTRODUCTION

It's common to think of empathy as a straightforward matter: Either I can or cannot feel what another person is going through, and that's where empathy ends. But empathy is a highly complex concept that encompasses a variety of emotional states as well as several physiological and psychological conditions. It influences how we perceive and interact with the world, encouraging us to take on helpful behaviors but sometimes giving rise to "amoral" or surprising viewpoints.

Many behaviors have an underlying cause that is not generally considered; for instance, powerful sympathetic impulses may be the source of our solid convictions or feelings of hate. The split of empathy into two main categories—affective empathy and cognitive empathy—shows the phenomenon's complexity.

The ability to react correctly to the mental states of those around us is called affective empathy. This enables us to comprehend a person's feelings differently from ourselves and, in a sense, be impacted by their "emotional contagion" (Shamay-Tsoory et al., 2009).

The ability to conceptually comprehend another person's state of mind despite not experiencing the same emotional state and understanding the logical justifications is known as cognitive empathy (Gerace et al., 2013). Both affective and cognitive empathy play a role in how we react to, experience, and learn from the world around us.

We will briefly discuss the idea of empathic rage and distress to highlight how much empathy affects our lives. According to Hoffman (1990), empathetic fury is an emotional state that occurs when someone else is harmed and prompts actions to either help or punish (Hoffman, 1990).

The degree and experience with empathy play a crucial role in defining the individual's response. The bigger one's capacity to adopt various viewpoints, the less enraged one was in response to aggression and provocation (Hoffman, 1990). To elaborate on this, sympathetic fury is a type of empathetic distress in which a person's reaction to the suffering of others neither elicits nor ends with the expression of sympathy; instead, it is a powerful aversive reaction that is fundamentally self-centered (Dowling, 2018).

The intensely unfavorable feelings could prevent people from offering assistance or encourage them to leave the situation to protect themselves. Guilt or unjust feelings are two more distressing emotions. A different philosophical discussion is necessary to determine whether or not these feelings are viewed as pro-social or moral.

We can investigate the idea of empathy from various angles and fields, and it plays a significant part in understanding how humans understand the world in each field, from philosophical conundrums to scientific phenomena.

# CHAPTER 02

# WHAT IS EMPATHY

Over a century ago, the English word "empathy" was developed to translate into the German word Einfühlung. The word is made up of the Greek letters em, which means "in," and pathos, which means "emotion, feeling, or sympathy" (Lanzoni, 2015).

Despite this background, most essays, novels, and other writings on empathy start by stating that there is no universally accepted definition. Anyone may see from a cursory search on empathy that there are potentially as many definitions as there are authors in the field (Decety & Jackson, 2004).

There are many implications of unclear definitions, particularly in the field of research. Readers need to understand quickly what the author intends by empathy, what and how the outcome is being measured, and to what extent it is connected to other relevant concepts when reading research papers on empathy. This makes it very difficult to replicate or compare studies.

Secondly, much research on empathy is conducted to apply findings to educational initiatives that foster empathy. As a result, there are numerous inconsistencies in the study on and applications of empathy in various circumstances, which profoundly impact the efficacy of these programs. Finally, many therapeutic fields, including counseling, medicine, and social work, use empathy as a fundamental framework and critical ability. Some understandings of empathy have demonstrated higher therapeutic results than others, as it is understood differently within and within each field (Cuff et al., 2016).

Numerous elements contribute to the concept of empathy's complexity. One is that it is impossible to say which definition is more or less "right." It is impossible to say who the foremost expert on empathy is because so many philosophers and scholars have offered different definitions of empathy.

## SOME DIMENSIONS OF EMPATHY

In and of itself, empathy is a complicated, multifaceted term. These dimensions include, but are not limited to:

1. Is empathy inherently compelling (i.e., behavior-related), cognitive (i.e., thought-related), or both?
2. Are the emotions of the empathetic observer and the target required to be "congruent" or the same?
3. Can the observer tell the difference between their feelings and the emotions of the target?
4. Is empathy a bottom-up or top-down process directed by the brain, or is it automatic?
5. Are the behavioral results of empathy—crying, rage, taking action in reaction to another person's feelings, etc.—part of empathy?
6. Can one feel empathy for something or someone who does not exist (such as in their imagination, novels, fictional characters on television, etc.), or does the stimulus or target need to be honest?
7. Is empathy a natural quality, or is it influenced by the circumstances surrounding the parties involved?

Each question has a different response according to various conceptualizations of empathy. Answers to these questions may also identify a thought as one of the numerous similar ideas frequently mistaken for empathy or asserted to be a cause, consequence, or subtype of empathy. Will examine these ideas in the next portion of this chapter. It isn't easy to formulate a clear, succinct, and straightforward definition in light of all this intricacy.

A review article examined 43 different definitions of empathy from various research fields. Their findings were compiled into one clear, albeit lengthy definition of empathy:

> *"Empathy is a form of emotional response (affective) that is influenced by a combination of intrinsic skills and environmental influences. Although automatically elicited, top-down control systems also influence how empathy develops. One's perception (directly experienced or imagined) and understanding (cognitive empathy) of the stimulus emotion are comparable to the resultant emotion, with the realization that the source of the emotion is not one's own (Cuff et al., 2016).*

We will use this definition to refer to empathy throughout this chapter.

## CONCEPTS RELATED TO EMPATHY

It is straightforward to confuse empathy with several related ideas described in the preceding section. In this section, we will try to define these related ideas and set them apart from empathy.

In our everyday language, the terms sympathy and empathy are essentially interchangeable. The differences between them are subtle, though. "Feeling as" another and "feeling for" another are described as the contrasts between empathy and compassion, respectively (Hein & Singer, 2008).

For instance, while experiencing someone else's sadness, empathy will result in a congruent sadness in the observer. In contrast, sympathy will involve incongruent responses, such as anxiety or concern. Empathy is much more than sympathy in therapeutic relationships. For instance, a therapist who is sympathetic to a client's loss or grief sincerely attempts to comprehend what the client may be going through without forgetting that these feelings are not their own.

While SYMPATHY, in its ideal form, can express compassion and support, it is sometimes expressed as pity for the struggling person. It can even establish a hierarchy in the relationship. In other words, empathy fosters connection, whereas sympathy might lead to a separation of two people (Jacobson, 2015).

The following ideas are rarely applied and have not been thoroughly researched in recent studies. It is essential to distinguish between empathy and these concepts as we currently understand them to prevent any misuse.

MIMPATHY is defined as the imitation of emotions or the sharing of feelings on a subject with another person while not necessarily feeling sympathy for them. Other philosophers have suggested that, in contrast to empathy, mimpathy remains in the realm of cognitive actions; that is, while mimpaths may mimic emotions, they are unable to understand the other person or, even to some extent, sympathize with them (Becker, 1931).

The following concepts were connected to sympathy but had many similarities to our modern definition of empathy, according to German philosopher Max Scheler, who identified them in the early 20th century. Becker mentioned Scheler's work in his paper from 1931.

COMPATHY, often known as emotional solidarity, is the immediate sharing of one person's emotion, frequently their suffering. Both sides deeply comprehend one another's emotions without consciously trying to empathize with them, a characteristic frequently observed in parents of departed children.

TRANSPATHY, often known as emotional contagion, is the spontaneous and sometimes unconscious way in which people are affected by the emotions of others. As the term implies, this occurs when an emotion is "contagious" and most frequently occurs in group settings.

For example, people could be "taken away" at a party by someone else's enthusiasm without paying attention or thinking about it. Similar to a virus, it can repeatedly spread among people from those who may have previously been "infected" with the feeling using expression and imitation. Thus, group settings are where this process is most noticeable.

The fundamental difference between transpathy and empathy is that during transpathy, people tend to take on the target's feelings but fail to recognize that these emotions are not their own; as a result, the self-other distinction, which is a critical component of empathy, is impaired.

UNIPATHY: Transpathy that is more intense and uncontrollable is referred to as unipathy (Runes, n.d.). The identification is involuntary but all-consuming, similar to transpathy. Becker gives an example of a charismatic leader or "hypnotizer" who captivated a group of people to the point where they were all preoccupied with his ideas, gave his moral principles any weight, and followed only his instructions (Becker, 1931). This could manifest as folie à plusieurs ('madness of several,' also known as shared psychosis or shared delusion disease (SDD)).

Hallucinations and delusional ideas can spread from one individual to another in this psychiatric syndrome. This is frequently related to people who are socially isolated from one another without a third party pointing out that their delusions might be flawed (Al Saif & Al Khalili, 2021). The concepts of unipathy—contagious emotions and social isolation, for example—then clarify how they can affect members of cults and religious organizations.

Given the significant overlap and connections among these linked ideas, it is not unexpected that empathy has proven to be incredibly challenging to define and separate. However, we intend to avoid using these terms interchangeably in future studies by highlighting the essential differences between these ideas and empathy in this exploration.

# EMPHATIC ANGER AND DISTRESS

Empathy can make the target (person in distress) feel less alone and more connected to the empathizer. However, those who work as doctors, nurses, lawyers, or therapists may experience empathic anxiety due to their constant exposure to unpleasant emotions.

According to definitions of empathy distress, *it is "a significant unpleasant and self-oriented response to the suffering of others, accompanied by the desire to disengage from a situation in order to shield oneself from excessive negative sentiments"*(Singer & Klimecki, 2014).

When practicing empathy, empathic suffering reveals a lack of self-defense. Contrary to the prosocial character of empathy, empathic discomfort causes empaths to withdraw into themselves and act out unfavorable emotions against themselves. People who experience empathic distress are more likely to suffer from various mental illnesses, including anxiety and depression, as well as physical symptoms like exhaustion and insomnia (Vu & Bodenmann, 2017).

Consequently, it is possible to argue that being sympathetic for a long time can be bad for those in these professions. But a lack of empathy in the medical profession can also negatively affect their practice (Derksen et al., 2017). Compassion is better in these instances. As was previously said, compassion is the emotion of caring for someone who is suffering and the desire to make that person feel better.

Contrary to empathy, compassion is goal-oriented, upbeat, and prevents burnout by shielding the viewer from experiencing those shared emotions on a deep level. This avoids forsaking those who might be in need (Dowling, 2018). Therefore, learning compassion at the same time as empathy is essential if someone wants to be able to defend himself adequately.

Empathic anger is a distinct type of empathic anguish experienced when someone else is harmed. This is frequently felt in response to circumstances perceived as ethically wrong towards looked-after persons, such as those close to the individual or others who might be weak and need protection.

Thus, empathic fury may manifest when a person's loved ones have been harmed or are experiencing hardship, as well as in response to a news article that may have included children being mistreated. This response is less about moral transgression and more about concern for other people's well-being (Hechler & Kessler, 2018).

Empathic anger may directly affect two particular types of elements:

(1) A desire to assist the sufferer(s)

(2) A desire for retribution against the aggressor(s).

There isn't much proof that empathetic rage has anything to do with prosocial behavior. However, one could claim that at least the helping desires are prosocial (Hoffman, 1996). Similar to empathy, fury fueled by empathy can also be influenced by a person's trait or state of mind (situation at hand). While trait empathic anger had beneficial effects (via state empathic anger) on both helping and punishing goals, state empathic anger had direct, positive impacts on both desires (Vitaglione & Barnett, 2003).

More study in this field is needed to demonstrate the connection between empathic rage and prosocial behavior. However, both empathetic stress and anger demonstrate that empathy is not always beneficial and has drawbacks.

# CONCLUSION

One of the most complex ideas to understand completely is empathy. Due to empathy's intricacy, multidimensionality, and ambiguity in the relationships between numerous related ideas. Researchers have developed varying conceptualizations of the notion over time. The dimensions that make up empathy had significant variances when examining these related concepts.

This led to the conclusion that empathy is a typically automatic process (which may occasionally involve top-down processing). It involves the sharing of congruent emotions between two or more parties, where the observer recognizes these emotions as not their own and may be influenced by trait or state elements.

Then demonstrated the potential drawbacks of empathy through exploring two distinct notions related to empathy: empathic distress and empathic fury. Instead of using compassion, it was advised to counteract empathic distress since it can be self-protective, upbeat, and problem-focused, reducing fatigue. Since many of its elements and relationships are still unclear, it has been accepted that more research on empathy and anger is necessary.

Empathy has emerged as a sophisticated and potent technique that may be used to connect with others in daily life. This is especially true for occupations that call for therapeutic and caring connections. To ensure one's self- and peer-preservation, one must avoid experiencing empathic distress and instead employ other skills at their disposal.

# CHAPTER 03
## CLASSIFICATIONS OF EMPATHY

## WHAT IS EMPATHY?

*Empathy is the capacity to experience what other people feel on an emotional level, see things from their perspective, and put yourself in their shoes. Essentially, it involves placing yourself in another person's shoes and experiencing their feelings.*

You might be able to instantaneously put yourself in another person's shoes when you witness their pain and feel empathy for what they are going through.

While most people are well aware of their sentiments and emotions, it can be more challenging to understand the thoughts and feelings of others. People who possess empathy can "walk a mile in another's shoes," as the saying goes. It makes it possible for people to understand how other people feel.

For many, it is inexplicable to witness another person suffering and act with indifference or even downright hate. But not everyone reacts to other people's suffering with empathy, as evidenced by the fact that some people do.

## THE IMPORTANCE OF EMPATHIZING:

Being empathic can be seen as a solution to many problems and issues one may face. In reality, studies have demonstrated that empathetic behaviors have a wide range of advantageous effects ("Empathy Definition: What Is Empathy," n.d.). In a study where white individuals exhibited "reduced racial bias" against an African American person after empathizing with them, researchers found that expressing empathy can diminish racist acts.

(Dixon, 2011; "Empathy Definition: What Is Empathy? (n.d.)) This is crucial in light of recent shocking discoveries about the persistence of racial bias in organizations like the government and sports. Furthermore, the police task force can benefit from empathy (Suttie, 2016).

According to a study on the Seattle Police Department, one set of officers received training on how to carry out their police duties using the fundamental ideas presented in the program Listening and Explaining with Equity and Dignity (LEED) (Owens et al., 2016; Suttie, 2016).

A better relationship between the public and the police was established, and police confidence levels were raised when resolving issues. And there was a decrease in police brutality when the group using LEED principles was compared to another set of officers who were following standard protocols, according to the results (Owens et al., 2016; Suttie, 2016).

Since the police officers who implemented LEED demonstrated behaviors like actively listening to the community, respecting their opinions and feelings, and understanding diverse perspectives from those engaged in the incident, LEED essentially hinges on the fundamentals of empathy.

This example exemplifies the significance of empathy and its potent effects on touchy subjects like police brutality. These activities are all examples of empathy. Considering the controversy surrounding the murder of George Floyd, this is incredibly pertinent today.

Additionally, it has been demonstrated that empathy helps to address inequality issues (Batson et al., 1995; Batson et al., 1997). People acting out of empathy are more likely to assist others who are perceived as weaker or outside of their social circle. Reaching out to the underprivileged is an example of this (Batson et al., 1995; Batson et al., 1997). It's interesting to note that another describes empathy and its benefits to healthcare.

According to a study ("Empathy Definition: What Is Empathy," n.d.; Krasner et al., 2009; Suttie, 2015), patients were happier with the treatments they received from doctors who showed empathy because it helped them better manage their emotions. All of the above examples support and give hope to the idea that sympathetic behavior might further improve racism, police brutality, inequality, and even healthcare.

## SIGNS OF EMPATHY

Some indications that you have a sympathetic personality include:

- You are good at being attentive to what people are saying.
- People refer to you about their issues all the time.
- You have a real sense of what people are thinking and feeling.
- You frequently consider how others are feeling.
- You get requests for advice from people.
- Tragic situations frequently cause you to feel overwhelmed.
- You attempt to help those that are in need.
- You have a real sense of when someone is lying.
- There are moments when you feel tired or overpowered in social settings.
- You give folks lots of thought.
- You struggle to determine limits in your interactions with others.

When you have plenty of empathy, you care about other people's pleasure and health. Additionally, it implies that continually considering other people's feelings may occasionally leave you feeling overwhelmed, worn out, or maybe overstimulated.

## HOW TO DEVELOP EMPATHY?

An exceptional human quality that emerges naturally in infancy is empathy. Babies frequently show emotional mimicry of their parents. While this can be true, as people mature, their levels of empathy might fluctuate. It's interesting to notice that research has shown that certain traits and behaviors might promote empathy in people. The subsequent could be a list of them, in no particular order:

1. Puzzling over the sensations a selected victim or someone who has endured hardship would have felt after they were picturing their face.
2. Make an inventory of all the items you would possibly have in common with someone radically different from you.
3. Engage in active listening by paying close attention to the opposite person's speech and expressing your understanding of their circumstances and emotions.
4. Use appropriate visual communication, like eye contact, posture, and facial gestures, to convey friendliness, warmth, and a readiness to concentrate on the opposite person.
5. Concentrate solely on the opposite person to interact in mindfulness and meditation. These methods have improved one's ability to tolerate different points of view from other individuals.
6. Changing one's mindset to incorporate the conviction that empathy will be understood and further developed. This has proven accurate since people who adopt this approach stress the previously described qualities, like active listening and understanding another person's viewpoint, irrespective of the challenges which will arise.

## TYPES OF EMPATHY

Putting oneself in another person's shoes could be a common way for people to talk with empathy. The definition of empathy encompasses four types: cognitive, emotional, and compassionate, and although this is often partially true, there's more to it. Will cover each thoroughly within the sections that follow.

- Cognitive Empathy:

Cognitive empathy is the capacity to assess the circumstances in which another person finds themselves and to recognize their feelings and thoughts at that exact instant. Put differently, it shows the opposite individual that you understand their predicament and may relate to what they're prying on because you have had a similar experience. As a result, you'll guess their spirit.

The expressions "I know what you mean" and "I've been there" are a pair of typical expressions that are frequently employed when exhibiting acts of cognitive empathy.

*Examples Of Cognitive Empathy:*

1. Use an example to connect the concept to understand it better. Imagine John telling Kevin, his roommate, that they had lost their job when John gets home late at night. When Kevin approaches John and says, "I understand how you are feeling, I lost my job last year, and I was feeling the same way,"
2. Cognitive empathy would effectively be on exhibit. When doctors converse with their patients, they exhibit another typical instance of cognitive empathy that frequently goes unrecognized. It is typical for doctors to evaluate conditions when patients disclose their signs and symptoms during their session exclusively based on what they observe rather than considering the patients' feelings.

These examples all have one thing in common: they emphasize understanding the other person's perspective rather than their feelings.

Although many people would assume that cognitive empathy would have benefits, such as assisting a person during trying times by connecting with their experiences and viewpoints, it has drawbacks. For example, some people use cognitive empathy to influence others.

However, the benefits of cognitive empathy exceed the drawbacks. Other classifications, including emotional empathy, must be considered to comprehend the fullness of the umbrella term empathy.

- Emotional Empathy:

The ability to experience the same emotions as another person when you see them is known as emotional empathy. In other words, emotional empathy is the capacity to comprehend the circumstances and emotional states that another person is going through and to go through those same emotions yourself (Arnold, n.d.; Spitz, n.d.).

Additionally, it is frequent to overlook the distinction between emotional and cognitive empathy. Emotional empathy is cognitive empathy plus true emotional sharing, whereas cognitive empathy merely involves using knowledge to evaluate another person's emotional state.

It is crucial to clarify the relevance and relationship of this particular sort of empathy (i.e., emotional empathy) to a group of mirror neurons, which are the brain's essential functioning cells. Mirror neurons, thought to be a novel finding in the 1990s, have been the subject of numerous investigations (Winerman, 2005). Researchers looked at mirror neurons in macaque monkeys in a preliminary investigation connected to an animal study.

It was discovered that a group of similar neurons named F5 in the premotor cortex of a monkey became red when it picked up an arbitrary object, such as a peanut, and then watched another monkey complete the same action.

Another experiment revealed a connection between a researcher and a monkey (Winerman, 2005). More specifically, when the monkey performed the identical behavior as the researcher, the same neurons lit up in red. The success of these trials allowed for the establishment and identification of the neurons as mirror neurons (Winerman, 2005).

Additionally, additional investigations were made to see whether mirror neurons in people behaved similarly (Winerman, 2005). One such instance is a 1995 paper written by two neuroscientists named Dr. Giacomo Rizzolatti and Dr. The hands of a person were examined by Luciano Fadiga to examine their muscles.

The participant was explicitly instructed to watch an investigator pick up an object. During this process, the participant's motor evoked potentials (i.e., electrical signals indicating the stimulation and readiness of the muscle to contract/relax) were recorded (Legatt, 2014; Winerman, 2005). The scientists discovered that the participant's motor evoked potentials while being observed were identical to those induced when they physically grabbed an object.

Although more research is needed, basic human and animal tests have already significantly contributed to identifying mirror neurons as distinct brain cells that uniformly fire when one does the same activity and watches it perform.

Researchers have noted that emotional empathy occurs using the basic features of mirror neurons by allowing one to truly experience the sentiments and emotions of another person upon witnessing them, making the process by which mirror neurons function significantly.

*Examples Of Emotional Empathy*

To help one understand emotional empathy better, it's also essential to provide a few examples:

1. Imagine coming home one day to discover a close friend crying hard at the news that they have been fired. After seeing this, your mirror neurons will start to work, and you'll start to feel for your friend and cry in response (Spitz, n.d.).
2. When you are at your first cousin's wedding, your cousin starts to recite a speech about how much they love and support the entire family and how many challenges they overcame to be where they are now. Through the activation of mirror neurons, as your cousin sobs throughout the speech, the audience members who care about them will also cry and experience the same emotions (Spitz, n.d.).
3. When you see someone sit on a row of sharp nails or press their toes against a wall, you immediately "cringe" because you know it will hurt because of previous experiences (Spitz, n.d.; Villines & Morrison, 2019).

Emotional empathy has been found to have benefits and drawbacks, just like cognitive empathy. When nurses, doctors, and palliative care professionals care for patients, for instance, this can favor the patients because emotional empathy enables one to connect with others in terms of their perspectives and emotions. This is so that they can provide patients with better care and therapy by better understanding what they are going through by exhibiting emotional empathy.

In addition, outside of the healthcare industry, this empathy can aid job seekers in building positive rapport with their hiring supervisors, better marketing their unique contributions to other businesses, and forging deep connections with career coaching professionals and brand ambassadors. On the other hand, emotional empathy comes with a few drawbacks.

For instance, there can occasionally be an "empathy overflow" when a person connects with another person's perspectives and starts feeling the same emotions. In essence, this happens when someone empathizes with another person and experiences too many emotions, which leads to stress, feelings of overwhelm, and an inability to maintain an emotional balance.

- Compassionate Empathy:

Compassionate empathy is the third category of empathy. Renowned psychologist Daniel Goleman previously defined compassionate empathy: "With this form of empathy we not only understand a person's plight and feel with them but are impulsively inspired to aid, if needed." (From "About Daniel Goleman," n.d.; from Spitz, n.d.)

Essentially, this kind of empathy combines cognitive empathy (i.e., understanding others' perspectives based on their situation). Emotional empathy (i.e., experiencing the same emotions as those distressed upon observation) and additional genuine help to the person during their difficulties to relieve their challenging experience and emotions (Spitz, n.d.). This type of empathy considers the person's condition on a social and emotional level and deliberate actions.

# ELEMENTS OF EMPATHY
According to Daniel Goleman, there are three key elements.

1. Understanding Others
2. Developing Others
3. Leveraging Diversity

## 1. Understanding Others
Perhaps this is what most people mean when they talk of "empathy": "seeing others' feelings and viewpoints, and taking an active interest in their worries," in Goleman's words. Whoever does this:

- Pays attention to your emotions. They are good listeners, aware of nonverbal clues, and unconsciously pick up on them.
- Is sensitive and aware of other people's viewpoints.
- Based on their comprehension of those individuals' needs and emotions, they are capable of assisting others.

You can acquire all these skills, but only if you want to. Some people may turn off their emotional antennae to avoid being overwhelmed by others' emotions.

For example, there have been several controversies involving the National Health Service in the UK, when nurses and doctors have been charged with showing no concern for their patients. They may have isolated themselves out of concern that they couldn't handle the demands of the patients who needed them so much without proper assistance.

## 2. Developing Others

The development of others means attending to their wants and worries and assisting them in reaching their most significant potential. Those with this expertise typically:

- Give individuals positive feedback that focuses on getting better while praising them for their accomplishments and abilities.
- Help people reach their most significant potential by mentoring and coaching them.
- Give your teams challenging assignments to help them grow.

## 3. Leveraging Diversity

Utilizing diversity is developing opportunities through various types of people, acknowledging and enjoying that every one of us brings a unique perspective to the table.

Leveraging diversity does not entail treating everyone equally; it entails adapting your interactions with people to suit their wants and requirements.

Regardless of their origin, people with this competence respect everyone and get along well. They typically view diversity as an opportunity since they know that various teams perform significantly better than more homogeneous ones.

A respectful environment is created when people adept at utilizing diversity question intolerance, bias, and stereotyping when encountering them.

## Uses

There is no doubt that selfish and even cruel behavior is possible in humans. You may swiftly peruse any daily newspaper to find several instances of cruel, self-centered, and terrible behavior. Why don't we constantly act in such a self-serving manner, then, is the question. What makes us empathize with another person's suffering and act kindly in return?

Being able to feel empathy contains a range of advantages:

- People can form social ties with others because of empathy. People are better able to behave in social circumstances once they know what others are thinking and experiencing. in keeping with research, social relationships are critical for physical and psychological well-being.
- You can learn to manage your own emotions by empathizing with others. Emotional regulation is crucial to regulate your emotions and avoid feeling overwhelmed, even under extreme stress.
- Helpful behavior is inspired by empathy. After you feel empathy for others, you're more likely to act in helpful ways, and when people feel empathy for you, they're more likely to help you.

# BARRIERS TO EMPATHY

Cognitive biases, dehumanization, and victim-blaming are some reasons people occasionally lack empathy.

- **Cognitive Biases**

Multiple cognitive biases can sometimes affect how people view their environment. People frequently blame their shortcomings on external reasons while attributing the failures of others to their internal traits, as an example.

These biases can make it challenging to know all the weather in a situation and reduce the likelihood that somebody is ready to view a situation from the attitude of another.

- **Dehumanization**

Many people believe that folks who are different from them don't experience identical emotions or behave in the same ways. When other individuals are physically far-flung, this is often very typical.

People could also be less likely to feel empathy once they see news stories of a disaster or conflict in a distant country, for example, if they believe those suffering are fundamentally different from themselves.

- **Victim Blaming**

Some blame the victim for their circumstances when another person goes through a horrific experience. It explains why people frequently question crime victims about what they may have done differently to prevent the incident.

This propensity results from the need to think the globe is simple and fair. People wish to assume that they deserve what they get because it makes them want such dreadful things that could never happen to them.

## GUIDELINES FOR DEVELOPING EMPATHY

Fortunately, you'll develop your empathy as a skill. There are some things you can do to extend your capacity for empathy:

- Practice not interrupting others while they're speaking.
- Pay close attention to nonverbal cues like visual communication.
- Even if you trouble someone, endeavor to know them.
- Inquire about people to discover more about them and their life.
- Put yourself in the shoes of the opposite person.

## FINAL THOUGHTS

To conclude, empathy is often misconstrued as a quality like helping others. But as was previously mentioned, it's a highly complicated concept that could also be divided into three primary categories: cognitive, emotional, and compassionate. Someone can accomplish wonders for one more person by guiding them through difficult situations after they demonstrate acts of empathy. As a result, empathy can increase happiness when it's demonstrated positively.

# CHAPTER 04
# THE DEVELOPMENT OF
# EMPATHY THROUGHOUT HISTORY

In all human interactions, empathy is a crucial component. In addition to being a crucial skill that "promotes being in tune with others and caring for those in need," empathy is frequently referred to as "the glue" that holds communities together (Segal et al., 2017). Therefore, it is not unexpected that research on and continuous interest in the subject of empathy persists.

*The two components of the emotional definition of empathy are the ability to detect other people's emotions and the capacity to envision what another person could be thinking or feeling.*

However, the definition of empathy in psychotherapy is more nuanced and lacks a comprehensive definition of the term (Elliot et al., 2011). The history of the phrase and notion of empathy and how we might agree on a concept will be covered in the following chapter.

## EMPATHY IN EARLY 1900

The German word Einfühlung, which means "feeling-in," was offered as a translation for the English word empathy in 1908. (Lanzoni, 2015).

The word's structure is derived from the Greek words "em" (which means "in") and "pathos" (which means "feeling"). Being empathetic meant being able to "enliven an item or to transfer one's imagined sensations onto the world" in the early 1900s. This concept included "cognitive effort and body sensation thought" to distinguish various aesthetic experiences (Rae Greiner, "1909: The Introduction of the Word 'Empathy' into English," 2011).

For example, sympathetic theatergoers might experience the abstract dance moves seen on stage as if they were performing them themselves. Despite the lack of the word "empathy" in official dictionaries, Rebecca West, a novelist, was one of the first people in the general public to use it. West described her experience of "soaring with a bird as it soared into the skies" in 1928 using empathy.

## EMPATHY IN THE MID-CENTURY 1900S

By the middle of the 20th century, more psychologists were becoming interested in the topic of empathy, primarily concentrating on its function in social interactions. Rosalind Dymond Cartwright and Leonard Cottrell were two of the first psychologists to experimentally focus on interpersonal empathy in 1948.

After their original study, Cartwright's subsequent research focused on rejecting the previous definition of empathy and redefining it as "when he says others possess a quality in issue and others genuinely do have it when speaking of themselves." Or the perspective-taking type of empathy (Cartwright, 1958). Cartwright and other psychologists improved psychotherapy by further implementing this definition.

For example, research by Cartwright and Barbara Lerner examined factors such as "a patient's need to change, the therapist's level of experience, and the therapist's empathetic understanding" (Cartwright et al., 1953). Among the study's other findings are a correlation between the patient's overall progress and the therapist's "empathetic knowledge of the patient."

Numerous psychologists started to adopt Cartwright's difference between the two definitions of empathy. In contrast to the old definition of empathy, now known as "projection," psychologists have started to distinguish between projection and "genuine empathy," defined as "the accurate appraisal of another's ideas or feelings."

Psychoanalyst Heinz Kohut added cognition through introspection to the concept of empathy in 1959, expanding it further (Segal et al., 2017). In other words, empathy now refers to more than simply feeling, but to the process of thinking about the emotions of others.

# THE MODERN DEFINITION OF EMPATHY IN PERSPECTIVE

Researchers from fields like neurology, medicine, counseling, and social work were also drawn to the topic of understanding and developing empathy because of its complexity (Segal et al., 2017). The idea of empathy was widely adopted as a possible way to advance these disciplines' methods.

Despite talking about the rising interest in and analysis of empathy within these activities, it is evident that empathy lacks a precise definition or conceptualization.

Fortunately, during the first decade of the twenty-first century, developments in neuroscience (namely neurobiology) helped to clarify the idea, which continues to influence our present research and discussions on empathy.

In the sentences that follow, we'll go over many elements that help us come to terms with the idea of empathy. Affective response, affective mentalizing, self-other awareness, perspective-taking, and emotion regulation are the components of empathy.

### 1. Affective Response

One definition of an effective response is a quick reaction to a stimulus. For instance, an external stimulus may cause an affective reaction. Our five fundamental senses—touch, sight, smell, taste, and hearing—can all be used in this situation.

Hearing someone cry, for example, can behave as an external stimulus since it rapidly activates cerebral networks. Often, this immediate emotional reaction happens unknowingly. Other stimuli, including the process of envisioning an event, can also elicit a response, as was already mentioned. Affective mentalizing is the next aspect of empathy, which is where we will go from here.

### 2. Affective Mentalizing

Affective mentalizing can be defined as "the practice of cognitively evaluating someone's emotional situation." Or the capacity to envision or reflect on a specific experience. Additionally, effective mentalizing can take place even in the absence of a direct stimulus.

For example, reading a sad story conjures images in our minds and causes a passionate reaction. Thus, emotional mentalizing is a "bridge between affective experiences and cognitive reasoning."

The brain will start to go through various processes after being urged to have an emotional reaction to comprehend the mirrored feelings felt. It brings us to the following three interrelated parts that describe our cognitive processes.

### 3. Self-Other Awareness

*"The ability to identify with another while keeping a distinct sense of self" is how self-other awareness is defined.* The ability to recognize and comprehend another person's experiences and feelings while consciously distancing them from one's own experiences and feelings are necessary for this process. This kind of awareness is prevalent in fields like counseling since it calls for the capacity to establish "strong boundaries" to keep another person's experiences or emotions apart from one's own.

Additionally, self-help literature frequently contains self-other awareness, frequently mentioned as a caution to readers. It cautions readers against getting too caught up in another person's circumstances since doing so can "blur the line between what is my experience or worry and what is yours."

Self-other awareness is crucial for developing empathy. By adequately establishing the necessary boundaries, we can avoid being sidetracked by our own emotions and instead maintain our attention on the other person's feelings and experiences.

For example, a close friend might ask to go out to lunch with you because her relationship is having issues. In this case, the friend is seeking help and needs you to see things from her point of view. It would help if you worked to comprehend your own and her feelings to acquire self-other awareness. If boundaries between the two are not established, and you get too preoccupied with your feelings in the scenario, you are not experiencing empathy.

Emotional contagion may result from an affective reaction that is not followed by a self-other awareness. Mimicry, feedback, and contagion are the three stages that make up the process of emotional contagion (Raypole, 2019).

Mimicry is the imitation of another person, most often through body language. For example, if your friend's face appears comfortable in a circumstance that makes you feel anxious or stressed, this will probably cause your facial expression to do the same.

The feedback stage follows the imitation stage, which happens when you start to feel the feeling you previously imitated. For example, you feel calmer after copying your friend's carefree face. Contagion is the last stage of this process when the emotion initially imitated has entered your own experience. To put it another way, you can actively "express it and relate to others," completing the cycle of emotional contagion (Raypole, 2019).

To conclude, the ability to discern "between the self and other when effectively responding to external stimuli" distinguishes emotional contagion from empathy (Segal et al., 2017).

### 4. Perspective-Taking

*The ability to actively acquire the perspective of another is referred to as perspective-taking.* Empathy requires self-awareness and understanding of what you were made aware of, though self-awareness is a critical component. Putting oneself in another person's shoes to gain an understanding of their life and experiences is another way to describe perspective-taking.

It's crucial to remember that taking another person's perspective is just one of many elements that go into the idea of empathy. Understanding the critical distinctions between these two words is essential. The emotional content of the two is their primary distinction.

Perspective-taking, as previously said, is the capacity to "see someone's side" or "take on another's point of view" (Empathy Versus Perspective, 2018). However, empathy is simply the "emotional response of accepting someone else's suffering" or perspective. Setting boundaries when demonstrating self-other awareness is similar to doing so when picturing another person's experiences while setting them apart from your own.

Perspective-taking can also take place when self-other awareness is absent or impaired. This can happen when you can comprehend another person's viewpoint, but you cannot distinguish between yourself and others. Thus, you may analyze the experience in terms of what it means to you personally.

In other words, you can think you have empathy for someone else because you're looking at the issue from their point of view, but you respond from your perspective. Instead of visualizing myself going through the target's experiences, as psychologist Coplan suggests, "imagine becoming the target and going through the target's experiences" (Segal et al., 2017). This brings up the topic of the theory of mind (ToM).

The theory of mind (ToM), which is related to perspective-taking, is the "capacity to assign mental states — beliefs, intents, de- sires, emotions, and knowledge – to ourselves and others" (Ruhl, 2020). ToM uses perspective-taking to comprehend the experiences of another person. It incorporates data from our experiences to better understand what is most likely to happen.

In other words, "we risk misinterpreting the meaning of the experience for the other when we perceive the other's reality via our own experiences because we can never fully know what the other is thinking in a given scenario."

Let's present a straightforward scenario to comprehend better how the theory of mind functions. Imagine sitting down on the park bench after taking a stroll around it. By chance, you come upon jogging at the park. You also enjoy it, especially the sense of accomplishment it gives you afterward.

An emotive reaction to this discovery may include "an increased heart rate, labored breathing, or even the sensation of the ground beneath your feet" (Segal et al., 2017). According to the ToM, you may project your enjoyment of jogging onto the jogger by picturing how terrific the activity must make the jogger feel.

The jogger then stops and sits on the same park bench, murmuring about how difficult it is to jog and promising never to do it again. It "tells you that your interference based on your experience does not apply to the experience of the other person," according to this information.

Self-other awareness is crucial because it reminds the other person may not be thinking exactly how you assume they are. Thus, empathy "pushes us to remain open to different interpretations of what an event may entail" by incorporating self-other awareness and perspective-taking (Segal et al., 2017). It brings us to the second aspect of empathy that we'll discuss: emotion regulation.

## 5. Emotion Regulation

According to Segal et al. (2017), emotion regulation is the "capacity to react to another's experiences and comprehend what those reactions might entail without being overwhelmed or caught up in someone else's feelings." When sustaining perspective-taking and self-other awareness is challenging, this crucial skill to control emotions can be seen as having a "calming impact."

In addition to its role in the concept of empathy, emotion control is frequently unknowingly used in our daily struggles. Conversations with friends, rest, exercise, meditation, and more are some typical illustrations of healthy emotion regulation techniques (Rolston and others (2015)).

## THE FULL SCOPE OF EMPATHY

This contemporary definition of empathy may initially appear complicated, but if all of its elements are comprehended, it gives us access to the "whole breadth of empathy" (Segal et al., 2017). Let's cover each of the main aspects of empathy with an example so that everyone may fully understand it.

A close friend calls to tell you his mother has passed away. This stimulation will immediately evoke feelings you once had when you learned of your mother's passing; this reaction is known as the emotional response.

You start to mentally see your mother being treated in the hospital, which is an instance of affective mentalizing. One of your initial reactions might be to start crying as you reflect on your loss, but you are warned not to let your emotions get the better, especially when your friend is going through a similar tragedy.

This is what it means to be self-other aware. When you realize your friend needs your aid, you try to "walk in their shoes" while thinking about your loss. The element of perspective-taking is this. This is the aspect of empathy referred to as the theory of compassion, and you do it to better comfort your companion with the appropriate words of consolation.

You are seeking to balance the various processes of empathy as all these varied thoughts are running through your head. Put another way; you are controlling your emotions, which is another aspect of empathy.

These aspects of empathy, according to neuroimaging, include various brain regions, "some overlapping, some sequential, and some occasionally stronger at one time than the other" (Segal et al., 2017). We now understand the idea of empathy as an "umbrella phrase" that encompasses all of the previously covered elements.

## CONCLUSION

In conclusion, from its inception in 1908, the definition of empathy has undergone several revisions. Empathy is a concept that was first used to define aesthetics, particularly in the fields of dance and art. We must understand the complexity of empathy as more academics from various fields get interested in the topic. Empathy is a dynamic and "moving target," as was mentioned. Analyzing the components of empathy is crucial if one wants to comprehend its total reach.

# CHAPTER 05
# EMPATHY IN HUMAN DEVELOPMENT

We like to believe that morality is something humans excel at and that part of what makes us unique in this vast evolutionary tree is our existential awareness of ourselves and other people. Our physical and emotional relationships with people, which are strong enough to aid in the development of civilizations and propel us to other planets, come from this awareness. But as scientists continue to understand more about the brain and its evolutionary past, we find that traits we see as uniquely human, like empathy, precede humanity.

This chapter examines the role of empathy development in evolution and how it impacts natural animal selection intending to trace the origins of what we now understand as human empathy. Additionally, we will look at how empathy develops in people—in its early stages during childhood and as it matures with more social encounters as we age.

## EMPATHY'S EVOLUTIONARY ORIGINS IN THE ANIMAL WORLD

While this may seem to contradict the theory of natural selection directly, Charles Darwin proposed that empathy occurs in non-human creatures and that such traits are essential to evolution. Modern theories and research experiments support Darwin's theory (Preston et al., 2002).

Similar to altruism, there are several fundamental reasons why animal empathy development is advantageous or even necessary, even though these reasons aren't always easily discernible.

First of all, the function of parenting becomes more crucial as animals go along the evolutionary tree. To give their children the finest care and ensure the family survives, mothers must be sensitive to the needs and distress exhibited by their children. This shows where empathy comes from in families (de Waal, 2005).

Second, more advanced creatures like mammals and primates frequently exhibit the emergence of social groups and cooperation. Animals quickly understood there was a limit to how much they could accomplish independently. Therefore, this community-originated trait may be beneficial in guaranteeing the species' survival.

An animal and its conspecific must share some emotional state to engage in this kind of cooperation. Depending on an animal's evolutionary proximity to humans and the level of brain evolution, varying levels of empathy have been seen in that animal (Pérez-Manrique & Gomila, 2018; Preston et al., 2002).

Additionally, social animals or those whose survival depends on collaboration, like lions, elephants, or primates, exhibit sympathetic behaviors more frequently. According to scientific theory, the growth of empathy is a bottom-up process (de Waal, 2005; Mafessoni & Lachmann, 2019).

Empathy depends on the existence of a shared emotional state to function, which is accomplished through the spread of emotional contagion. The basic definition of empathy is that it is possible for the observer to feel similar emotional arousal to that of the actor without actually experiencing the event. The less developed a species' brains are and the more phylogenetically distinct it is from humans, the more primitive its empathic actions are.

In trials with rodents and pigeons, for example, the animal can exhibit significant suffering when another animal in the same cage is exposed to a distressing stimulus, such as an electric shock. This can be seen as a primitive kind of empathy because it is clear that the animals can share some emotional states with their distressed subjects. But for such emotional excitation to occur, certain stimuli must be present. Hence this might be categorized as affective empathy.

One can find more complex sympathetic behaviors in more advanced mammals and primates. When a companion is under stress, rhesus monkeys have been seen to alter their behavior to lessen their companion's suffering.

For example, a monkey will immediately stop reaching for treats if doing so might cause one of its companions to receive an electric shock. This protects the other monkey (Preston et al., 2002). Since they share a close evolutionary relationship with humans, bonobos, sometimes known as miniature chimpanzees, are also widely studied regarding their empathy behaviors.

When a wounded or otherwise disabled bonobo is introduced to a new community in a new setting, the majority of the resident bonobos welcome their new member and provide a helping hand—possibly in a pretty human-like manner (de Waal, 2005).

Aside from the numerous instances of spontaneous aid and selfless behavior, many other bonobos will come and support their newest member if they make a distress call, sometimes even holding them by the hand (Preston et al., 2002). However, not all members share this compassion, as some bonobo looks for this chance to intimidate the newcomer. Surprisingly, the most senior bonobo would frequently intervene and defend the newcomer with its arms.

As long as they develop the appropriate cognitive capacity observed in elephants and cetaceans, the creatures can experience empathy without being phylogenetically related to humans (dolphins). However, empirical data on these animals are more complex to get by and less common than data on primates (Pérez-Manrique & Gomila, 2018). These instances demonstrate that empathy does exist across species, however, to varying degrees of complexity depending on the animal's cognitive capacity.

Animals can create a more shared emotional and mental state than the straightforward experience started by an emotional contagion as brain complexity increases in the evolutionary tree. In reality, only two species—humans and apes, the most cognitively advanced land mammals we have ever studied—are capable of cognitive empathy, which allows us to see past our own emotions and understand how others think.

It's interesting to note that animals can only exhibit so much empathy. Empathy can be activated but quickly turned off, mainly when the other animal is unfamiliar or viewed as a threat. There are several instances of animals acting cold-bloodedly and destroying other species, such as bonobos striking an injured monkey in the head.

Examples of situations where other vital mental factors suppress empathy include the innumerable wars and acts of violence throughout human history. According to the wise Darwin, *"this virtue (empathy), one of the best bestowed upon man, seems to come indirectly from our sympathies getting softer and wider spread till they are extended to all sentient beings."*

His theory has been supported by human research findings, which show that as our phylogenetic distance from other species increases, so does our ability to feel empathy for them. The more different an animal is from us in evolution, the less compassion we have for them (Miralles et al., 2019).

Overall, we can trace the evolution of empathy along the evolutionary tree and learn from biology that it is not just a trait of humans. Bottom-up development creates the many aspects of empathy, with less cognitively developed creatures merely able to react to emotional contagion. And more cognitively evolved species can exhibit more sophisticated kinds of empathy.

## EMPATHY AND HUMAN DEVELOPMENT

Many theories discuss how the human mind functions, how we perceive and produce emotion, and how we engage in social interaction going back to ancient times due to human beings' unending fascination with ourselves. Without a doubt, these ideas have also frequently examined the phenomenon of empathy.

Just a few notable philosophers of the contemporary era who have included empathy in their most important theories include Sigmund Freud, Carl Jung, and Jean Piaget. By monitoring the behavior of newborns and toddlers, they largely came up with innovative theories about how empathy develops.

Nowadays, with the help of cutting-edge tools like functional magnetic resonance imaging (fMRI), fantastic technology, and a better grasp of neuroscience. We have made exciting progress in understanding how empathy develops during our early childhood and how it may go awry.

Numerous theories of cognition and philosophical approaches to the mind have incorporated many of the concepts underlying the development of empathy. One of the most well-known child development psychologists, Jean Piaget, asserted that the kid is still egocentric during the first two phases of development, The sensorimotor stage and the preoperational stage.

This means that the child can only understand their own opinions and ways of thinking. But empirical research refuted Piaget's assertion. Children have three different levels of empathy. Rudimentary emotional connection is its most basic form and the first to emerge. Researchers have discovered that the experience of emotional contagion can cause the development of primitive empathy or shared emotional states as early as a few months after birth.

Children can feel agitated and distressed when put among other crying or distressed newborns, for instance, due to the so-called emotional contagions from their distressed neighbors (McDonald & Messinger, 2011). Children increasingly acquire more complex empathic capacities throughout the first year of life, reaching the second level of empathy development and starting to deliberately pay attention to the emotions and thought processes of others (Ornaghi et al., 2020).

For example, a 12-month-old can be seen soothing a distraught person, and by 14 months, they can pretend to be helpful to others (Decety, 2010). Infants typically establish communication with others before learning complex language by reading face. The next step is to comprehend the emotional connections made with individuals.

The children can be said to have attained a complete range of empathetic capacities after this. When it comes to assisting the youngsters in understanding their emotions, the last two stages are when socializing and parenting are most crucial. This precise sculpting process may last well into the child's first ten years of life (Levy et al., 2019).

Since the discovery of mirror neurons, we have been able to more thoroughly examine how empathy develops cognitively (MacGillivray, 2009). Mirror neurons are distinct motor neurons that carry out actions that mirror the observed movement, as the name suggests. It is present both when an action is being performed and when it is being observed, producing the mirroring effect. The foundation of empathy could be the perception of emotion only observed when the same principle is applied to emotional states.

An observer can reach partial activation in the same brain area as the actor displaying a given emotion in fMRI and brain activity investigations, producing an essential shared emotional experience. These fundamental connections can develop more sophisticated cognitive processes, which lead to the compassionate actions we observe in modern humans.

As previously mentioned, a wide range of circumstances affects how empathy develops. Scientists have discovered that genetic variables and heredity significantly influence a child's potential level of empathy before they are even born through twin studies and family studies (McDonald & Messinger, 2011). Additionally, genetics has an impact on a child's temperament, which is a contributing factor to how empathic a person is.

For example, naturally timid children may behave with above-average empathy in familiar settings but avoid displaying any empathy in challenging social situations. Parenting, as an environmental component, is just as crucial for developing empathy as the hereditary influences from the parents. It's interesting to note that emotional empathy seems to be influenced by how much the mother and baby behave similarly (McDonald & Messinger, 2011).

A child's ability to show empathy correlates with how loving and connected their family is. Additionally, researchers discovered that parents' explanations of their motivations for their feelings and behaviors could hasten a child's cognitive empathy development (Ornaghi et al., 2020).

However, much like every other developmental stage in a child, the environment can also negatively impact a youngster's ability to acquire empathy. Adversity or negligence in their care and any other early life stress can hurt the child's ability for empathy, especially when compared to good parenting (Levy et al., 2019). Because empathy serves as a weak foundation for human social conduct, young children consequently struggle to participate in and integrate into society more.

## CONCLUSION

In the end, empathy is a fundamental aspect of our social behavior and must be adequately developed to integrate into society successfully. After all, it is regarded as a quality of a decent person. Contrary to particular early influential views, empathy develops from the very first moment of life and is influenced by the emotional contagion of other distressed infants.

After that, we continue to think at a higher level of complexity while using an increasing number of brain areas to process this information. Both hereditary and environmental factors influence the appropriate development of empathy.

# CHAPTER 06
# INDIVIDUAL DIFFERENCES IN EMPATHY

*The human mind's capacity to relate to other's feelings and experiences is known as empathy.* Empathy is not precisely defined. However, it can be loosely divided into two sections (Lockwood et al., 2017). The first component, cognitive or intellectual, implies the ability to understand others' perspectives. The second component is an affective or emotional response to the first.

In the past, they conducted psychological research on empathy in two different directions because they believed that empathy came in two different forms. However, there has recently been a shift to the notion that these forms are two aspects of empathy, allowing for the simultaneous conduct of both types of research (Davis, 1983).

Most people assume that empathy is a human trait that comes naturally, but this may not be the case because several circumstances, including motivation, personal suffering, and seeing other people's behavior, can have a significant impact on how empathetic a person ends up being (Lockwood et al., 2017).

The idea of empathy has become very popular as a multifaceted idea (Davis, 1980). Empathetic qualities have been connected to personality traits and interpersonal behavior, explaining individual variances (Powell, 2018). Certain desirable traits in an individual are being measured in various methods to understand better how individuals differ from one another.

This chapter will go over observed individual differences, potential causes of such differences, and current methods for quantifying them. The following chapter of this book deals specifically with psychiatric conditions affecting a person's empathy capacity.

## WHAT ARE INDIVIDUAL DIFFERENCES IN EMPATHY?

Like any other talent, different people display empathy to varying degrees. On one extreme, some people are constantly thinking about others, and on the other, some people are indifferent to the pain of others.

People who fall into the spectrum's extremes are highly uncommon, probably for good reasons, since those who have difficulty empathizing with others' feelings may have trouble integrating into society. At the same time, those who are overly sensitive may do so at the expense of their mental health and well-being (Hodges & Klien, 2001).

People also respond to stimuli physiologically differently depending on how empathic they are. In a study conducted in 1984 by Wiesenfeld, Whitman, and Malatesta, it was discovered that those with high empathy exhibit more expressive facial expressions and had more considerable heart rate variations and skin conductance (Mehrabian et al., 1988). More sympathetic people have a higher propensity to cry, which shows their emotional receptivity (Mehrabian & Epstein, 1972).

Aggression differs negatively from empathy in a person; these people frequently volunteer and work for charities, score highly on social qualities, have better moral standards, and are more tolerant and helpful to others (Mehrabian & Epstein, 1972). In a study that revealed violent criminals scored poorly on the empathy scale, higher empathy was linked with a greater sense of remorse and responsibility (Mehrabian et al., 1988).

To explore a broad spectrum of sympathetic behavior demonstrated by people in society with varied personality types, Davis used the Interpersonal Reactivity Index (IRI) to measure four aspects of empathy, namely perspective taking, fantasy, empathic concern, and personal pain. Females outperform males across the board regarding all aspects of empathy (Davis, 1983).

People who are better at understanding other people's perspectives tend to be more socially connected and have higher self-esteem. People who score highly on the fantasy scale exhibit more robust verbal intelligence and moderately higher emotional sensitivity. Higher degrees of anxiety, shyness, and low levels of ego were related to higher levels of empathy in persons (Davis, 1983).

Intelligence and empathetic worry did not correlate, but the empathetic concern was associated with increased emotionality and unselfish concern for others. Social anxiety and shyness, low self-esteem, and higher levels of emotion, vulnerability, and fear were all linked to higher degrees of personal suffering (Davis, 1983).

# FACTORS THAT AFFECT PEOPLE'S EMPATHY

Various factors might work together or separately to diminish a person's capacity for empathy. Following is a list of some of the factors:

1. Genetics:

A 1986 study on identical twins found that 68 percent of diverse empathy qualities are inherited, indicating a genetic basis for the emotional component (Mehrabian et al., 1988).

2. Motivation:

The degree of empathy demonstrated by members of society is strongly influenced by motivation. More vital cognitive or intellectual empathy has been linked to higher social, emotional, and behavioral motivation levels. It was discovered that a more potent emotional motivation was linked to a more robust emotional component of empathy.

People with higher levels of cognitive empathy claim to be quicker and more likely to figure out which of their activities will benefit others, which increases their desire to help others in society (Lockwood et al., 2017).

3. Child-rearing Practices:

Parents of those who had higher levels of empathy were found to have spent more time with them, expressed their emotions verbally more, and showed them more affection. Higher empathetic mothers were less likely to abuse their children and tolerate crying children better (Mehrabian et al., 1988).

Empathy development in youngsters is greatly influenced by how mothers treat their children and how the family is socialized. According to a study by Trommsdorff, moms of children with more empathy tended to understand their offspring more and had more socially conscious aspirations (Trommsdorff, 1991). Children's empathy levels are higher when parent-child interactions are more intense and early (Mehrabian et al., 1988).

4. Sex:

Numerous studies have revealed that women are generally more empathic than men (Davis, 1983). Females are believed to have this inclination because they have more paid emotional proceeds (the ability to be emotionally influenced by the emotions of others) than their male counterparts.

Also, adult females have greater empathy which is less linked to their upbringing from their parents than adult males (Mehrabian et al., 1988).

5. Emotions:

Adult males and females were asked in Williams' 1982 study about their propensity to cry in scenarios like the death of a close friend, ending a romantic relationship, seeing a movie, receiving negative feedback, feeling lonely or undesired.

People who cry more frequently have greater emotional openness and empathy in their personalities (Mehrabian et al., 1988). Higher empathy is also correlated with better emotion identification (Lockwood et al., 2017).

6. Environment And Personal Experiences:

Individuals develop empathy as they interact with their environment, connect with the cultures and people around them, and relate the feelings and emotions of others to their own experiences.

Individuals' efforts to comprehend the circumstances or feelings of others and the amount of information they are exposed to that prompts an empathic response control how much empathy they display (Hodges & Klien, 2001)

# MEASURING INDIVIDUAL DIFFERENCES IN EMPATHY

## 1. Hogan Empathy Scale (HES)

According to the Hogan Empathy Scale (HES), empathy is "the intellectual or imaginative understanding of another person's circumstance or state of mind" (Hogan, 1969). The HES examines four characteristics in a person: social self-confidence, even-temperedness, sensitivity, and nonconformity (Spreng et al., 2009). It was one of the first scales to be used widely.

The scale consists of 64 items, including eight by Hogan and colleagues and 25 from the California Psychological Inventory (CPI), and 31 from the Minnesota Multiphasic Personality Inventory (MMPI) (Hogan, 1969).

Hogan selected the questions based on the participants' responses, which would categorize them into two categories based on how empathic they were or weren't (Stueber, 2019). Due to intrinsic discrepancies and doubtful test-retest repeatability, numerous academics have questioned the HES's reliability (Spreng et al., 2009).

## 2. The Emotional Empathy Questionnaire By Mehrabian And Epstein (QMEE)

Emotional empathy is a vicariously emotional reaction to the perceived emotional experiences of others, and it is quantified by the Questionnaire Measure of Emotional Empathy (QMEE). The 33 items are rated on a 9-point scale, with -4 being the most disagreement and +4 being the most robust agreement.

The following seven subscales of QMEE are taken directly from Mehrabian & Epstein (1972):

- Susceptibility to emotional contagion
- Appreciation for the emotions of distant and unfamiliar persons
- Extreme emotional responsiveness
- Tendency to be moved by other people's pleasant emotional experiences
- Tendency to be moved by other people's distressing emotional situations
- Tendency to be sympathetic
- Willingness to interact with others who are struggling

The scale was created based on the idea that someone more empathic will be less inclined to act aggressively toward others and more willing to offer assistance to those in need. It demonstrated strong reliability and validity and suggested that it could be a helpful tool for predicting success in people who work in specific environments or professions, such as therapy, nursing, or medicine (Mehrabian & Epstein, 1972).

## 3. Interpersonal Reactivity Index (IRI)

Empathy is defined by the Interpersonal Reactivity Index (IRI) as "one person's responses to another person's observed experiences" (Davis, 1983). By taking into account all of a person's significant characteristics at once, IRI evaluates the relationship with measures of social functioning, self-esteem, emotional state, and sensitivity to others.

The 28-item questionnaires used in IRI have classified measures into four scales: the personal distress scale, the perspective-taking scale, the fantasy scale, and the scale for empathic care (Davis, 1980).

Twenty-eight items are considered while considering thoughts and feelings in various circumstances, with responses ranging from "Does not describe me well" to "Describes me very well" on a 5-point Likert scale. The assessment comprises four subscales, each with seven unique items. The following description of these subscales is taken directly from Davis (1983):

- Perspective Taking: the propensity to unprompted take on another's a psychological viewpoint
- Fantasy: examines respondents' propensity to creatively place themselves in the thoughts and behaviors of fictional characters in plays, movies, and books.
- Empathic Concern evaluates "other-oriented" emotions such as compassion and worry for unfortunate individuals.
- Personal Anxiety: measures "self-oriented" sensations of Anxiety and discomfort in complex social situations.

The IRI's temporal stability was deemed adequate since the test's dependability (test-retest reliability) was established by a sample of University of Texas students of both sexes who took the test twice with an interval of 60–75 days.

IRI shows statistically significant sex differences, with females scoring higher than males on each subscale. This index is a beneficial tool for thoroughly examining empathy and its constituent parts, and it was discovered to be compatible with earlier research findings (Davis, 1980).

## 4. Other Measures Of Empathy

The Scale of Ethnocultural Empathy, the Jefferson Scale of Physician Empathy, the Nursing Empathy Scale, the Autism Quotient, and the Japanese Adolescent Empathy Scale are only a few self-report measures of empathy that have been employed in specific populations or professions.

The 16 items on the Toronto Empathy Questionnaire (TEQ) assess various theoretical components of empathy. TEQ is a quick, simple, and straightforward assessment instrument with solid test-retest reliability, internal consistency, and concept validity (Spreng et al., 2009).

Self-reports of empathy may not accurately reflect how one felt in a situation; instead, one's attitude may have been modified by societal expectations of how one should feel in a particular situation. Self-reporting tools may have a wide range of results depending on how well people can describe themselves (Stueber, 2019).

## RELATION OF FACIAL EXPRESSION AND EMPATHY

The psychologists distinguish between situational empathy, which gauges a person's reactions when placed in a particular circumstance, and dispositional empathy, which gauges a person's fundamental personality features.

Situational empathy is measured by asking participants about their feelings quickly after exposure to a particular situation while observing their facial expressions, hand gestures, or physiological readings like their heart rate or skin conductance. The limitation of physiological techniques for measuring empathy is their inability to differentiate between empathy, sympathy, and personal sorrow (Stueber, 2019).

A person must have the ability to recognize appropriate facial expressions to display appropriate empathy. The empathetic reaction is positively impacted by improved identification of facial expressions that represent emotions of fear and distress. The amount of time a person is exposed to a particular facial expression affects their empathic reactions; short exposures result in automatic reactions, whereas prolonged exposures include cerebral circuits and result in deliberate, conscious responses (Basel & Yuille, 2010).

Another study discovered that the Interpersonal Reactivity Index' (IRI) empathy subscales—perspective taking, personal anguish, and empathic concern—were significant predictors of how people rated fear and anger together.

Later stages of facial expression interpretation may be influenced by empathy because individual differences in empathy appear to have a role in the decision-making processes involved with perceiving ambiguous facial emotions (Graham et al., 2010). When compared to inhibitors (those who exhibit fewer facial expressions), expressions (those who exhibit more facial expressions) are proven to be more empathic (Mehrabian et al., 1988).

## CONCLUSION

Empathy is said to be a fundamental aspect of human nature that enhances fairness and justice, as well as our ability to relate to others and form social bonds. People who display varying levels of empathy may behave more compassionately and charitably. While also experiencing higher despair and psychological distress (Powell, 2018). Because of these expenses, one must control empathy appropriately depending on the circumstances (Hodges & Klien, 2001).

A person's degree of compassion depends on their personality, past experiences, gender, and surroundings. Different scales can be used to evaluate variances in empathy levels, but no single rating system can accurately capture all of the nuances of empathy. When interacting with others, one must consider individual differences to ensure psychological well-being and prevent discomfort (Powell, 2018). Understanding individual differences can also help understand healthy processes and diseases linked to decreased motivation and empathy (Lockwood et al., 2017).

# CHAPTER 07
# DISORDERS IMPACTING EMPATHY

*Understanding, sharing, and responding to emotional states regarding oneself and others depends critically on one's capacity for empathy.* To see, comprehend, and relate to another person's feelings as if you have personally experienced them is to be empathetic. It is crucial to interact with people and participate in social situations. Having a personal understanding of the feelings of the people you speak to aids with behavior management and developing positive relationships.

Because empathy is so individualized, it can be challenging to comprehend its real potential and assess a person's capacity for it. Empathy is a source of altruistic motivation, which in some instances, may result in behavior that can be deemed immoral and, in others, may demonstrate the moral character of the person (Decety & Moriguchi, 2007).

The selfless part of empathy creates an understanding between people in social interactions that the other person understands them. And is not using their emotions to manipulate them; it is intrinsically intersubjective that people moderate and is directed by other people's behaviors. Since humans will alter their behavior to obtain the response they seek from members of their social circle, this inherent social regulation emphasizes empathy.

Most of the time, this action occurs unconsciously (humans do not actively control their emotions; they flow through the brain as the neurotransmitters accept the hormones). However, people unable to process other people's emotions must consciously modify their reactions and actions to fit into societal norms. As a result, empathy disorders affect all facets of a person's life.

As the issue of nature vs. nurture significantly influences human behavior and emotional capacity, empathy is a heavily discussed topic in psychology and developmental science. The nature vs. nurture controversy is a highly contested subject in the natural and social sciences because it has implications for how much influence we have over our lives and behaviors. This could alter how scientists see the developmental process. The argument from nature contends that heredity determines our human character and the course of our lives.

According to the nurture camp, each individual can become whoever they choose because our upbringing, social connections, and developmental experiences significantly impact who we are on the inside than our genes do. It is simplest to discuss the subject using identical twins. Let's imagine that a family only desires one child, so when a set of identical twins is born, the other child is adopted by a family on the other side of the country.

The difference between baby A and baby B will depend on their upbringing and social circumstances, according to the nurture theory, which contends that because their genetic makeup is identical, baby A and baby B will share similar likes, interests, motivations, and behaviors. For example, if baby A's biological family has less access to resources, education, and extracurricular activities because they are at a lower level of the economic and social hierarchy, this would affect how the child develops. The nurture theory states that if baby B is adopted into a caring and supportive family with financial and social resources, the two children will be completely different because they were raised in very different environments. And their genetic makeup won't have much of an impact on who they are.

The consequences of the nature vs. nurture controversy are wide-ranging and crucial for understanding empathy and the diseases that impact it. It is still uncertain whether these empathy disorders are genetic, causing children to be born with the disorder or if they arise due to trauma during developmental stages. Scientists have not yet reached a firm conclusion regarding a genetic basis for these disorders; there is still speculation about a broader cause.

Understanding the causes of empathy disorders will have a significant impact on social work and how to decide when to remove children from abusive and neglectful homes. We will concentrate on comprehending the symptoms, effects, causes, and therapies of personality and developmental disorders where empathy is severely impacted because the etiology of these diseases is currently poorly known.

## MENTAL STATE ATTRIBUTION (MSA) VS. SHARED REPRESENTATIONS (SR)

Empathy is understood in two primary ways it is being examined. Empathy is a shared representation (SR), in which "we co-represent another person's affect by involving brain and physiological mechanisms supporting the first-hand experience of the emotion we are empathizing with during the event."

Shared representations of empathy happen when you have experienced something similar to what the other person is going through and can recall it; you share their emotion because you have experienced it before.

The other method taken by empathy is mental state attribution (MSA). The cognitive capacity of a human to recognize and assess their own and other people's mental states is explained by the concept of mental state attribution. This entails being able to interpret, comprehend, and relate to another person based on their actions, expressions, and words used in conversation.

When employing the MSA pathway to empathize, misperceptions can result in poor communication and occasionally hostility because MSA dramatically influences how we perceive ourselves and others (Brune et al., 2007).

## DEVELOPMENTAL DISORDERS VS. PERSONALITY

Disorders that impact a person's mood and behavior have drawn more and more attention from the scientific community. And the media on mental health has grown in importance as the stigma associated with it is gradually eliminated. "Mood disorders" as a collective phrase and "personality disorders" tend to mean different things.

The psychology of personality disorders and traumatic childhood experiences that require a person to change their behavior to live are frequently linked. The most well-known personality disorders include obsessive-compulsive disorder, borderline personality disorder, schizoid, narcissism, and antisocial personality disorder. Because the exact origin and form of developmental disorders are not fully understood due to the lack of knowledge regarding their genesis, treatments for these illnesses typically focus more on managing symptoms than addressing the underlying causes.

Medical professionals and researchers have proposed that heredity and prenatal activities like drinking and smoking can contribute to developmental issues. These behaviors have demonstrable developmental repercussions that may hurt the child for the rest of their lives.

The two most prevalent and well-known developmental disorders are attention deficit hyperactivity disorder and autism spectrum disorder. The capacity to recognize one's feelings and those of others is impacted by personality and developmental issues.

## AFFECTIVE VS. COGNITIVE EMPATHY

The autonomic nervous system facilitates affective empathy, which is a quick process. The shared representation model of empathy is used to describe it, and it is "described as one's emotional, sensorimotor, and visceral response to the affective state of others" (Yu & Chou, 2018). Affective empathy notices others' emotional expressions on their faces and internalizes them to understand and interact with them.

Cognitive empathy is a slower process involving conscious thought and analysis of the intentions of self and others during communication to relate to emotions and feelings. Cognitive empathy employs perception to understand and guess how the person you are interacting with feels. Since it is impossible to comprehend the thoughts and intentions of another fully, this type of empathy is frequently misconstrued (Yu & Chou, 2018).

Affective empathy is impacted by some empathy disorders, while others impact cognitive empathy. Cognitive disorders tend to lead to more chaos in a person's life because they lead them to misunderstand and misinterpret the motives of others, which makes them distrustful of those around them. As the person has trouble adopting other people's emotions as their own, affective empathy disorders frequently hurt close relationships. It can be challenging to sustain close relationships because of this stressful situation.

## HYPO VS. HYPER EMPATHY

It is crucial to comprehend how empathy can be impacted while considering diseases that affect it. Hypo-empathy, or the inability to understand the emotions and feelings of others, is a symptom of most disorders, meaning that the person in question lacks the capacity for empathy. With numerous personality and developmental abnormalities, this condition is more prevalent.

Hypo-empathetic people react differently and with less warmth and caring than the average person because they do not register the emotions or feelings of others, giving them the appearance of being cold and heartless.

Hyper-empathy is another option, albeit it is less common. People who suffer from hyper-empathetic disorders have heightened empathy and a propensity to internalize other people's emotions. As the person struggles to cope with both their feelings and the intense emotions of those around them, hyper-empathy can be crippling.

## BORDERLINE PERSONALITY DISORDER (BPD)

The cause of borderline personality disorder (BPD) is uncertain. Some people with BPD have symptoms from an early age, indicating that it is a developmental disease; however, many people with BPD start displaying symptoms after experiencing some trauma (generally occurring in mid-to-late childhood).

However, all people with BPD typically exhibit the following symptoms: affective instability, interpersonal dysfunction, mood swings, self-uncertainty, rapid changes in values and beliefs, extreme views, a fear of abandonment, unstable social relationships, impulsive behavior, tendencies towards self-harm, uncontrollable anger, and a tendency to dissociate. Depending on the individual's history, they may react differently in social situations.

The wide range of symptoms has a significant and frequently incapacitating impact on the person. It is challenging to interact with people and form lasting relationships because of the severe fear of abandonment, unstable emotions, and mood swings. BPD sufferers frequently oscillate between idealization and mistrust; in one instance, they might only be able to notice a person's positive traits, in which case they elevate them and have a tendency to devote themselves entirely to them.

The person can suddenly distrust those in their lives and accuse them of being the cause of all their problems and suffering. As the person with BPD may be motivated to quickly change their attitude and actions based on what another person says or does, this rapid fluctuation has strong ties to empathy. Since the person with hyper-empathic functioning is highly tuned in to and sensitive to other people's feelings, stress may speed up transitions.

Severe BPD symptoms, according to the study, "occur in the setting of social threat, contributing to brief episodes of paranoia, erotomania, or detachment. Relationships characterized by projective identification and conflicted dependency; emptiness and identity diffusion; and impulsive suicidality or aggression" (Ripoll et al. 2013). People with BPD experience negative emotions and perceptions intimately related to how they perceive other people's emotions and how naturally they tend to empathize with those emotions.

According to Ripoll et al. (2013), people with borderline personality disorder transition between shared representations and mental state attribution far more quickly and inaccurately than people without mental disorders. "SR processing relies on visceral recognition of mental states via similarity in brain activation in both social targets and perceivers," they claim. Due to their extreme resemblance to other people's mental states, people with BPD are more likely to hyper-focus on little fluctuations in other people's facial expressions and mistake them for their feelings.

Their autonomic system overreacts, causing unpleasant effects, where they apply the feelings and reactions of others to themselves at a rate too rapid for their brains to grasp the differences between themselves and others, which can make it difficult for them to interact in social circumstances (Rippol et al., 2013). BPD seriously harms those who have it because it assaults the affective empathy system.

## ANTISOCIAL PERSONALITY DISORDER

The term "antisocial personality disorder" (ASPD) refers to many disorders. Antisocial personality disorder includes psychopathy, sociopathy, and narcissism, all of which have significant adverse effects on the lives of those affected. As a result of their highly manipulative personality and callous indifference to others, these disorders impact a person's life duration as a whole.

1. Psychopathy

Psychopathy is a neuropsychiatric condition characterized by inadequate emotional reactions, a lack of empathy, and poor behavioral controls, frequently leading to persistent criminal and antisocial behavior. Psychopaths find it challenging to sustain intimate personal connections (Anderson & Kiehl, 2014). Because psychopaths have little regard for the impact of their behavior on others, their lack of empathy makes it difficult for them to comprehend the emotions of others and frequently culminates in illegal behavior.

According to research, psychopaths can grow and are both born and made; the development of psychopathy is strongly linked to a genetic risk factor; yet, environmental variables and early trauma can combine with genetic risk to produce an individual's lack of empathy. Most psychopathy symptoms start around the age of 10 when kids can generally grasp and distinguish between good and wrong. Psychopaths are more likely to exhibit this comprehension, being erratic and lacking in emotional expressiveness. There are two types of psychopaths:

- The one of which exhibits more predatory and deliberate criminal behavior, planning out their crimes in advance.
- The second kind of psychopath is referred to as impulsive-reactionary and exhibits higher levels of anxiety regularly.

According to research, psychopaths have high executive function and prefrontal impairments, which results in highly clever people with no sense or understanding of emotions and no capacity for empathy. There are no known therapies or cures for psychopathy's environmental and developmental components.

Empathy cannot be acquired through a pill, and there is no way to learn how to comprehend and interpret social signs in a way that will result in genuine empathy. Although some psychopaths have learned to act "normally" in social situations, they will never fully understand or experience empathy.

2. Sociopathy

An antisocial personality disorder is also known by the word "sociopath," which is more frequently used in movies and other forms of media. Sociopathy is closely related to psychopathy, but it differs because a sociopath may be aware of the distinction between good and wrong but lacks empathy, making it difficult to comprehend how their actions will affect other people entirely.

A sociopath is also less likely to use violence because they have a strong sense of morality (Pemment, 2013). The empathy circuit in the brains of sociopaths has been shown to activate in studies employing functional magnetic resonance imaging (fMRI).

They cannot experience or comprehend empathy, but they may witness it and adapt their behavior to those around them. Sociopaths lack the amygdala and frontal cortices damage that psychopaths do, allowing them to feel empathy and recognize right and evil (Pemment, 2013). After brain injuries are caused by trauma or sickness may develop antisocial behavior and tendencies.

As a result, acquired sociopaths who may have originally been healthy people who developed sociopathic traits due to a disease or injury are produced. Comprehending how empathy and disorders of empathy are depicted in the media requires understanding these fundamental physical and behavioral differences between psychopaths and sociopaths.

3. Narcissistic Personality Disorder

Although narcissism and antisocial personality disorder share a lack of empathy, they differ in the lower crime rates and propensity for violence. A distorted and highly fragile sense of self is a typical characteristic of people with a narcissistic personality disorder. Low self-esteem and an unhealthy sense of self result in frequent disappointment, difficulty maintaining relationships, and a tendency to react violently to even minor inconveniences.

Their lack of empathy for others perpetuates their lack of meaningful relationships and raises the likelihood of outbursts. They frequently use dishonesty as a strategy to elevate their social or economic status. Grandiose narcissism and communal narcissism are the two basic types of narcissism.

- Grandiose narcissists think they are superior to and more significant than everyone else. They tend to utilize other people to advance their status because they think they are entitled to all forms of power. They are without regret, don't give a damn about the suffering they cause others, and aren't even aware of it. How they handle the people in their lives, who are merely stepping stones on their path to power, demonstrates their complete lack of empathy (Nehrlich & Gebauer, 2019).

- Conversely, communal narcissists benefit much from other people's compassion. Although they cannot experience emotions themselves, they can observe them and profit from other people's perspectives. They desire to be viewed as solid and affluent within their social circle. Nehrlich and Gebauer (2019) discovered that while communal narcissists seem to empathize with others, clinical research has revealed through brain scans and social testing that they are merely emotional mimics rather than genuine empathizers.

The ability of many narcissists to mimic the feelings of those around them, giving the impression of empathy without actually understanding or feeling those emotions, distinguishes narcissistic personality disorder from other personality disorders. Their intricate brain activity suggests a genetic, environmental, and neurological origin. The condition is a contemporary and fascinating subject of study due to its complexity and many-faceted causes.

Personality disorders are complicated and necessitate a multifaceted approach to diagnosis. They must exhibit more than just one or a few symptoms to be diagnosed. They must exhibit substantial deficits in various facets of their lives and many of the symptoms. A psychiatrist or psychologist must diagnose any personality disorder. This analysis typically entails psychotherapy due to the complexity of these diseases and the symptoms they share with other disorders.

It's essential to remember that although the popular media refers to criminals and fictional television characters as psychopaths, sociopaths, or narcissists, they are not such until they have received a diagnosis from a doctor.

We may use these phrases loosely when judging the actions of others based on what we observe and how they treat people. Still, an accurate diagnosis requires a trained expert for several months and numerous observations.

## ATTENTION DEFICIT HYPERACTIVITY DISORDER (ADHD)

The developmental disease known as attention deficit hyperactivity disorder (ADHD) has significant behavioral implications and restrictions. It is characterized by impulsivity, hyperactivity, and inattentiveness, which create developmental difficulties.

According to studies looking at their neuroanatomy, the cerebellum and the cortex of people with ADHD have anomalies. These anatomical anomalies indicate empathy deficits seen in social and cognitive contexts. When combined with the inattentive symptom, these deficiencies often lead to inappropriate social behavior and frequent conversational disruptions.

ADHD patients with empathic disorder often have social cognitive deficits that influence how they perceive other people's emotions. Some people with ADHD have trouble reading facial expressions, making it difficult to empathize with those around them.

Those with ADHD are not able to grasp the emotions of others, which leads to the theory that they are unable to empathize. This is because they are inattentive, frequently interrupt, and have difficulty reading and understanding nonverbal communication. However, some ADHD kids have horrific childhoods that taught them to empathize too much with their violent or emotionally damaged parents.

The empathy deficit that affects people with ADHD has a vital hereditary and environmental component. This reaction is partly caused by a shift in brain structures and partly by the deliberate efforts of the child to avoid pain. Some children who grow up in abusive homes and experience childhood trauma will become closed off and lose the ability to empathize.

People with ADHD who exhibit excessive empathy are typically girls who experienced some form of abuse from their parents as children. To protect themselves from experiencing the same sorrow they had, they absorb the suffering of those around them. Although it is a very overpowering illness, psychotherapy has been demonstrated to lessen its effects (Kessler, 2019).

## CONCLUSION

Empathy is a crucial component of human existence in a world where personal connections are paramount in both our personal and professional lives. Disorders that interfere with our ability to empathize with those around us lead to substantial communication gaps and make it difficult for people to build meaningful connections.

Hyper-empathic illnesses produce people who are overwhelmed by other people's emotions and find it challenging to sustain genuine relationships. In contrast, hypo-empathic disorders often result in coldness, isolation, and a lack of meaningful connections.

# CHAPTER 08
# THE ECONOMICS OF EMPATHY

The common characteristic and subject of modern business is empathy. Businesses and their marketing actively promote it, highlighting the value of empathy as a subject. Through empathy in their marketing, businesses create emotional appeals to connect with their customers on a deeper level. Notably, empathy as a talent can help people understand other people's viewpoints and strengthen customer relationships.

A happy world is made possible by having an open mind to other people's perspectives. Furthermore, it promotes company success since consumers connect with compassionate brands. Coca-Cola's -marketing, for instance, effectively communicates this.

As a business, they heavily rely on empathy in their marketing to advance their brand. Notably, Coca-Cola has recently had success as a result of this. However, businesses like PepsiCo have fallen short in applying sympathetic concepts to their brand. The subsequent chapter will contrast these examples to show how marketing empathy may be successful.

Barack Obama stated to American schoolchildren in 2006 that there is an "empathy deficit" in the nation. He said people should have broader concerns and worry about others because the world does not revolve around them (Obama, 2008). When addressing their marketing campaigns, companies take this into account. Companies want to show their customers that they care about them and are invested in their personal development.

Coca-Cola launched an awareness campaign emphasizing how the COVID virus has impacted many people's lives (Coca-Cola: Open, n.d.). Their business thoroughly grasps these ideas and successfully incorporates empathy into their brand's core values. However, take Facebook as an example. Singled out their company for exploiting sympathy and profiting off misfortune. The company leveraged the damage caused by Hurricane Maria in Puerto Rico to display its new technology. For empathy to impact a crowd, it must be genuine and meaningful.

Examples of companies that failed to accomplish this goal include PepsiCo and Facebook; this topic will be covered in more detail in the following section. PepsiCo, Facebook, Coca-Cola, and other businesses influence empathy as a critical marketing strategy. A brand must have a simple and impactful message to benefit from empathy marketing.

## THE EFFECTIVENESS OF MARKETING EMPATHY

Marketing today places a lot of emphasis on the topic of empathy. Businesses strive to put themselves in other people's shoes to be more understanding. Companies, their employees, and customers all become more interconnected as a result.

Unfortunately, several businesses, like Coca-Cola, have developed ads centered on the concept of empathy. Take the Ekocen terms kiosks from Coca-Cola as an example. Coca-Cola, a multibillion-dollar company, created its Ekocenters to give anyone in need access to safe drinking water, food, and supplies off the grid ("Coca-Cola Ekocenter," n.d.).

Since the firm values the concept of charitable activity, Coca-Cola is sympathetic. People in disadvantaged areas may use the Ekocenters' services and safety, which is crucial. Coca-Cola strategically placed these kiosks in Southeast Asia, Africa, and South America.

A statement from Coca-Cola's website reads, "Ekocenter is part of our mission to do business the right way by doing what's suitable for people and our world. Giving underserved communities a helping up will help them develop more quickly on the social and economic fronts. We established a social company to give The Coca-Cola Company and our partner growth opportunities (Coca-Cola Ekocenter, n.d.). It had a positive effect on underprivileged communities.

Coca-Cola's implicit emphasis on its approach to empathy is seen in this. According to Coca-Cola, empathy is crucial to establishing new connections and fostering economic expansion as a brand. Additionally, the corporation contributes resources to underprivileged areas as part of its programs ("Coca-Cola Ekocenter," n.d.).

Empathy plays a primary role in Coca-Cola's Ekocenter kiosks to reflect the brand's operations. Coca-Cola as a business has successfully incorporated the concept of empathy into its marketing and image. Coca-Cola is aware that people are more likely to associate with businesses they can relate to (Fauconnier et al., 2014). The business released an advertisement criticizing the lockdown concept in light of the spread of COVID-19. Coca-Cola enlisted the spoken word artist George the Poet to address the issue in the "Open like never before" campaign. "What is normal," "what if I listen," and "what if my aspirations never take the backseat again" are just a few of the queries George the Poet poses in this passage ("Coca-Cola Embraces, n.d.").

In this commercial, Coca-Cola displays empathy for the lockout scenario. The lyrics by George the Poet reference all the various incidents that have happened throughout the pandemic. The company's message to its customers is that they can depend on them in good times. Here, Coca-Cola as a brand seeks to put itself in another person's position and demonstrate its concern.

Coca-Cola promotes empathy-based marketing, which emphasizes viewing the world from the consumer's perspective. The business is making use of the subject by considering the lifestyles of its clients and creating an advertisement in response to the exceptional times. Modern firms must embrace empathy-based marketing since it fosters customer loyalty. Coca-Cola illustrated this idea in their "The Great Meal" commercial, which debuted on June 30, 2020.

Coca-Cola's commercial stresses the significance of setting aside time to dine with your family while once more stressing the circumstances brought on by COVID and the lockdown. Coca-Cola says their drink is a family member and is there for you when things are hard.

"Now that we know to appreciate the moments that were always there, we won't leave anything on our plates. According to the advertisement ("The Great Meal," 2020), they have never tasted this nice. "The Great Meal" addresses issues of empathy when it is claimed that family is important and required in difficult circumstances.

The commercial demonstrates how foods and beverages, such as Coca-Cola, assist families in making the most of their situation. It is no coincidence that themes of empathy are prevalent in many of Coca-marketing Cola's efforts Notably, Coca-Cola announced in 2020 that their future campaigns would be empathy-driven. About their most recent campaign, Coca-Cola said,

> *The campaign builds on Coca-134-year-old Cola's brand objective of bringing people together and inspiring optimism for a happier world. The realization is that everyone can empathize. However, sometimes we simply are not listening and frequently want to reaffirm our opinions rather than seeking to understand one another's viewpoints (Coca-Cola: Open, n.d.).*

Coca-Cola conveys its support for both business and empathy in the statement. As has been mentioned thus far with Coca-Cola's commercials, the company recognizes the need for businesses to establish themselves in consumers' minds. By doing this, Coca-Cola can better understand its customers' wants and meet them.

Last but not least, Coca-Cola's advertisement "Open" illustrates how the business has shifted to empathic marketing (Dan, 2020). In the advertisement, there is a globe filled with individuals debating who is right and who is wrong. As a result of the arguments, chaos breaks out and starts to self-destruct in the form of automobiles, buildings, and streets.

Actress Natasha Lyonne approaches the conclusion of the advertisement and asks, "What if we pondered if we were incorrect. Maybe then everything would turn out better?" (Dan, 2020). The motivational message is directed toward today's dialogue, where everyone is constantly disputing and trying to be correct.

The commercial's theme is that if people occasionally admitted they were wrong, perhaps they could avoid mayhem. The new wave of sympathetic marketing from Coca-Cola reflects new business ideas. Companies nowadays are looking for new methods to connect with their customers. Said, a business will be more successful in selling its goods if it demonstrates that it cares about the needs of others.

Although this may not be Coca-Cola's primary priority, it does show how they can sell their brands more effectively as a result.

## WHEN EMPATHY IN MARKETING CAN FAIL

Companies may successfully promote the values of empathy, as shown by Coca-Cola's successful usage of empathy in their campaigns. Businesses like Coca-Cola's success show how empathy can be included in marketing strategies while also engaging their audience and demonstrating that they care. It is crucial to remember that if empathy is not shown naturally, it might work against a corporation. Take the controversial Pepsi commercial "Live for Now Moments Anthem," for instance (Smith, 2017).

The premise of the advertisement drew immediate criticism after it was released. Kendall Jenner is pictured here joining a group of protesters of different races. Jenner and the gang make their way around a line of police officers who are in their way while displaying gestures of peace. The demonstrators applaud when Jenner gives one of the police officers a Pepsi at the end of the commercial. People who felt PepsiCo was trying to distract from a serious issue by airing the advertisement criticized it.

People thought the scene in which Jenner handed the authorities a Pepsi resembled the Baton Rouge protests, where officers apprehended Ieshia Evan in a well-known photograph (Smith, 2017). assumed that the advertisement was an attempt to cash in on the Black Lives Matter (BLM) movement. The following day, they took down the advertisement due to the uproar.

In response, PepsiCo issued the following statement, saying that the company "tried to reflect a global message of harmony, peace, and understanding. [They] regret having missed the mark. The intention was never to make light of a serious subject. [They] stop all subsequent rollouts and remove the content. [They] also apologize for placing Kendall Jenner in this predicament" (Smith, 2017). Here, PepsiCo's attempt to impose and profit from empathic marketing was the main factor in the commercial's failure.

The concept that Pepsi was trying to promote their product by using the BLM movement did not find favor with the public. According to activist DeRay McKesson, "[the] add trivializes the urgency of the concerns, and it lessens the seriousness and gravity of why we first entered the street" (Smith, 2017). People could see that the commercial didn't have sincere intentions, which was its primary problem.

People still recall the iconic Pepsi commercial in the wake of the scandal. As a result, Pepsi's abuse of empathy was made fun of in popular culture. For example, Saturday Night Live's comedy program made a segment about the incident. In the sketch, Beck Bennett, who plays the campaign's writer, is shown putting the advertisement together. He is shown being reprimanded by his family and friends as the premise is being developed. Although he is aware that what he is doing is cruel, he continues doing it.

On the other hand, Cecily Strong's portrayal of Jenner seems unaware of what she is doing. On the phone with a friend, she is shown unwittingly disclosing the immoral aims of the commercial (Saturday Night Live, 2017). People harshly attacked Pepsi as a result of this because they understood the purpose of the advertisement. Finally, when more individuals became aware of the controversy, they expressed their worries about the advertisement on social media.

When Dr. Martin Luther King Jr.'s daughter Bernice King commented on the situation, she said, "If only Daddy would have known about the power of #Pepsi" (Smith, 2017). As a result, if a corporation does not express intentional empathy, it will come under fire and work against it. Building off of this idea, Facebook has also generated debate.

In 2017, Mark Zuckerberg showed off Facebook's brand-new virtual reality (VR) technology. This happened after Hurricane Maria hit Puerto Rico. Zuckerberg demonstrated how the new "Facebook Spaces" VR technology might give users a real-time perspective on events occurring across the globe. Users may "build 3-D avatars for Facebook video calls and the virtual reality gear Oculus Rift" using Facebook Spaces (Tarnoff, 2017).

Facebook, though, faced criticism for how it promoted the technology. In the virtual reality environment, Zuckerberg's avatar was grinning as he saw the flooded streets of Puerto Rico. People didn't respond well and felt it was disrespectful given the circumstances. Nobody wanted to see a millionaire make money out of the relationship.

People were saying that Zuckerberg was "exploiting a tragedy," even though it is doubtful that this was his objective (Tarnoff, 2017). People who want to be empathetic must see themselves in another person's position. In this case, Zuckerberg didn't, and as a result, the event had a disastrous outcome. In response to the allegations, Zuckerberg said,

> "Empathy is one of VR's most potent properties. Here, I wanted to demonstrate how virtual reality (VR) may increase awareness and allow us to view what's happening worldwide. Additionally, I wanted to let you know about our

*collaboration with the Red Cross to aid in the recovery. I'm sorry if this offended anyone; after reading some responses, I see this wasn't obvious (Tarnoff, 2017).*

Facebook failed to understand its audience in this situation. Facebook did not consider how people would respond to the issue because it focused on showing off its technology. Based on Zuckerberg's comments, Facebook may have sought to show its sympathies. Others believed that Zuckerberg was attempting to capitalize on the catastrophe and did not see it that way.

In general, individuals oppose dishonest marketing tactics. Businesses like Facebook and PepsiCo must consider other people's realities. Brands like this risk rejection if they don't take the time to consider the consumer. The companies were able to bounce back from the events as a result. However, it illustrates the need for businesses to pay attention and ensure they are stressing with their consumers.

## CONCLUSION

A corporation must show that its care is genuine and significant to benefit from empathy marketing. Companies like Facebook and PepsiCo could not connect this concept with their audiences. Companies must ensure their advertising is truthful because each occurrence receives criticism for profiting off tragedy.

The PepsiCo commercial, "Live for Now Moments Anthem, " does not convey this message." People have noted how strikingly similar the Kendal Jenner and police officer's commercial ad is to the BLM Ieshia Evans photograph. The outcome was that the advertisement was taken down within a day, and the company suffered. The commercial's failure can be attributed to the message's lack of authenticity. It proved that there were several protests then, and PepsiCo issued the advertisement to profit from the situation.

People were aware of this and shunned the business as a result. Facebook unveiled its VR technology while looking at the damage inflicted in Puerto Rico by Hurricane Maria, another example of a non-empathetic marketing campaign. Zuckerberg, in particular, faced outrage and criticism for his actions after taking advantage of the occasion. People believed he was taking advantage of the catastrophe in Puerto Rico to help Facebook.

*Empathy needs to be genuine to be positively appreciated. A company must be sincere in its approach if it wants to use empathy as a marketing strategy.*

# CHAPTER 09
# EMPATHY IN SOCIAL SETTINGS

We constantly encounter the word "empathy" in our daily lives. Empathy is crucial to success in various contexts, including leadership, healthcare, courtrooms, and even relationships.

Who defines empathy? Empathy is the capacity to understand the thoughts and opinions of another person by placing oneself in that other's situation. You have been trained to be kind to those around you since childhood. You have also been taught to put yourself in their position and consider how your words can affect their day.

Early on in childhood, we are taught how to be empathic. Empathy is a vital energy that enables us to connect and understand one another. An important quality being studied in practically all spheres of life is empathy. Nathalia Gjersoe and Krznaric (2012).

## BEING A LEADER REQUIRES EMPATHY.

When asked to define a leader, someone might respond, *"A leader is someone who commands his people to execute a given work in hand."* What if I told you that I wasn't a good model of a leader? An exciting, dynamic, and motivating process is leadership. It is a force that makes it possible for society to function. Someone who inspires their people to achieve is a leader. Good leader convinces their followers that they deserve to be defended.

The five practices of excellent leadership that leaders who are at their most acceptable adhere to are: "Model the Way," "Inspire a Shared Vision," "Challenge the Process," "Enable Others to Act," and finally, "Encourage the Heart." ("THE FIVE PRACTICES OF EXEMPLARY LEADERSHIP® MODEL", n.d.). "Set the Example" – Set a positive example by acting in a way that demonstrates your suitability for the position of leader. Show the public that you are trustworthy. Be a strong advocate for your beliefs. Clarify your values to find your voice.

As a leader, it would be up to you to establish relationships with those around you to convince your followers that they can rely on you. To lead by example, a person must demonstrate to their followers how similar these two groups are.

Empathy is needed in this situation. You must empathize with your followers if you want to establish their faith in you as a leader. You share your followers' feelings by empathizing with them. Their concerns and troubles have now been replaced by your own. As a result, to "Model the Way" and lead effectively, one must have compassion for their followers.

Develop a Shared Vision - Consider empowering possibilities. Consider goals that you and others would be motivated to pursue. Consider how you can influence the world. Try persuading others to join your cause by outlining the advantages of their assistance. To inspire others, you must have a clear goal, collaborate with your followers rather than dictating to them, support their growth, give them recognition, and take the time to listen.

It would help if you comprehended what is significant to your supporters to motivate them to support your vision. What benefits would your followers experience if they adopted your vision? The technique that can be utilized to comprehend people's viewpoints in a particular circumstance is empathy.

As a result, by having empathy, a leader may comprehend the community's requirements and, using that understanding, create a vision that will benefit the community. Making the process complicated: One must never be scared to make mistakes if one wants to become a successful leader.

Leaders look for chances to advance and change the way they operate. They try new things and take chances, but they know failure is always possible. This process seeks to find more effective ways to realize the vision. Although empathy is not a requirement for this leadership practice in particular, "Challenging the Process," it does make it simpler. Empathy builds trust, which is essential for healthy partnerships.

The followers would continue to trust their leader and welcome risk if they built up the trust rather than criticizing the leader's choice and trying to avoid danger. Only if their followers continue to support them can leaders challenge the process.

Providing others with the means to act: Leaders interact with their followers. Leaders give themselves the best chance of realizing their intended goal by working with their followers and fostering spirited relationships. To improve their chances of realizing the intended goal, a leader must find strategies to assist their followers in developing into stronger people. One approach to inspiring others to act is through empathy.

It conveys to followers that their feelings matter when a leader tries to understand their emotions. When a leader demonstrates empathy, it conveys to the followers that they are valued as individuals rather than mere tools to be used and forgotten. Trust results from empathy, and trust encourages productive employees to put up their best effort to achieve the desired outcome.

Encourage the Heart: Effective leaders recognize and appreciate each team member's achievements. As long as everyone is recognized for their effort, the group may work diligently with a positive outlook. This display of leadership is a perfect illustration of empathy. Concern for the followers' successes demonstrates to the followers that their sentiments are essential.

The leader shows empathy for the followers when they can put themselves in their position and do actions they would benefit from (such as praising the followers' accomplishments). (THE FIVE PRACTICES OF EXEMPLARY LEADERSHIP® MODEL, n.d.)

In the leadership process, empathy is essential. A great leader must adhere to excellent leadership techniques. Empathy is needed for each of these procedures.

# EMPATHY IN HEALTHCARE

One of the critical motivations for pursuing a profession in healthcare is a person's concern for those around them and want to assist them in their time of need. Two of the most frequent reactions of a healthcare professional who sees someone in agony are pity and empathy.

When a healthcare professional demonstrates to their patients that they care about their health, they are demonstrating sympathy. This allows them to say the right things when they observe a patient in pain.

When a healthcare professional tells a patient that they understand what the patient is going through, even though they are only doing it out of politeness, that is an example of sympathy. Another response a healthcare professional may have upon witnessing their patients' pain is empathy. Healthcare professionals can guarantee they are sympathetic to their patients by using various strategies.

Here are a few of these methods:

- Pay close attention as you listen to learn what is bothering the patients. Please refrain from accusing the sufferer of "making things up" or "imagining their suffering." It is not your body; it is the patient. As a result, they are more knowledgeable than you about what they are going through. Your ability to determine what upsets people increases due to how attentively you listen to their difficulties. (Bradley et al., 2018)
- Imagine your patients as members of your family, and treat them accordingly. You would want to keep doing your best to provide for the patients if you considered them your parents, grandparents, siblings, or kids. If these patients were members of your family, you would do all in your power to ensure that they are treated with respect, that their dignity is preserved, and that they are aware of their course of treatment. (Bradley et al., 2018)
- Think about your reaction if you were in the patient's current position. Put yourself in the patient's position and respond to them appropriately. It is frequently simple to overlook how uneasy patients and their families may feel in a hospital. If that is the case, you should be aware that it would be simple to switch roles and treat the patients in line with how you would want to be treated. (Bradley et al., 2018)
- It is critical to recognize the various patient populations' cultures. It not only increases societal knowledge of the diverse cultural backgrounds present but also offers the healthcare professional a fresh perspective on patient treatment. (Bradley et al., 2018)

## Why Is Empathy Important In Healthcare?
While compassion enables medical professionals to speak appropriately to a patient in pain, empathy enables them to form relationships with their patients that cover the patient's mind, body, and spirit. Empathy can reduce anxiety and increase trust. Patient satisfaction is significantly higher when a doctor demonstrates empathy for their patients. It results in fewer malpractice cases, fewer errors, and improved levels of treatment compliance.

Empathy with the patients' experiences makes it easier to provide care for them because of how much better the patients' experiences are made by the caregiver. Patients who seek the assistance of a healthcare provider do so out of fear, anxiety, and a desire to receive the finest possible care.

Exacting this message to the patients—that the medical professionals care about them and would do all in their power to assist them—is what empathy and compassion accomplish. (Stone, 2019, Jeffrey, 2016, The Difference Between Empathy & Sympathy, 2016, respectively).

## SHOULD EMPATHY EXIST IN THE COURTROOM?
The use of empathy in a courtroom is one of the more contentious issues under discussion. Barack Obama, the concurrent president of the United States of America, stated in 2009 that "I regard that trait of empathy, of understanding and identifying with people's hopes and hardships, as a crucial factor for arriving at just decisions and results." As the phrase shows, Barack Obama was a big fan of showing empathy in court.

People who supported empathy suggested that less wealthy people would receive lenient punishment from sympathetic judges. Empathy could lead to bias or favoritism in the courts, according to those who opposed it. The 2016 Stanford Swimmer Case is one example used by the detractors to support their argument. Brock Turner, a freshman at Stanford University at the time, was convicted of rape in this case.

However, Judge Aaron Persky gave him a lesser punishment. Turner and Persky were of the same race and gender. Turner and Persky attended the same university. But none of these traits were present in Persky or the rape victim. When pronouncing the punishment, Persky appeared to have more sympathy for Turner than the rape victim, possibly due to the similarities between Persky and Turner. (Do We Need More Empathic Judges? n.d.).

## IMPORTANCE OF EMPATHY IN A RELATIONSHIP
People frequently assert that while relationships can be challenging to maintain, they are not difficult to begin. Empathy is one of the critical elements of any fulfilling relationship. The importance of empathy in relationships cannot be overstated, and ignoring it will not result in a happy outcome. After saying that, let's talk about several behaviors that could present you as an empathic person in a relationship. (3 Ways to Build Real Empathy for Others in Your Life, n.d.)

- *Listening to your partner:* Although it can seem simple, we overlook this simple yet essential responsibility. Any relationship is put under stress by this. We could discern the speaker's emotions by listening and then reacting appropriately. It is not sufficient to only listen; you must also make an effort to observe the clues and gestures that the speaker uses in addition to their words. Having preconceived notions or an underlying emotion on the subject the speaker is discussing could obstruct your ability to discern their feelings.
  You might not be able to make the necessary effort to comprehend the turmoil of the other person if you are already too preoccupied trying to catch up with your sentiments. To effectively participate in a conversation, active listening is essential. Although it is impossible to put yourself in another person's shoes truly, you can at least try to understand their emotions by paying attention to what they are saying. This is what it means to be genuinely sympathetic.
- Due to the worry of being judged, it can be challenging to open up about your weak mental condition or genuine beliefs in any interaction. You become frustrated if you keep quiet. In addition to not being honest with yourself, you are also preventing others from seeing the true you. In a relationship, a partner will find it easier to open up and be themselves if one is sympathetic to them, regardless of personal judgment. Honesty is the first step in building a great relationship.
- Keep in mind that empathy is not personal. It is more important to step back and empathize with the speaker's feelings than to express your feelings. According to research, the mirror neuron in our brains drives neuronal activity. It creates neural networks while responding to stimuli and when we observe another person responding similarly. People frequently need someone to lean on while they are going through a difficult

period. Sharing the complex emotions, they are going through while you share your shoulders provides them with moral support. By letting them know they are not alone, you can make someone else's unpleasant experiences more bearable.

- It is not sufficient to identify the emotion. After identifying the feeling, we must apply what we've learned to improve the speaker's well-being. When the speaker feels heard and understood while speaking, it offers them a sense of belonging and happiness. Utilizing this information to your advantage is also essential. You are in a stronger position to assist them because you are not experiencing the circumstance firsthand but are merely experiencing their feelings. Even if you believe your efforts are insignificant, they may significantly affect the other person.

## CONCLUSION

In the current context, empathy frequently has a positive impact. We want to assist them in whatever manner we can when we observe their suffering. This then fuels our desire to alter the course of the modern world.

What are some instances of changing the world? It might be as straightforward as giving money to a worthy cause, like alleviating poverty in Africa or comforting a friend going through a difficult breakup. In many social contexts throughout daily life, empathy has been employed repeatedly. Empathy may be used in a productive way to improve situations from the courtroom to the hospital, from leadership to relationships.

Therefore, try to be sympathetic and concerned for those around you so that you might benefit from a brighter tomorrow.

# CHAPTER 10
# EMPATHY IN INTERCULTURAL CONTEXT

Many attributes and qualities reflect who we are as people. Some people are more likely than others to exhibit particular traits, whereas those same individuals may show less development of another critical quality. Additionally, people acquire particular abilities that are classified as positive and inadequate skills.

Throughout a person's lifespan, it's necessary to build and strengthen the many promising talents that would be useful in social and non-social contacts while also restricting the usage of the negative skills that have regrettably evolved. These abilities can start in childhood but can also be developed as we get older and are exposed to increasingly complex situations.

## EMPATHY

Empathy is a critical ability that has been studied and employed by people for a very long time. A great deal of time has been spent studying and developing this skill. Being empathic would entail being in a position to comprehend another person's emotions and consider the situation from that person's perspective (Borody, 2020).

Empathy is an exceptional quality because to demonstrate empathy; one must figuratively put themselves in the other person's shoes to comprehend what is happening in that particular situation.

Three distinct aspects of empathy—emotional, cognitive, and compassionate—have been studied and identified when looking more closely at the idea of empathy. One aspect of affective (emotional) empathy that many people do not realize they display regularly. This aspect of empathy can be defined as the capacity to physically experience another person's emotions since those emotions are intense, transferable, and contagious (Borody, 2020).

For example, most listeners flinch and wince when footage of someone getting punched in the groin is aired. While that illustration focuses more on the potential bodily emotions of a circumstance, emotional empathy generally enables one to experience feelings comparable to another person's circumstances. Another aspect of empathy someone could exhibit is cognitive empathy. Simply comprehending another person's feelings might be used to define this aspect of empathy. They can consider a situation from another person's perspective (Borody, 2020).

However, there is a disadvantage to someone only demonstrating cognitive empathy for another person. When you use cognitive empathy, you are not experiencing the scenario from the same emotional perspective as the other person.

Compassionate empathy is the final aspect of empathy. This element refers to someone's capacity to comprehend another person's issue and, if necessary, to provide practical assistance (Borody, 2020). It makes sense that engaging all three elements of empathy, as opposed to just one or two, has certain benefits.

If someone only exhibited cognitive empathy, they would comprehend another person's point of view. Still, they would be unable to identify the specific feelings that person is experiencing since they view the situation differently. They would also be unable to assist.

Empathy does not necessarily need to be specifically assigned to a person's early years when examining its development throughout their life. Empathy is a talent created through attachment and connections during childhood, but it can continue to grow as an adult (Krznaric, 2012).

Empathetic people incorporate specific practices into their daily routines. One particular trait, for example, is their natural curiosity for strangers and the unknowable details of their lives. They do this to comprehend particular situations from the perspective of another person. Another distinctive trait of highly empathic individuals is their capacity to listen while sharing personal information about themselves (Krznaric, 2012).

Because you are listening to someone else's concerns or situation and only providing them with someone to talk to, the listening component of this habit is reasonably visible and empathic ability. It's crucial to realize that sharing information and discussing our circumstances are also facets of empathy. You are opening out to someone else and expressing your emotions by doing this (Krznaric, 2012). Ultimately, this forges a link and trust between the two people that did not exist initially.

Another aspect of highly empathic people is their capacity to comprehend and respond to the numerous prejudices around them. They cannot bring about change on their own, but they can learn about the perspective of the disadvantaged group, inform others, and share their understanding of the issue (Krznaric, 2012). Although not exclusive to them, highly empathic individuals are better equipped to use these habits in their daily lives.

## INTERCULTURAL CONTEXT

Why are some people more empathic since empathy can emerge as early as the first two years of life? We all possess the capacity to love and care for one another. As we age, every one of us develops our talents and skills in a setting that is unique from others. The degree of empathy that a person can display can vary depending on their surroundings.

Culture is an illustration of an environmental component that varies amongst groups of people. People from different backgrounds have different cultural views and perspectives, which causes environmental differences between groups.

Different cultures have different approaches to dealing with particular circumstances, but this does not imply that one culture is right and another is wrong. It denotes a cultural difference that might influence a subject's disposition differently. The parallels and contrasts between cultures, as well as how they express empathy, will be examined in this chapter. If there are discrepancies, we will examine how, where, and why they developed.

## EMPATHY VARIES BETWEEN COUNTRIES

Several variables have been tracked and measured to compare different nations in the world. Numerous studies investigating the possibility of regional variations in the empathetic response have employed this concept. Any scenario a person is put in is impacted by the culture they are exposed to daily.

This happens because the actual cultures worldwide differ, creating a unique and distinctive environment for everyone.

## EMPATHY AND PHYSICAL AND SOCIAL PAIN

Numerous investigations have been done to determine how empathy differs throughout cultures. The problem with such research is that the majority of their sample sizes were made up mostly of Caucasian people. Second, given the connection between empathy, social interaction, and suffering, additional attention to those studies.

A 2016 study by Atkins et al. examined the differences in empathic reactions to certain painful stimuli amongst individuals from various ethnic backgrounds. This was one of the few publications addressing social and physical suffering.

Atkins et al. decided to conduct two investigations that would lead to a more in-depth examination of empathy for both physical and social distress. In the first study, researchers wanted to know how people from other cultures would react if they witnessed someone in physical agony (Atkins et al., 2016). They needed to choose a subgroup of participants who represented a variety of cultural backgrounds to do this. Thirty-eight persons who identified as British and 33 people who identified as East Asian were used (Atkins et al., 2016).

Each participant in the exam was shown four different movies as the actual testing procedure. The movies were significant because they included three "control" videos in which one punctured a tomato with a needle and one in which a hand was punctured with a needle to cause physical discomfort. This study looked at felt pain and affected ratings across cultures to see whether there were any changes (Atkins et al., 2016). Affect rating as a self-reported tool for evaluating feelings experienced during social encounters was considered.

The perception of the pain component was added to determine whether the participants could accurately detect the intended pain in each movie. The affect rating allowed the researchers to see how the participants felt about each movie regarding their affective empathy.

As previously said, affective empathy is defined as our capacity to feel particular emotions in response to a particular circumstance another person is experiencing. After experimenting, they had specific outcomes for the sense of pain and the affect rating.

Firstly, compared to the other three control movies, the needle puncturing the hand video caused more pain to be reported by all participants. Participants also reported increased pain at the tomato piercing site after seeing movies that pierced the tomato with a needle instead of videos in which they punctured it with a Q-tip. In the end, scientists concluded that both British and East Asian individuals perceived target pain similarly (Atkins et al., 2016).

They discovered more concrete proof of cultural variations in terms of affect assessment. First, scientists noticed that the subjects reacted more negatively to the pain video than in other situations. They noticed that individuals also had a higher unfavorable reaction to the tomato needle movie after watching it, as opposed to the Q-tip film.

After watching the physical pain movies, they found that the British participants felt more negatively than the East Asian participants when comparing the different cultural groups (Atkins et al., 2016). This observation was significant since it corroborated earlier research findings that showed Easterners have less emotional experience than Westerners.

In their second study, Atkins et al. sought to determine if there were any cultural variations in how people responded to social suffering. They utilized 41 participants who identified as East Asian and 45 participants who identified as British to carry out this investigation.

Each participant watched videos with particular British residents discussing difficult social experiences they had to endure. The participants were required to self-report specific criteria both during and after seeing each video. They had to document their emotional state and empathy for the persons in the video (Atkins et al., 2016).

Additionally, they had to detect their target's discomfort and extrapolate the speakers' emotions. After finishing the approaches, they compared the outcomes for the British and East Asian subjects. For each specific movie, both cultural groups reported the target pain at comparable levels, corresponding to Study 1's findings (Atkins et al., 2016). Study 1's findings were replicated when both cultural groups analyzed the effect rating data.

They observed that British participants responded more emotionally and empathically to the movies than East Asian ones. In analyzing the data for empathic concern, Atkins et al. found that British participants expressed more worry about the social suffering of the persons in the movie than East Asian participants (Atkins et al., 2016).

Finally, they saw that the East Asian participants made their empathetic predictions more accurate compared to the British participants (Atkins et al., 2016). Even though Atkins et al. only examined two distinct cultural groups, the fact that they did so by contrasting affective and cognitive empathy between Eastern and Western populations can serve as a starting point for further comparative research.

## LARGE SCALE STUDY OF CULTURAL DIFFERENCE
Chopik et al. did a study in 2017 to see whether there were cultural variations in empathy. They looked for specific psychological features that explain these variations based on the findings. This study's distinctive feature was the use of a sizable sample size.

Notably, 104,365 adults from 63 different nations participated in the study (Chopik et al., 2017). They compiled all of their results following the completion of various statistical tests. One of the study's key findings was that collective societies exhibited greater empathy than individual societies.

China, Japan, and Indonesia are general collectivistic nations. At the same time, the United States, Germany, and Australia are examples of individualistic nations. This may seem like a simple conclusion because individualism emphasizes working alone to solve issues and achieve goals, whereas collectivism contends that self-sacrifice is beneficial if it benefits others. Another significant discovery was that nations with higher levels of volunteering also had higher levels of empathy (Chopik et al., 2017).

It's crucial to remember that high empathy levels were not associated with nations that received a lot of humanitarian donations. They discovered that empathy correlated favorably with several factors, including self-esteem, subjective well-being, prosocial behavior, and others (Chopik et al., 2017). The findings are creditable because participants came from 63 different nations, but it is still vital to find other research that might support these findings.

## CONCLUSION
All humans can possess particular skills that could benefit both ourselves and others. If properly developed, empathy is a skill that can foster fruitful interactions with others. Affective and cognitive empathy work together to let us

experience other people's emotions and see the world from their perspective while putting ourselves in their circumstances.

However, an individual's susceptibility to particular contextual circumstances can impact how they develop empathy. One area where empathetic disparities might occur is in culture. A few instances of published research that have sought to determine if cultural variations affect can find empathy in the studies discussed in this chapter.

In the end, regardless of whether there are differences in empathy between other cultures, everyone should attempt to be more sympathetic because we are all members of the human race.

# CHAPTER 11
# ETHICAL & PHILOSOPHICAL DILEMMAS SURROUNDING EMPATHY

## UNDERSTANDING PHILOSOPHY AND ETHICS

According to its definition, philosophy is the "study of basic natural knowledge." A philosopher is a person who studies philosophy. A philosopher typically asks many questions, provides multiple perspectives on issues, and challenges commonly accepted viewpoints. Numerous subfields exist within this academic field, including metaphysics, epistemology, ethics, and others. The medical field is one of many other areas that incorporates philosophy.

Other academic levels provide philosophy courses, which promote soft skills that can apply to many fields of study. Additionally, a significant number of individuals studied philosophy and created several ideas. It is typically a core subject that emphasizes improving critical writing abilities, communication abilities so one can transmit arguments clearly, and thinking abilities (What is Philosophy, n.d.).

The word ethics, which comes from the Greek word "Ethos" and means "way of living," is one of the subfields of philosophy that is stated. Ethics examines how people behave in social contexts. This could examine how people interact with other people, groups, or social situations.

Applied ethics is a branch of ethics used to guide decisions in several spheres of life, including philosophical, political, and educational ones. Our ethics, combined with the values we acquire from our environment, help to shape who we are as people today (Government du Canada, 2015).

We will cover what empathy is from the perspective of Heinz Kohut's self-psychology theory in this chapter, as well as what morality is, how morality interacts with empathy, moral issues, and "final words."

## REVIEWING EMPATHY THROUGH THE SELF-PSYCHOLOGICAL LENS

Heinz Kohut created the self-psychology thesis in the 1970s. There were four essential parts to it.

- First: The nuclear self, which dealt with the biological structure a person was born with, was the first component.
- Second: The second idea was the virtual self, which represented the person their parents or other legal guardians had of them while they were young. According to the upbringing raised the child, if terrible treatment-experienced, it could weaken this region.
- Third: The third component was the cohesive self, a combination of the nuclear and virtual self (Good Therapy, 2011).
- Fourth: The egocentric self, which valued a person's ego and was focused on them believing they were superior to the people around them, was the final element (Good Therapy, 2011).

According to Kohut, psychological issues may develop due to developmental requirements not being satisfied by a parent or guardian, which may result in a problem with oneself (Good Therapy, 2011). Empathy is one of the essential instruments in self-psychology for recovering from the lack of developmental needs or preventing them from occurring in the first place (Baer, 2017). According to Kohut, empathy was a way of receiving information because it allowed one to comprehend and value another person entirely.

When empathy is present, the person providing care may be better able to anticipate the needs of the person being looked after (Baer, 2017). The doctor or therapist can have a deeper understanding and form a closer link of trust with the patient whose developmental needs weren't met, which can be helpful later when mending a developmental need declared deficient (Good Therapy, 2011). It employs the adage "put yourself in their shoes," which fosters newfound respect and understanding (Baer, 2017).

Since pain is thought to be caused by unmet developmental needs, the self-psychology idea was more "empathetic" toward the person who may be experiencing it. As a result, the idea gained acceptance and is still considered a significant contribution to psychology today (Good Therapy, 2011).

# WHAT IS MORALITY -DESCRIPTIVE VS. NORMATIVE MORALITY:

The term "morality" is vast and contains numerous intricate theories. When it comes to creating experiments and collaborating with others, it is crucial. Descriptive and normative morality are the two categories into which morality is divided (Gert & Gert, 2020).

## Descriptive Morality.

Let's start with descriptive morality. This kind of morality relates to the guidelines and standards established within the community a person is a part of or their ideas and convictions (Gert & Gert, 2020). Extracurricular activities for students, religious organizations, communities, etc., are a few examples of groups. Diverse communities may have different moral sensibilities; thus, even while one community may think one way, another may feel another.

While Sam, a person who thinks people should stop smoking, illustrates a person's own opinions. This is Sam's belief in this situation; everyone may not hold it, but it is significant to him. Comparative ethics is another name for descriptive ethics, and sociological disciplines like anthropology, psychology, and sociology are typically used to research descriptive ethics (Hasa, 2019). The conclusions drawn from descriptive ethics can be used in various professional fields.

## Normative Morality.

The second category is normative morality. Depending on a person's situation, this kind of morality is flexible. It supposes that the decision-maker is logical and considers how people ought to behave in a particular circumstance (Gert & Gert, 2020). It is possible to consider the ethics found in normative morality to be timeless and applicable to all communities.

# MORALITY WITH EMPATHY

It is common to use the phrases empathy and morality interchangeably since it is believed that moral decisions require empathy. This article argues that while empathy includes several subfields, some significant distinctions between it and morality should be considered (Decety & Cowell, 2014). Empathy has been employed in various circumstances, from animal-related research to biological sciences, making it challenging to come up with a simple definition when someone asks the fundamental question of what it is.

When considering morality, one must choose between engaging in good or bad behaviors, regardless of the morality listed above (Decety & Cowell, 2014). The ventromedial prefrontal cortex, among other frontal lobe regions, is primarily responsible for moral judgment. Morality may not always be followed by empathy because one's environment can influence how one responds to a given situation.

A young child is more likely to exhibit behavior with empathy threaded into it toward parents or the social circles where they are more familiar than toward groups or persons who are strangers, which can be perceived as an imbalance in who empathy is shown (Decety & Cowell, 2014). Additionally, studies have shown that socioeconomic class can significantly impact whether or not a person is empathic.

According to the specific study mentioned in this article, higher socioeconomic status individuals tended to be much less sympathetic and more calculating in their decision-making compared to lower socioeconomic status individuals who considered what was best for the people around them. It is also acknowledged that this relationship might not always hold, demonstrating that morality and empathy are not synonymous and might vary depending on the circumstances (Decety & Cowell, 2014). Numerous historical examples can help to illustrate this concept further.

Given the numerous disputes and protests that have occurred over the years, many included broadly similar individuals on both sides. However, this situation had an environmental impact, such as persuading others to injure innocent people through manipulation (Baer, 2017). Take World War Two as an illustration.

Following the 1939 invasion of Poland, Germany, led by Adolf Hitler and the Nazi Party, declared war on Great Britain and France. This destroyed numerous properties and human lives, particularly the roughly four million Jews that Hitler claimed he had to exterminate to establish his authority. This implied a widespread genocide in which numerous concentration camps were set up to detain and murder Jews (A&E Television Networks, 2009).

The Gwangju Uprising, a significant event in South Korean history in the fight for democracy, is another illustration to consider. Martial law is when the military temporarily rules an area, which was declared by Chun Doo-Hwan, the head of the Korean Central Intelligence Agency at the time (Han, 2021). Many people protested a lot in favor of democracy and against martial law. Gwangju was one of the focal points of this movement.

From May 18 to May 27, just a few days, all of this transpired. At that time, several residents vanished, and the military thrashed the protesters who took part in them. When it came to the military assaults, there was no bias. More than 600 students came to Chonnam National University to demonstrate, but government security forces beat them in the end. A retreat caused a brief respite until May 27, when the military retook the area in full force and destroyed much of it (Han, 2021).

Since the military personnel in both cases significantly harmed others, the argument that morality and empathy are two separate concepts is brought up again. This is because of how much the environment influences each quality, which supports the idea that morality and empathy are two different concepts.

## MORAL DILEMMA

Many different scenarios have been used in philosophy to help people grasp the ideas. One such scenario is the well-known Trolley Problem, which was first created by the philosopher Philippa Foot and then amended by philosopher Judith Jarvis Thompson. You are stationed at a railroad yard close to a switch in this puzzle.

The tracks come to a point where they cross; one direction has one person fastened to the track while the other has two. The approaching train is currently traveling toward the section of track that has been secured with twenty persons. As you watch the situation unfold from a distance, you have the choice to flip a switch so that the train instead strikes the single person who is fastened to the rails.

Another well-known scenario problem is the Foot-bridge Dilemma, referred to as Trolley Problem #2. (Bizarro, 2020). This happens at the railroads, but things are a little different this time. A train is approaching, and you are stationed on top of a bridge that spans the railroad lines.

There are 20 persons tied to the tracks who are about to be hit by a train (Bizarro, 2020). You have two options: stop the train and save the twenty people, or throw one person off the top of the bridge. This circumstance might be referred to as a moral dilemma since it involves two moral requirements that are equally significant and present a difficult option.

Now that we have examined this scenario from a practical standpoint, we can see that the utilitarian would opt to flip the switch and save the seven individuals rather than just the one. The utilitarian viewpoint typically chooses an option based on which results in the most happiness for the most significant number of individuals.

The Footbridge Dilemma predicts that one person would have to be sacrificed once more to free the twenty individuals bound below. Of course, there is discussion as to the legitimacy of this arrangement and the reasons it might be immoral. Saving suitable individuals in the first situation is morally justified. Still, there is more significant hesitation in the second because you are the one who forced the other person to their death (Kadreva & Hristova, 2016). But before we plunge much farther, let's take a step back and examine how all of this relates to the idea of empathy.

The practical perspective about these events argued in a journal article by Gleichgerrcht, and Young (2013) lacks empathy. Although it is widely believed that people are logical creatures, numerous studies show that feelings like empathy influence moral judgment. The Footbridge Dilemma indicates that in theory pushing one person over to save the other is justified because it saves more people. Still, if humans were put in the pushing circumstance knowing the outcome, they would be less willing to push.

Since the degree of emotional involvement in a situation is crucial when discussing a moral quandary, the emotion of empathy would conflict with the utilitarian viewpoint in these situations (Gleichgerrcht & Young, 2013). This introduces the dual processing model, which describes two separate processing systems that become active when faced with a moral choice. Abstract thinking and cognitive control are the two processing modalities.

In the utilitarian perspective, judgments for both scenarios would be heavily reliant on the cognitive control system, and specifically, a highly functioning cognitive control system, as the cognitive control system can occasionally become confused when making decisions based on factors like time (Gleichgerrcht & Young, 2013).

# FINAL WORDS

Finally, empathy extends to various academic fields, including philosophy. Although empathy is a difficult concept to define, we concentrated on Heinz Kohut's self-psychology idea in this chapter. Kohut's idea divided self-psychology into four sections and linked those elements with empathy to aid in people's success.

As we continue to think about the philosophical topic, we start to consider the idea of morality, which was developed and then studied about empathy. When there is a moral quandary, empathy is crucial in determining the right course of action. Philosophy and ethics have a lot to say about empathy.

# **CONCLUSION**

Many aspects of our lives and the modern world are based on the incredibly complex concept of empathy. We rarely consider the significant impact it has on our actions, behavior, choices, and the state of the world today.

Modern research has mainly focused on this area, using cutting-edge technology to investigate anything from the molecular and physiological components that might contribute to empathy to the social ramifications of empathy. The categorizations of empathy, the nature vs. nurture debate, the individual development of empathy, and the individual variations in empathy all examine the function of this complicated feeling in a person.

Exploring these personal facets helps us comprehend how they affect a person's personality and cognitive abilities. Since it is hard to understand someone else's consciousness or frame of reference, further research and studies in this field aim to create as much understanding as possible. The impact of empathy on important institutions like the economy and the ethical and moral problems it raises can all be explored about international differences. Here, we can see the universality of empathy and how all people share it.

It gives insight into the function of empathy in contemporary society, from the material objects we have created to the social structures and processes we follow. We will never be able to comprehend the idea of empathy fully; all we can know about it is how it affects us and how our mindset affects it. We will never be able to fully understand empathy because it is entwined with everything and leaves traces everywhere if we look carefully.

# PART 03
# SHADOW WORK JOURNAL

# INTRODUCTION

Within every one of us, there is an angel and a devil. We need to accept and face this fact of life. Because we are spiritual beings living a human experience, we have two faces. The ego is the initial façade we present to the outside world. The shadow is the name given to the second face we hide. Because our shadow selves are so hidden, we frequently aren't even aware they exist. We only glimpse them when we experience fits of fury, nightmares, pettiness, retaliation, paranoid thoughts, drug and sex binges, and other behaviors that border on "crazy." Our shadows are kept secret and hidden within the gloomy recesses of our psyche for a purpose.

Everything deemed undesirable, "bad," humiliating, odd, forbidden, or socially unacceptable resides in our shadows. As we grew up, our shadows represent the aspects of ourselves shunned, denied, rejected, or otherwise adversely judged by our parents, other family members, and society.

To be accepted and loved, we learned as youngsters, to hide the aspects of ourselves that lacked praise and acceptance and only to adopt the characteristics and actions that were well-received. Certain pieces of ourselves had to be severed and buried to survive. But a very significant to suppressing portions of ourselves is that they start to rot and get worse, ruining our lives.

Our shadows yearn to be pulled into the light of consciousness, like ravenous monsters clawing their way out of a dank dungeon. The more we put off confronting our shadows, the more subtly they govern and rule our lives. In times of rage, stress, temptation, or exhaustion, we become susceptible to the power of our shadows like puppets on strings. They become our worst enemies instead of helping us learn to meet, acknowledge, and befriend our shadows. If you've ever felt at odds with yourself or like your greatest enemy, your shadows control you, not the other way around.

We can refer to The Shadow as "The Dark Side" of our personalities. The conviction that we are not enough, capable of loving, or deserving of love is a reflection of our most painful wounds. It comprises instincts from the animal kingdom, bad feelings, and impulses. Shadow Work will increase your sense of strength and self-assurance once you've mastered it.

Shadow is always just out of sight, directly behind us. We leave a shadow in any direct light. The term "shadow" refers to everything about ourselves that we are unable to see. When I published a biography of a spiritual teacher, I realized how crucial it was to be aware of my shadow. Most of us will often go to considerable lengths to shield our self-image from anything unfavorable or strange. Therefore, it is simpler to see someone else's shadow before realizing one's own.

This Shadow Work Journal was made to serve as a guiding light for you as you explore the enigmatic and shadowy corners of your unconscious mind. I could better comprehend how someone could exhibit talents in one area of life while being blind to terrible behavior in other areas after seeing the teacher's shadow. Every person is vulnerable to this.

Working with my shadow is a rewarding but challenging process for me. More excellent honesty, creativity, energy, and personal awakening can result from exploring your darkness. Introspection is crucial for developing into a mature adult (which is rarer than most think). In this shadow work journal and workbook, let's examine what the shadow is and how it manifests.

# CHAPTER 01
# WHAT IS THE HUMAN OR PSYCHOLOGICAL SHADOW

## WHAT IS SHADOW?

The "dark side" of our psyche is known as the shadow because it is mainly composed of irrational, adaptive human emotions and impulses, including fury, envy, greed, selfishness, want, and the drive for power.

(We also isolate ourselves from many of our better attributes, though. I discuss the "positive shadow" in a different psychological projection guide.)

The shadow comprises everything we reject about ourselves, including what we consider wrong, evil, or unacceptable. This dark side is everything that conflicts with our conscious attitude that we have decided about ourselves.

The disowned self is the individual shadow. It stands for the aspects of us that we no longer consider to be our own, including our innate virtues. These new or rejected facets of our personalities remain. We try to cast them out by denying them, but we cannot do so. They are a part of our unconscious that we suppress.

Consider whatever we are not aware of as belonging to our unconscious. The shadow won't go away. It remains with us as our dark sibling. When we fail to recognize it, trouble results. For sure, it is standing just behind us at that point.

When you follow someone on your first day at new work, you use the shadow as an action. Depending on their context, shadow organs be used wrongly or positively. Children frequently play with their shadows and view them as lifelong friends, like in the song line "just me and my shadow." You can be such a wimp that you are afraid of your own shadow or, at the very least, of what lurks in the shadows.

A spy might secretly follow you if they used you as a verb. Alternatively, your devoted dog may follow you around the house while your pace. You could be tired of constantly feeling that your elder sister is the focus of attention, keeping you out of the limelight.

## HOW IS A SHADOW CREATED?

Every young child exhibits kindness, love, and charity but also resentment, ego, and avarice. These feelings are a component of our shared humanity. But something changes as we mature. Regarding "being good," specific characteristics are valued while rejecting others. All share basic human needs. Physical requirements, security requirements, and needs for belonging are a few of these requirements. They are innate and biological demands.

We experienced negative indications from our environment as children when we expressed certain aspects of who we were. It's possible that we had a tantrum out of anger. Sent us to our room after our parents admonished us for the outburst. We might have also been brave, lively, impromptu, or silly in our first-grade classroom. Our teacher called us out in front of the class for acting impolitely and then told us to sit down.

Every time that happened—and it may have happened frequently—it put one of our fundamental requirements in danger. Would our parents' disapproval endanger our security? Would our desire to fit in be compromised if our teachers and classmates disapproved of us?

We learned to adapt to the outside world and changed our conduct to suit our needs. In the first 20 years of our lives, all pieces of ourselves that are rejected or discouraged are packed up and hidden (outside our conscious awareness). In A Little Book of the Human Shadow, poet Robert Bly writes, "The child packs all these undesired pieces into an invisible bag and pulls it behind him."

As described by psychologist Carl Jung, the personal shadow results from repressing undesirable portions of oneself.

## HOW IS A SHADOWS FORMED? THE SCIENCE OF SHADOWS

To define a shadow's purpose? Transparent things and opaque materials must be understood and learned.

Because the shadow is a patch or region where the opaque substance may hinder the light from entering by its race, the characteristics of that particular location where a kind of shadow is formed are known as the shadow. Since the shadow can be created by the Sun or light, understanding how a shadow is made and knowing what kind of shadow it is simple.

## Shadow- Formation by Sun

The sun is where shadows are created. A shadow is created when the sun's rays are directed directly at the earth. The sun's rays are directed outward, moving toward the earth at a speed of almost 300,000 km/sec in a straight line. It only takes 8 minutes for these light rays to reach us. It makes direct contact with the ground's path. The generation of a shadow won't occur if the path is a transparent object.

On the other hand, if it only hits a portion of the opaque substance, it prevents the race from entering the area and causes shadows to appear. They will strike anything that is in the way of these beams. When these rays strike an opaque item, the opaque object blocks the light and does not permit the rays to pass through, resulting in a shadow. An object casts a shadow on the other side when light cannot pass through it. It is not a reflection even though the shadow is identical to the object.

## Shadow- Formation by Light

Let's talk about light now and how shadows develop.

There are numerous light sources besides the sun, such as light bulbs, candle flames, computer screens, and glow worms. Numerous types of light can be seen, including candles, lamplight, electric light, computer light, etc. Each type of source can cast a shadow in a variety of situations.

The sharpness of the shadow is seen about the size of the light. Because light allows for the movement of particles, shadows are created. The particles move and choose a location, much like the sun. Depending on the object's size, it produces a fuzzy image if the destination is an opaque substance. When we use a phone as a spotlight, the shadow it casts is small. This could assist in clarifying how shadows are created.

The light from these sources likewise travels in a straight line, much like the light from the sun, but it does so over a shorter distance. The shadows cast on a white surface are easier to perceive because they are more distinct when there is a strong contrast between the shadow and the light surface. The size of the light source affects the shadow's sharpness and blurriness. In contrast to more giant lights, small lights cast definite shadows, while more giant lights cast less distinct shadows. The position of the light affects the size and shape of the shadows.

## Size and Shape of a Shadow

We learned how the shadow is created by talking about shadow generation in physics. However, understanding a shadow's size and shape is also beneficial. It entirely depends on the size and form of the receiving and source objects.

The shape of The Shadow can be seen when the reflecting item casts a shadow. It will cast a circular shadow if it is a ball. The shadow will be either rectangular or square if it's a book. If it is a person, the shadow will take the form of a human being. Similarly, the object's size that casts the shadow might affect how sharp it is. The shadow is sharper if large light beams, such as those from sunshine or tube lights, hit the path. The shadow will be fuzzier if the light source is slight, such as a cell phone or an aura lamp.

## Seasons

The size and shape of the shadow are also influenced by the seasons. The days are bright and sunny if the shadow is generated in summer. The shadow will then be more acute and last for a more extended period. Light cannot penetrate the water when there are shadows during the rainy season. Hence we cannot see distinct shadows. It can show up as a blur.

## THE SHADOW – CONFLICT WITH THE PERSONA AND EGO RESPONSIBILITY

Shadow: Good and terrible elements of oneself that are hidden or unconscious and that the ego has either repressed or never acknowledged.

Suggestion: It is frequently beneficial to begin a process of Jungian analysis with a trained Jungian analyst to work with the shadow.

The shadow is a moral issue that puts the entire ego-personality to the test because no one can become aware of the shadow without making a significant moral effort. It requires acknowledging the harmful components of one's personality as actual and present to become mindful of them. The shadow effectively represents the entirety of the unconscious before the differentiation of its components. People of the same sex as the dreamer frequently personify it in dreams.

## Unacknowledged Characteristics

The majority of the shadow comprises suppressed urges and desires, immoral motivations, immature fantasies, resentments, etc. - all the aspects of oneself that one is not proud of. Through the projection technique, we frequently encounter these unacknowledged personal traits in others.

Although can partially integrate the shadow into the conscious personality with understanding and goodwill, experience has shown that some traits present the most stubborn opposition to moral control and are virtually challenging to alter. These resistances are typically connected to projections that are not acknowledged as such, and their discovery is an exceptional moral accomplishment. While some characteristics unique to the shadow can be easily mistaken for a person's particular qualities, in this instance, both insight and goodwill are ineffective because the other person seems to be the only one who can be responsible for the emotion.

## Conflict with the Persona

The persona prevents the shadow from becoming manifest. The shadow is black in proportion when we identify with an upbeat persona. Because of this compensating link between shadow and ego, their friction is always present when neurosis flares up. The typical depression during these circumstances signifies that one must accept that one is not all one hopes or claims to be.

## Acceptance of the Shadow

There isn't a method for absorbing the consistently effective shadow. It is always a personal concern and is more akin to diplomacy or statesmanship. One must first acknowledge and take the shadow's existence seriously. The second step is to become conscious of its attributes and goals. This is accomplished through paying careful attention to one's feelings, fantasies, and urges. Third, protracted negotiations are inevitable.

The need for consciousness to face its shadow is therapeutic. It is the primary requirement of any comprehensive psychological approach. Even though the union initially consists of an open battle and frequently does for a considerable time, it must ultimately result in some union. It is an uphill battle that reason alone cannot end. When something is willfully suppressed, it persists in the unconscious and only expresses itself inadvertently, which makes it much more hazardous, yielding no benefit. The fight continues until one or both of the parties becomes exhausted. It is impossible to predict the outcome in advance. The only thing we can be sure of is that both parties will change.

We learn about aspects of our nature that we would not allow anyone to show us and that we would never have admitted via this process of accepting the Other within us.

## Ego responsibility

The ego bears responsibility for the shadow. The shadow is a moral issue because of this. One thing is realizing what it looks like and what we are capable of. To decide what we can live with or out of is quite another.

When the shadow is faced, it initially creates a dead equilibrium, a standstill that prevents moral judgment and renders beliefs ineffective or unattainable. Everything turns into a question.

## Not only dark

However, the shadow is more than just the personality's shadow side. It also consists of morally sound impulses, skills, and attributes that have either been dormant or never came to consciousness.

The shadow isn't entirely horrible; it's just a little inferior, archaic, unsuited, and awkward. In some ways, it even possesses childlike or primordial aspects that would animate and adorn human existence, but convention prevents it!

Suppose previously thought that the human shadow was the root of all evil. In that case, it is now clear from closer examination that the unconscious man, or his shadow, possesses a variety of positive traits in addition to morally repugnant tendencies, including common instincts, appropriate reactions, realistic insights, and creative impulses, etc.

Both the positive and negative aspects of a person—those traits and behaviors they are ashamed of—as well as previously unimagined possibilities—are constellated by a neurotic episode.

### The Archetypal Shadow

Jung made a distinction between the individual and the group or archetypal shadow. When the shadow is personal, one can see through it with a bit of self-criticism. However, the same issues as with anima and animus arise when it manifests as an archetype. In other words, a man can see the relative evil in himself, but seeing the face of absolute evil is a rare and terrifying event.

## BRING YOUR SHADOW INTO THE LIGHT.

Carl Jung's concepts of the "Persona" and "Shadow Self" significantly impact how we comprehend the phenomena above in the field of psychology.

The aspect of ourselves we like, accept, and want to portray to the outside world is our "Persona" or "Mask" in Jung's terminology. It comprises ideas about who we recognize, admit, and attach to; these ideas are frequently shaped by what society and upbringing have taught us. We feel at ease with these names and descriptions: "I am a guy," "I am a devoted mother," "I am a law-abiding citizen," and "I am a kind someone who truly wants my friends to be happy." Although these are proper elements of who you are, they may not be the whole picture.

*"The persona, appropriately described as a kind of mask intended to both leave a lasting impression on others and conceal the individual's true nature, is a complex system of relationships between individual consciousness and society"-Jung.*

On the other hand, we often repress or disavow aspects of ourselves that we deem "indecent," As a whole, these aspects make up our Shadow Self. We keep these parts dormant and unspoiled in the unconscious because we do not like to conceive of them as parts until one day when unexpected persons or situations set them off.

You start behaving out in ways that surprise or even alarm you at those times. For example, when you feel weak or reliant, you can be taken off guard and experience internal conflicts if you identify as a tough person and deny your vulnerability. When you notice yourself getting irrationally upset or disgusted by a person's actions, it may be a sign that you are terrified of what you see or possess in yourself. This is known as projecting our shadows onto others. (On the other hand, you may have abandoned your Light if you find yourself strongly drawn to certain qualities in others!)

*Everyone has a shadow; the darker and denser it is, the less it is embodied in the person's conscious life. If one is aware of their deficiency, they always have a chance to improve. Nevertheless, it never gets fixed if it is suppressed and removed from consciousness. — Jung*

Your Shadow can become destructive when it is repressed or projected; it may manifest as depression, inward aggressiveness, or interpersonal animosity. Pushing certain aspects of ourselves down all the time also consumes a lot of energy. In reality, psychological Shadow work can be helpful for many persons with chronic fatigue.

Your light and darkness are revealed during therapy and self-development; holistic health and true self-esteem result from our ability to accept all of these aspects of ourselves. By practicing self-compassion, you can learn to integrate your own Shadow, to be angry, self-preserving, needy occasionally angry, self-preserving, needy, and burned with envy.

The first and last steps of self-love are learning to embrace who you are in all your complexity. One of the most effective measures you can take towards genuine peace and aliveness is shadow work, which is both the starting point and the basis.

## HOW TO WORK WITH YOUR SHADOW?

To connect with your Shadow successfully, you must make a significant imaginative leap and keep up your wholehearted effort. Since science favors logic and the quantifiable, we modern creatures have inherited a predisposition that prevents us from developing a relationship with the enigmatic, fluid, symbolic, and lyrical Shadow.

If you bring the critical analysis of the left brain and Ego, shadow work won't produce anything. The Shadow requires an attitude of openness, curiosity, humility, and faithful attention to show itself and reveal its many gifts. To legitimize and animate this alienated part of the Self, you must find a way for your Ego to suspend judgment and disbelief.

Here are some considerations to bear in mind as you begin to build a relationship with your Shadow:

- Consider the Shadow a distinct entity with its awareness that resides inside you.
- Building genuine connections and trust takes time, just like in any relationship. It could take considerable wooing and persistence to get through the Ego's defenses because they have historically rejected the Shadow.
- When you first begin working with the Shadow, it's common to be unsure of whether you are creating the responses or the Shadow is speaking. Just keep going. One day, with constancy and honest effort, you will hear the Shadow speak for itself.
- The Shadow is more concerned with consistency and effort than the total time spent.
- As you proceed, trust your gut. As you show up to it, the intuitive process of working with the Shadow will get easier. No action is ever right or wrong.

## VISUALIZE YOUR SHADOW IN 3 STEPS

1. Bring to light a person in your life who is critical of you. Imagine this guy mockingly staring at you. You are exposed before them. They can see all of your flaws. They are already evaluating you.
2. Now adopt their viewpoint. How do they perceive it? How do they perceive you? How do they perceive you? Connect with the negative emotions you encounter when you are around this individual. Do an honest accounting while being fearless. Your Shadow will become more solid as a result.
3. Once you have felt the emotions deeply, push them forward and give them a less-than-true representation of your face and body. Do you see anything? Take in as many specifics as you can. You have a Shadow.

If this doesn't work the first time, it's okay. Your Shadow will be more receptive to revealing itself as you get better at allowing it in. Never give up. This aspect of you cries out for your attention and recognition.

## WHAT TAKES PLACE WHEN YOUR SHADOW IS SUPPRESSED

What occurs to all the pieces of ourselves that we hide from view, then? We recognize in others the qualities we reject in ourselves. Psychologists refer to this as projection. Everything we bury within us, we project onto others. It's a safe probability that you haven't acknowledged your rudeness if, for instance, you become annoyed when someone is disrespectful to you.

This does not imply that they are not being impolite to you.

However, you wouldn't mind someone else being nasty as much if the rudeness wasn't lurking in your shadow. This procedure doesn't involve conscious thought. Our predictions are unknown to us. Our egos use this defense mechanism to protect how they see themselves. Our false identities as "good" people prevent us from engaging with our shadows. These psychological projections skew reality, separating how we perceive ourselves from how we act in the world.

## CONCLUSION

Psychological projection occurs when we mistakenly think, feel, or even possess something that belongs to someone else. When it comes to the shadow, there will be an apparent quality in another person that you find "unacceptable," and the projection frequently comes dressed in blame. The shadow sometimes referred to as the ego-dystonic complex, the repressed id, the shadow aspect, or the shadow archetype, is a subconscious element of the personality that does not fit the ego ideal, which causes the ego to fight and project the shadow.

# CHAPTER 02
# WHAT IS SHADOW WORK?

The elements of ourselves that have been suppressed and repressed, or those we are ashamed of, angry about, or uneasy about, are what we refer to as our "shadow self." The idea behind the shadow self is that we metaphorically bury those facets of ourselves that we worry won't be liked, accepted, or embraced by others. Therefore, we keep them hidden.

The parts of ourselves that we do not present to society are, in essence, our shadow selves. What precisely is shadow work, then? To be who we are is the practice of accepting things and letting go of guilt and judgments. The greatest delight in life, in the words of Victor Hugo, is knowing that we are loved—either for who we are or, more accurately, loved despite who we are.

## WHERE DID THIS CONCEPT COME FROM?
The concept "the shadow self," first used by renowned psychologist Carl Jung in the 20th century, is where the word "shadow work" originates. According to Jungian psychology, this phrase refers to the unconscious aspects of the personality that our conscious ego doesn't want to acknowledge.

According to Jung, everyone has a shadow; the darker and denser it is, the less it is embodied in the person's conscious life. The darker half of ourselves that we suppress or dismiss is, in essence, the shadow self. Imagine it as a backpack you drag behind you that is invisible.

## WHAT IS SHADOW SELF?
Swiss psychologist Carl Jung devoted his entire life to researching the psychology and personality of people. He made numerous contributions to psychoanalysis, such as the "shadow self" idea. At first glance, the word "shadow" in this statement can seem a little ominous, but there is nothing to be concerned about!

Our shadow selves frequently show up when we react negatively to others' words or actions, feel tense, have cognitive dissonance, feel uncomfortable, judge others, and are held back.

## WHAT IS A SHADOW WORK?
*Working with our shadow selves to change their negative impacts on our lives and integrate our disparate parts into a single, cohesive self is known as shadow work.*

Occasionally throughout our lifetimes, we push small parts of ourselves so far away that we become unaware of what is in our shadow selves. In a sense, we frequently are unaware of what we are unaware of. What defines shadow work—psych them analysis—is the bringing to the surface, processing, and re-acceptance of those minute bits to achieve a complete, whole, and integrated self (as psychoanalysis is at the core of Jungian psychology). Whatever language is chosen to express the fragmented selves, according to Jung, integrating them is a comprehensive process.

For example, a shadow rooted in apprehension about change may prevent you from leaving your unfulfilling 9 to 5 work and pursuing something new. Massi adds of shadows, "It transforms how you see the next steps." It alters your actions since you won't participate in potentially dangerous situations if you're terrified of them. In other words, our shadows prevent us from pursuing our goals, and shadow work enables us to develop the self-assurance and sense of security that will enable us to pursue those goals.

## HOW DOES SHADOW WORK PROVIDE?
Even though shadow work is difficult since the pain of previous rejection typically goes along with it, the process of closing the gap between the shadow self and the conscious self has the potential to improve one's life significantly. "Shadow work is the way of the heart warrior," according to Jung.

Such a procedure, according to Jung, could aid in developing a sense of harmony and balance within oneself. A new sense of freedom can be created when we feel entire rather than broken, allowing us to view life differently and engage in new experiences that we previously wouldn't or couldn't.

To better fulfill our obligations and relationships in life, whether as a husband, sibling, child, parent, teacher, mentor, friend, or any of the countless other roles we play, we must address the emotional baggage that has been long-hidden in our shadows.

Additionally, shadow labor gives us a stronger sense of personal agency and control in a constantly shifting and occasionally constricting reality. Shadow work almost always results in increased authenticity in everything we do because it helps us become the most authentic versions of ourselves we've ever been.

Finally, rather than suppressing those pieces of ourselves until they erupt in harmful, uncontrollable ways, By embracing and mend the aspects of ourselves that we've labeled as our shadows. We learn how to express those features in healthy ways (like lashing out at others in anger or creating a toxic body image and inner dialogue). This acceptance might even grow into a powerful love for oneself.

## SHADOW WORK METHODS

We can also do shadow work for ourselves, while therapy and outside assistance are sometimes the best options. Here are a few methods:

1. Refrain from judging yourself:

As a healing and self-development technique, shadow work necessitates acceptance and surrender. Instead of battling whatever you don't want to think, feel, or admit, approach this process with compassion for your experiences and yourself. Shadow work will be easier and more effective if you have patience and care for yourself.

2. Ask why:

Working in the shadows can be like trying to drag a rope out of a deep hole. We raise that rope higher and higher each time we ask, "Why?" and then respond with an answer. The shadow self is gradually revealed due to this iterative probing of our feelings, behaviors, and past experiences that have impacted us. We can investigate the precise emotions felt in a circumstance by, for instance, questioning why a given action by another person causes us to react in a particular manner.

Then, by investigating the causes of our sentiments (such as anger or anxiety), we may arrive at a more profound level of emotions (such as more significant, a reminder of past trauma or abstract fears). By enquiring as to the source of those stronger emotions, it can be developed further. The bottom line is to allow one discovery to lead to the next since everything is connected.

3. Journal:

To more effectively process our ideas and emotions, journaling enables us to perform a metaphorical "brain dump." These ideas and sensations are then more clearly perceived as a result of the processing.

Writing these down regularly can help us gain a more comprehensive drive, make connections, and detect patterns in our moods, habits, and past experiences. This can be done on paper or digitally in a place like the notes app on our phones.

Overall, journaling's reflecting quality makes it practical for self-development techniques like shadow work. Check out these shadow work diary prompts if you're prepared to plunge in.

4. Meditate:

Sometimes the most pleasing thing to do for ourselves is to sit motionlessly. One of the most valuable tools at our disposal to develop better self-awareness is meditation. Regular meditation practice may teach us to be more aware of our thoughts, behavior, and total selves. The conditions for essential discoveries and emotional healing are frequently created through meditation.

5. Talk with someone:

Talking to a close friend or member of your family can help you if you're having problems working things out on your own. or seeking professional assistance from a therapist may be helpful if you are having trouble making sense of everything.

Furthermore, the unbiased opinion of a third party could help you identify problems that you otherwise might not have noticed.

6. Break down limiting beliefs:

By meticulously deconstructing a lifetime's worth of challenging or unpleasant feelings, we can learn the roots of many of our self-limiting beliefs. Do you feel unqualified to apply for a job you want, for instance? Do you hesitate before departing on your ideal getaway? These issues often start with our shadow selves.

Addressing, comprehending, healing, and letting go of the foundations of these issues—rejectionists, insecurity, or other repressed emotions or experiences —can be incredibly liberating. Shadow work can help us evolve into more robust, more true versions of ourselves who have the resources to pursue our goals and desires by removing the power from the things that hold us back.

7. Individualize your approach:

Each of us has a favorite method for growing personally and gaining a more profound sense of self. The activity that makes you feel the most introspective might be going on a hike to spend some time by yourself, clearing your head and pondering. Another option is an EFT session. Whatever it is, go with it if it suits you! The process, not the method, is what matters.

Excellent self-awareness results in relief, progress, freedom, and authenticity, regardless of our route to get there. Additionally, the world now more than ever needs individuals who are powerful, confident, and aware of who they are.

## IS SHADOW WORK DANGEROUS?

This is when, for some, things could become a little too; how do we put this, paranormal? The shadow self is referred to as a demon in some circles. According to the theory, any aspects of ourselves that we reject turn on us and appear as some form of supernatural being. Without our knowledge, that entity may operate independently, leading to events we regret later. Everything is high, "Dr. Jekyll and Mr. Hyde,"... however evil.

## IS IT WORTH TRYING?

Listen, the idea of shadow work has enough appeal, even if the demon stuff is too much for you to comprehend. Healing might result from uncovering the issues that are plaguing underneath the surface. And completeness can result from healing, which translates into enhanced relationships and a more distinct sense of self.

Devout supporters of shadow work even assert that it can result in increased vitality and improved physical health. If you think about it, it makes logic. Being emotionally drained can leave you feeling physically and mentally fatigued. According to this line of reasoning, if you aren't embracing your entire authentic self, you're constantly experiencing emotional exhaustion. Weakness that never ends!

So yes, shadow work is a viable option. If it is not your thing, you can always consult an expert or decide to give up. However, who knows? You may find a source of untapped physical, emotional, and spiritual vitality when you unlock something within you.

## WHAT WAS THE ORIGIN OF SHADOW WORK?

To poetically express human depravity, Carl Jung used the term "shadow." With a grounding in Christianity, the concepts of "demonic possession" were made more intelligible by introducing the unconscious, the shadow, etc. The fundamental idea behind devilry is that you or other people do not intrinsically deserve God's love. So one must be instructed on how to live.

Evil occurs when you despise or dehumanize another person or group of people for no other reason than that your mind is projecting your shadow attributes onto them. And they are in opposition to your egotistical way of life. This is proof of psychological distortion. Unable to accept oneself and humanity for who they are—unable to see things as they are.

Shadow work comes from the desire to restore one's damaged psyche and respect one's inherent claim to wholeness. As a result, you learn to respect other people's right to wholeness.

# DO WE ALL HAVE A SHADOW SELF?

Yes, every one of us has a shadow self. Every human being has a dark side, as unsettling as that may sound. How come this is the case? All people have shadows because of how we were raised as children, frequently referred to as our "conditioning."

I'm a wonderful guy, though! You might be thinking, "I don't have a shadow side. The truth is that you might e a good person. You might even be the most kind, the selfish person on the planet. You could save puppies, give half your pay to the needy, and feed the hungry. However, it remains po for you to have a Shadow. Here, there are no exclusions. We must accept that having both a good and a terrible wrong is part of what is beginning, man.

There might be a lot of denials when someone is told they have a shadow side (or when it is brought up). We have been trained to have a two-dimensional and constrained view of ourselves. We have been taught that the only people with shadows are criminals, murderers, and thieves. One of the main reasons for our suffering is this "black and white" way of thinking.

Consider whether you have created an idealized and inaccurate picture of who you are if the idea of having a Shadow side worries you. The following attitudes are indications of an idealized or unrealistic perception of self:

- I'm better than those people; I'm not like them.
- "I have never wandered off."
- God is pleased with me.
- Criminals and bad actors are not people.
- "Even if everyone knows I'm good, I still have to remind them,"
- "I act as an example."
- "I deserve to be recognized and praised for my good deeds."
- "Why do others think awful things when I don't?"

Such views of ourselves are erroneous, unwholesome, and essentially deluded. Exploring our Shadows is the only way to achieve inner tranquility, joy, real love, fulfillment, and illumination.

## CONCLUSION

Finding those fearful aspects of yourself in the shadows and bringing them into the light are the goals of shadow work. It is a kind and careful process. Integration is the purpose of the shadow work. Unconscious integration results in totaled awareness. Bring your shadow closer to you by engaging in shadow work. When you connect with people, projection is lessened because of too much work. Other people's personality traits and eccentricities are less likely to set you off. Thus, you may feel more sympathetic toward other people as a result. The concept "the shadow self," first used by renowned psychologist Carl Jung in the 20th century, is where the word "shadow work" originates. According to Jungian psychology, this phrase refers to the unconscious aspects of the personality that our conscious ego doesn't want to acknowledge.

# CHAPTER 03
# SHADOW SELF: OWNING OUR DARK SIDES

## INTRODUCTION
You might not show the world your complete personality like many other people. It is common for undesirable or inappropriate features to be concealed.

According to psychoanalytic theory, this negative aspect of the personality is called the "shadow." Whether you are aware of it or not, it has the potential to have a variety of effects on your life. You might be able to comprehend all aspects of yourself by acknowledging and accepting your shadow self.

The aspect of our psyche is concealed in the depths of our "dark side" We are frequently shocked to discover its existence, and it is typically a facet of ourselves that we would prefer to forget.

## WHAT IS YOUR DARK SIDE?
Midway through the 20th century, psychologist Carl Jung coined the phrase "shadow self. According to Jung, a person's positive and negative traits make up their entire personality, but only the desirable traits are displayed in what is known as the "persona." According to Jung, you psychologically suppress those thoughts and feelings that you may unconsciously identify as harmful or unattractive.

They are still present despite this. It simply implies that most people have lost the ability to acknowledge them. You might grow apart from them. If someone points them out to you, you can even choose not to accept that they are a part of you or project them.

## ACKNOWLEDGING YOUR DARK SIDE
Everyone has a "dark side," or traits they frequently like to keep hidden from others. It's the characteristics we might feel embarrassed or ashamed about. the ones we could have been rejected by, or those we think to make us unlovable or undeserving.

Sometimes, you might display overbearing, egotistical, or furious behavior. These supposedly bad qualities about yourself may not be to your taste. Alternatively, you can have buried them so deeply that you aren't even aware they are there.

But according to Debbie Ford, accepting these attributes creates a pathway to contentment, fulfillment, and "genuine enlightenment" Our experiences include aspects of our dark sides. We may accept every aspect of ourselves by discovering and accepting our shadow side.

Ford, a speaker, teacher, and coach, writes that "every component of ourselves has a gift." Every characteristic and feeling we have guides us in the direction of enlightenment and oneness.

Ford tells the tale of Steven, a man concerned about being a wimp, in her book. Steven admitted to his father that he was scared of riding on a pony when he was five years old. What type of man are you going to make? His father said in response.

You're nothing more than a little wimp, and our family finds you embarrassing. Steven remembered these words. He exerted every effort to show that he wasn't frail, including lifting weights and earning a black belt in karate. He also detested observing weakness in others.

However, after speaking with Ford, Steven understood that he was still a "wimp" in several aspects of his life and that this trait had benefited him. For example, his wimpiness made him warier.

According to Ford, this not only "kept him out of conflicts" but also prevented him from going out with friends in college when he knew excessive drinking would be. The horrific event that killed his best friend and seriously damaged others could have been avoided if not for this.

Certain aspects of our daily lives can become complicated when we don't fully own ourselves. We could push ourselves so hard to hide our flaws or imperfections that we start going after goals we don't even want, making our days full of meaningless chores.

We could change into someone we don't even recognize while striving to establish our value. According to Ford, we exhaust our internal not when we try not to be something.

## WHAT DOES IT MEAN TO EMBRACE YOUR DARK SIDE?
From a psychological perspective, accepting your dark side does not entail giving up your other supposedly desirable qualities. You're not abruptly abandoning your current way of life in favor of more unfavorable attitudes, actions, and social groups.

You accept the negative aspects of yourself when you embrace your dark side. You're accepting responsibility for them and acknowledging their significance in your day-to-day activities.

## WHAT ARE THE BENEFITS OF EMBRACING YOUR DARK SIDE?
In the study, it might be challenging to measure personality. It is something ethereal that cannot be touched or quantified. As a result, there isn't much peer-reviewed research on shadow employment and mental health advantages.

However, studies on a process known as individuation can provide some insight into the potential advantages of embracing your dark side of Trusted Source. The process by which you feel like an individual self is known as individuation, another idea that Jung articulated. It entails uniting every aspect of your personality.

Primary individuation takes place during the formative years, but according to Jung and other adherents of his work, it is a lifelong process that molds a person's identity.

Shadow work was a part of individuation, according to Jung. When you consciously explore the dark aspects of your psyche, you engage in shadow work.

You can become aware of these hidden aspects of yourself by studying them, which may enable you to experience greater levels of perception, consciousness, and self-control.

## WHY IT'S IMPORTANT TO UNDERSTAND YOUR DARK SIDE
Were you frightened of the dark as a young child? The majority of us were. And I doubt we ever considered challenging this apprehension. Because so many unknowable things in the dark could hurt us, we were almost instinctively trained to be terrified of the dark.

However, what often occurred when you turned on the light? You discovered that the unknown was not all that terrifying. They weren't as obscure either. They made up a part of the surroundings.

We understood that the dark is terrible and unknowable and that it is best to keep our gloomy thoughts and feelings to ourselves. Turning on an emotional light is more complicated than turning on a physical light switch. Therefore, we steer clear of it. The superficial is simpler. But whether or not we choose to acknowledge it, this darkness in our spirit has a life of its own and thrives. It is present and potent.

## UNDERSTANDING DARKNESS
As we developed, this fear of our emotional complexity deepened and eventually turned into our shadow. A hidden aspect of ourselves affects our decisions more frequently than we realize.

Denying and hiding it from ourselves and others takes a lot of work. We have a shadow side. The flaws were embarrassed and afraid to display. But because of our denial, we fail to recognize that our strengths also lie in the darkness's obscurity.

We have chosen to ignore and conceal this dark side without further investigation for reasons that have their roots in the past. Consequently, it prevents us from genuinely expressing ourselves. In many respects, keeping our shadow hidden is the ultimate act of betrayal. We betray ourselves by hiding this aspect of ourselves and implying that we don't deserve to be fully revealed.

As previously noted, our shadow can manifest as either power or weakness. Being fully conscious of who we have given us a chance to exhibit our strength. But ignoring these attributes will always have a negative impact.

The more we suppress our dark parts, the more we experience personality disorders. This may appear as addiction, anxiety, willful failure in relationships or the workplace, or other actions that harm the self and others.

By recognizing our shadow, we can bring our earliest scars to light and give ourselves a chance for healing and growth. But if we ignore this, the wounds will worsen and release poison into our lives.

## WE NEED TO GO THROUGH THE SHADOW TO DEEPEN OUR SPIRITUALITY

Any spiritual endeavor requires acknowledging and understanding our shadow. When we are only concerned with finding our light, we are kept out of realms of guilt, shame, lust, resentment, and aggressiveness. But to access our lighter sides, must resolve these very feelings first.

Even spiritual practices such as meditation can become challenging when we attempt to ignore our shadow selves. Its repression becomes apparent when we close our eyes and are left with nothing but our thoughts.

Like all powerful emotions, avoiding what we see keeps us constrained and in rejection. We all have these traits and emotions inside of us, and trying to hide them makes us act inauthentically and even inexplicably self-destructively.

The depth of our spiritual and personal development will be constrained if our shadow is not acknowledged and welcomed. When we refuse to look at the darkness, we reject our urge to be entirely accepted by others.

We begin to identify too much with the aspect of ourselves that we have developed through our reality-perception. Our personality, or the aspect of us that the outside world sees, is then shaped by this.

Our personalities and roles do their best to make us feel deserving and lovable. Some people achieve success by being intelligent, successful, and influential, while the opposite is true for others. Regardless of how our personality tries to take control of life, it is still another effort to get people to love us for something we are not.

We maintain separation as long as this bad image of ourselves is constant. The message is, "I choose separation, inside and out. I don't want to look and feel certain things inside me, and I blame others for showing and living what I want to reject." It is a torturous cage of never-ending solitude.

## EMBRACING THE COMPLETE YOU

Our light is accessible only via darkness. The evil side of us is pretty active whether we want it to be, even though it is hidden and not visible from the outside. But we're aware that it exists because it keeps pleading for attention.

It is best to confront the shadow in a secure and caring setting. Otherwise, it is terrified of the destruction and isolation its visage will bring about. We can begin seeing, seeing, and expressing what has been kept from our awareness once it is safe to do so.

There are many unpolished diamonds of power, imagination, and beauty that we've kept to a minimum so that those who are near to us don't feel insignificant, intimidated, or afraid. Having a conversation with our shadow is a huge step toward healing and self-love.

When we first start on this fascinating and vital trip, we might not be entirely clear about who we are. However, this is only the case because we are so accustomed to wearing masks that being authentic feels like meeting an old friend. New options, choices, and impressions soon become apparent.

All Suddenly can approach all of the unanswered questions in our lives with courage and authenticity. Our ability to exist in this world more fully and ultimately is strengthened.

# CHAPTER 04
# WHAT ARE THE BEST PRACTICES FOR DOING SHADOW WORK

## WHAT IS SHADOW WORK?
It's a process of accepting our anger, jealousy, greed, and bitterness as "ugly" parts of ourselves and learning to love them regardless of how we may initially perceive them.

Created many of our shadows due to developmental or attachment trauma we experienced as children. These shadows are now stored in our nervous system and the stories we tell ourselves since we lack the tools to digest our emotions adequately. Shadow work is trauma work because it helps us heal the wounded parts of ourselves.

*"The encounter with oneself is among the more unpleasant things that may be avoided as long as we can project everything terrible onto the environment. This confrontation is the first test of courage on the inner journey, a test that is enough to scare off most people. However, if we can recognize and tolerate our own shadow, then a little portion of the issue has already been resolved—at the very least, the unconscious self has been brought to light. Since the shadow is a living aspect of the personality, it desires to coexist with it in some capacity. It cannot be reasoned away or made to appear harmless."* - Carl Jung.

## THE BEST PRACTICES FOR DOING SHADOW WORK
The following are suggested methods for reclaiming aspects of ourselves that we have rejected:

### A. Pay attention to your responses and work on being mindful.
What sets you off? What or who triggers a response in you? Being triggered is a programmed fight-or-flight response that starts in our brain and sends messages to our endocrine and neurological systems. Triggering is caused by unconscious behaviors.

Keep an eye on your interactions with others as you go about your regular activities and use social media. We can work on recognizing our shadow sides by practicing self-observation and mindfulness.

Although it may take some time for you to master this skill (it can be challenging to return to a mature, logical state of mind when we are triggered), just becoming aware of your reaction after the event and giving it some thought is a significant first step. The choice is enabled through consciousness.

Because remember: It's historical when it's hysterical. Meaning: Your reaction to an incident or someone else's actions is usually founded in your history and your shadow when it is out of proportion.

### B. Complete the emotional cycle and Practice emotional inquiry.
- How do I feel?
- Why do I feel this way?
- What myth or belief is associated with this feeling? (For instance, I am not good enough, my emotions are unimportant, I am unlovable, no one cares about me, and I will never be happy...)
- Does this emotion or circumstance make me think of something from my past or youth?
- Experiencing the emotion physically. Embrace it and give it the room it requires to finish its cycle.

It comes down to cultivating an interest in your inner emotional world and viewing your emotions as data.

### C. Daily journaling and writing from the heart
Continuum of thought Writing is like a raw, do-it-yourself window. As a result, we learn to be more honest with ourselves and unexpected things from our unconscious surface.

We are not allowed to bullshit ourselves on the pages.

The finest methods:

- Daily Pages
- Communicative Writing
- Technique for Internal Family Systems

Alternatively, you might begin by using these questions to determine your shadow parts:

- What sets off my relationships and life?
- How and when do I evaluate others?
- What about other people do you dislike?
- How and when do I evaluate myself?
- What about myself do I dislike?
- What or who do you harbor grudges against?
- What issues do I have complaints about?
- What qualities in others do I wish I had?
- What issues do I encounter?
- What about other people inspires and intrigues you?

### D. Sit with your shadow in meditation.

To indeed come to know yourself and your shadow, you must learn how to sit by yourself in solitude. For many people, it is also the most challenging thing to do. To come in touch with your (wounded) shadow parts, sit with your emotions, and go deeper into your triggers, it's essential to be just with yourself, your thoughts, and your feelings. Using Insight Timer is a must if you're just getting started.

### E. Dream analysis

Because dreams offer a direct channel to the unconscious, they serve as the perfect vehicle for facing the shadow. Your unconscious is communicating with you through your dreams. (Jung, incidentally, was a great fan of dream interpretation.)

Persistent dreams indicate that your shadow demands your attention and contains a wealth of valuable information.

1. The most challenging aspect of dream work is recalling even one of the roughly six dreams we have each night. Before you go to sleep, concentrate on recalling and comprehending your dreams. Make that your goal.
2. Keep a pen and a notepad by your bed. In this way, if you have a dream and wake up in the middle of the night remembering it, you can make a few notes on essential words or imagery that may help you remember the dream in greater detail the next day.

*Necessary: Include your feelings towards the dream and the events that occurred.*

### F. Examine your favorite myths, stories, and movies.

To explore your shadows more intuitively, seek symbols and archetypes in the narratives that speak to you the most. Without our knowledge, they communicate directly with the unconscious. We enjoy particular films and heroes because they represent a facet of our shadow selves.

Make a list of your favorite myths and movies, then scribble down a rough outline of each one's plot. Then consider how your heroes and heroines' traits might connect to you, your unrealized potential, or your hidden ambitions.

I also advise searching for myth/movie analysis or interpretations on Google to comprehend complex narratives and their significance better. I've completed this activity a few times, and I'm surprised by what I learn about myself every time. Try it!

### G. Inner Child Work

As most of our shadows are formed in childhood, this is the area with the most significant possibility for healing and integration. For our adult selves to take control of our lives, we must learn how to reparent ourselves.

## WHAT IS THE GOAL OF SHADOW WORK?

Your shadow is not a shortcoming or an error; instead, it is an inherent aspect of who you are.

The main goal of shadow work is to increase self-awareness, which leads to self-acceptance and compassion. You can perceive the various aspects of yourself through shadow work, which is frequently both therapy and more spiritual.

Shadow work is about admitting the existence of shadows and becoming curious about studying them for people who have been particularly successful at ignoring their shadows, perhaps because it differs too much from your self-perception or preferred impression.

This kind of work assists persons whose shadow is connected to trauma in embracing the aspect of themselves that has been repressed or shamed their entire lives. You can begin to understand how your ideas and emotions affect your actions by acknowledging your shadow self.

Knowing this gives you the power to take charge of your life and empowers you to lead a more purposeful and conscious existence. You can start presenting who you indeed are.

## CONCLUSION

Shadow work is a process of learning to embrace our wrath, envy, greed, and bitterness despite how we may at first consider them as being "ugly" elements of ourselves. Developmental or attachment trauma we encountered as children formed many of our shadows. Since we lack the resources to digest our emotions properly, these shadows are now stored in our neurological system and the stories we tell ourselves. Because it aids in our ability to mend our injured aspects, shadow work is trauma work. Finding your hidden and repressed sides also referred to as your shadow, is the goal of shadow work. You can work with the darker, more secretive, mysterious self by engaging in the discipline of introspection. We feel the most shame and avoid dealing with these areas of your existence that have been suppressed and rejected.

# CHAPTER 05
# THE BENEFITS OF SHADOW WORK
# (PLUS, ARE THERE ANY DANGER)

People have recently become quite interested in shadow work. Everyone appears to be engaging in it. Some people are interested in the advantages of working with their shadows, while others are concerned about the risks. Because it goes by the label "shadow work," you might be unsure whether you want to start doing it or even why you should. I'll discuss the benefits of doing shadow work in this chapter and touch on the contentious subject of its risks.

## UNDERSTANDING WHAT REAL SHADOW WORK IS
The therapeutic approach developed by Carl Jung, which emphasizes accepting and integrating the unfavorable facets of our personalities, gave rise to a sort of healing work known as shadow work.

According to Jung, we all have a shadow, or dark side, which includes undesirable personality traits, negative habits, dysfunctional behavioral or emotional patterns, unfulfilled wants, and hidden anxieties. He also believed that these characteristics, requirements, anxieties, and routines would control our lives from a subconscious perspective, destroying our aspirations.

For example, the dread of awkward circumstances can prevent someone from pursuing the career they want, or the fear of intimacy can prevent people from establishing fulfilling relationships.

Due to emotionally inaccessible parents as children, unmet demand for affection may manifest as the propensity to suffocate your relationship; for example, as human beings who have come to grow and develop spiritually, we all have a shadow or dark shadow side.

In the same way that avoiding the dirt in your home won't make it clean, ignoring the shadow won't make it go away. It needs to be cleaned; the same is true for the shadow. I believe everyone must engage in shadow work, but first, they must comprehend the benefits of doing it.

If people know the incredible benefits of performing shadow work, it will inspire them to do it diligently and persistently. Therefore, read the following primary advantages of doing shadow work if you are thinking about it or are just trying to understand how it might benefit you:

## THE BENEFITS OF SHADOW WORK
Shadow work is a skill that can be useful in many facets of your life. Here are the advantages of incorporating shadow work into your self-care routines.

- Getting To Know Yourself

To know what you want and to lead a happy and fulfilled life, in my opinion, you must have a strong sense of who you are.

Knowing yourself entails accepting both your positive and negative traits, having complete awareness of your personality, and being aware of the events and circumstances that developed your personality. No one is flawless; thus, we al. Thus good and "bad" sides.

You may identify why you struggle in some aspects of your life. You are succeeding by understanding your strengths and weaknesses. Love for oneself, self-esteem, and a positive self-image are all built on self-knowledge.

The first step toward creating healthy, genuine relationships with others is to have a positive relationship with yourself.

- Achieving Self-love

Another advantage of shadow work is self-love, which is a topic that everyone is discussing. Although that sounds nice, nobody ever teaches you how to love yourself. Or even if they do outline specific actions you must take to love yourself; it can occasionally be trickier than that because love is something that must be felt rather than comprehended.

As a result, shadow work can assist you in learning to love yourself by assisting you in realizing how all of your negative traits or behaviors result from trauma experienced during childhood or in a previous incarnation.

As a result, it will assist you in letting go of the notion that you are "evil," "broken," or that something is fundamentally wrong with you. You'll realize that your past has shaped who you are and that all of your adverse events have served as teachers for you to improve. Second, by enhancing your self-esteem, shadow work can help you love yourself.

- Increasing Your Sense Of Self

You can boost your self-esteem through shadow work by developing a better awareness of yourself. Since they did not show them unconditional love and acceptance, many people were conditioned to believe something was wrong with them, starting at a very young age. They were instructed to feel ashamed of their shortcomings, needs, and desires.

Additionally, many people lack a proper understanding of who they are, including their motivations, limitations, and unmet needs. You may reveal all these through shadow work, which can help you better comprehend who you are.

You can pursue what is suitable for you, leave what is wrong, set healthy limitations and boundaries, and more by discovering all this about yourself. This can help you respect yourself more as a person and embrace your good and bad traits.

- Feeling Whole As A Person

We accumulate many traumatic events throughout our lives, some of which are more agonizing than others. We are criticized, disappointed, and looked down upon, and we are taught that we are not good enough.

We suffer various forms of violence or lose the people we love. These traumatic events are kept in our soul, energetic body, and subconscious mind. Every unpleasant experience weighs heavily on us and has an effect later on.

For example, some people may unconsciously think they deserve to be miserable, hurt, used, etc., and they will manifest the necessary conditions for that to occur.

You will feel entire once more, just like you did when you were a young child, thanks to shadow work's ability to help you heal the experiences and feelings brought on by the traumatic occurrences.

You can only begin to experience true happiness and begin to construct a life based on authenticity and integrity if you have fully recovered and feel like you are entire as a person. According to the definition, integrity is "the attribute of consistently acting by the moral ideals that you believe in, learning respect and trust of others."

The issue is that when we have unresolved trauma, we occasionally stray from our moral standards because we can get to the point where we no longer know who we are or what our principles and values are.

It kike whatever was directing you through life has now evaporated as a younger compass has broken. As you work through each painful memory, reclaiming your power, and letting go of all the unfavorable ideas and feelings, shadow work can help you feel whole once more.

- Healing Generational Trauma

Another significant advantage is the ability to do shadow work to repair generational trauma. Due to the intense emotional connection between a parent and kid, we may have taken on many of our parents' traumas as children or acquired them ourselves. The traumas that our parents experienced came from their parents, and so on.

Trauma and specific ways of thinking, feeling, and behaving are passed on from generation to generation. "genetic equipment" is used in science, whereas "family karma" is used in spirituality.

We have energy cords that link us to all of our ancestors, so as we cure ourselves, we also heal our entire family tree. This reduces the amount of karma transferred to our children and clears much of our own.

- **Developing New Methods For Meeting Your Needs**

Through these exercises, you will better grasp the unfulfilled needs and desires you have carried with you throughout your life because a significant portion of shadow work focuses on your youth. When you were a youngster, you had to rely on your parents to meet your needs, whether emotional, physical, or otherwise.

Suppose your parents could not meet all of them or explain how you would feel unfulfilled. This also shaped your attachment style, which impacted how you felt about yourself and saw other people's needs.

As you complete shadow work, you learn which of your needs have not been satisfied and how you may do so to improve your mental health. The ability to recognize that, as an adult, you have the authority to meet your own needs and design the life you want makes shadow work tremendously empowering.

- **Setting Boundaries**

Relationship boundaries are crucial because they distinguish between healthy and harmful partnerships. How we connect with our parents or siblings as children shape our ability to create firm limits.

Suppose your parents were overly authoritarian or controlling. In that case, you might not be able to set limits as an adult since you were never allowed to do so when you were younger. By enabling us to see when and how our boundaries were crossed and, indirectly, how to stop that from happening in the future, shadow work teaches us how to set firmer limits as adults.

A person is unconsciously still thinking and feeling like a child who was not permitted to speak out when they cannot establish healthy boundaries in relationships. Shadow work aids in your understanding on all levels that you are now an adult and may reclaim your authority because you are no longer a little child who must obey his parents.

Without clearly defined limits, we are more likely to attract unhealthy relationships and others who take advantage of us, make fun of us, and ultimately demolish our self-esteem. People unable to set boundaries in relationships inevitably find themselves in unhealthy, toxic situations.

As a result, if you were not permitted to create boundaries when you were a child or adolescent, it is essential to start learning how to do so now. To achieve this, you can employ shadow work.

- **Seeing Others For What They Indeed Are**

We frequently commit the following two blunders in our interactions with others:

- The first mistake is when we either idealize someone or elevate them.
- The second standard error is demonizing them, treating them as inferiors, and emphasizing their negative traits exclusively.

We tend to idealize those who assist us or whom we like for a particular reason, and we tend to vilify anyone who doesn't fit our standard or who may have harmed us in any way.

Your ability to genuinely see yourself as a person with good and terrible traits will help you understand others in the same way that shadow work has helped you see yourself.

You won't categorize individuals as good or bad any longer, and you won't blame someone for making a mistake.

Simply by realizing that everyone has a shadow they need to face, you will be able to forgive and treat people with more compassion.

- **Better Relationships**

You will value the various ways that shadow work will enhance your connections. In the beginning, you will feel better by healing and loving yourself; when you feel better, you also attract better.

You will only select to surround yourself with individuals that respect and encourage you as your self-esteem grows. Knowing how to care for your needs can help you avoid becoming dependent on others and forming co-dependent relationships.

Egomaniacs and other people with bad intentions will stay away from you if you know how to set clear boundaries. Overall, you will grow in your ability to empathize with others and yourself as well as your communication abilities.

- Creating A Thriving Life

You will experience an overall improvement in your mental and emotional health due to shadow work, which also helps you heal generational trauma and your own.

We all carry significant baggage from trauma, which frequently keeps us from advancing. Additionally, you will discover many problematic habits through shadow work, including self-sabotage.

Once you address that, you will be more effective in most aspects of your life and more in line with your desired life.

- Shadow Work Helps You Break Free.

You can only say that you are genuinely stuck when unaware of what is occurring. To start solving problems and taking action to stop what is happening, you must be aware of what is happening. Shadow labor achieves that.

Many people believe that doing covert work renders them helpless. It doesn't; all it does is force them to acknowledge their helplessness.

You are not it because you are facing it and consequently perceiving it. You are no longer connected to it. It is no longer helplessness by definition if you choose to introduce consciousness to it since you have added the frequency of free will.

- Find Your Hidden Abilities

Shadow work can help you discover the inner strengths and resources you didn't know you had, or what some people refer to as the "gold in your shadow bags."

Some people might be concerned that the darkness in their shadow is too great for them to bear. However, most of the time, this golden shadow occupies most of the area. It simply never had the chance to prosper before.

Through shadow work, you can entice this aspect of yourself to come out of hiding and exercise all of your genuine abilities.

- Improved Clarity

You can more clearly see how your thoughts, feelings, and emotions influence how you act due to doing shadow work. Knowing this knowledge will enable you to present yourself with greater sincerity and clarity.

## CAN SHADOW WORK BE DANGEROUS?

It appears that many people wonder whether working in the shadows is risky. I think the origin of this query is that the word "shadow" is typically used to refer to anything ominous, misunderstood, and perhaps even associated with black magic.

I'm here to tell you that shadow labor is not necessarily evil and has nothing to do with wielding dark abilities. This phrase refers to a person's most minor appealing traits and originates from psychologist Carl Jung's understanding of the human psyche.

The only risk associated with shadow work is a result of not doing it. The generational trauma and dysfunctional tendencies cycle repeat when people are unaware of their shadow.

Some have been burdened their entire lives with unfavorable emotions and thoughts. I highly recommend that anyone new to spiritual development and self-improvement at least do shadow work, whether with a trained professional.

# CHAPTER 06
# SHADOW WORK: MEET YOUR SHADOW ARCHETYPES: 13 DARK ARCHETYPES

Let's be honest. Every story has a protagonist and an antagonist. You are both in your story; your life's song is composed of bright and gloomy sides. Many of us focus on only one side of the song when listening to it. You see, most people emphasize their positive retraits and repress their negative ones. But this shadowy aspect will always exist, frequently referred to as the dark side. In addition, it can appear small or large depending on your outlook on life. Accepting your shadow archetype: Are you ready for it?

## THE SHADOW ARCHETYPE'S ORIGIN
One of the rare individuals who attempted to unite the concepts of psychology and spirituality was prominent psychologist Carl Jung. He aspired to learn ways to transcend the human situation in this way. Jung made repeated trips to India, where he immersed himself in various spiritual activities. His research would develop continuously to analyze ideas like the ego, the shadow, the archetypes, and the anima and animus.

## UNDERSTANDING THE SHADOW ARCHETYPE
The shadow archetype is one of the four major categories of Jungian archetypes that impact behavior. These are innate personalities from the collective unconscious, as popularized by Mark and Pearson. The persona, the self or ego, and the animus are some of the other categories of Jungian archetypes.

In particular, the life and sex drive continuously opposing the ego-personality make up the shadow archetype. To become aware of your shadow, you must make a conscious moral effort. It involves accepting the negative aspects of your personality as genuine and present. Then and only then can we start comprehending who we are and have a personal awakening and authenticity.

## CARL JUNG AND SHADOW SYMBOLISM
Scholars continued to find the shadow to be a fascinating subject. Carl Jung describes it as a moral quandary that tests ego-personality. Additionally, he portrays this intricate understanding of the shadow archetype graphically and fluidly by using the symbolism of the shadow. Such visual imagery establishes anchors using ideas already known to the human intellect.

Jung, therefore, characterizes the shadow archetype as being mysterious, hard to pin down, and change in size according to your current life circumstances. Few of us are eager to face the darkness and distance it creates from the body. However, as light appears, the shadow disappears.

## THE FEAR OF EMBRACING OUR SHADOW ARCHETYPE
Most of us recognize that the shadow archetype is necessary for our existence. However, in a painful effort to preserve our sense of self, we choose to stay oblivious to it, hide it, or disguise it. It is an appropriate image for the story we choose to reveal.

Furthermore, social conditioning contributes to the misconception that we can maintain the stability of the foundation of our manufactured identities. We feel protected by disregarding the uncertain aspects of our existence and willing that they would go away.

However, how can we feel secure when the very thing we are trying to avoid has the power to enter our minds and emerge in our behavior without our consent? Must embrace the shadow archetype.

## IMPLICATIONS OF IGNORING OUR SHADOW SELF
We are as liberated as the mind will allow; take note. Additionally, illusions and neurosis may take control when the mind puts walls between a person's reality and the rest of the world. Have you ever seen someone who is obliged to remain ignorant? If so, you'll observe that individual is trying to maintain a particular status quo by denying their shadow archetype.

But ultimately, the suppressed shadow expands due to the enforced ignorance. As they project themselves into more areas of their lives, the negative features of their personalities become more apparent. Furthermore, since we can only control what we comprehend, the effect of the shadow can become out of control because the individual isn't even conscious of its presence.

## THE WAY FORWARD

### 1. Shadow Work

Shadow work is the most effective method for interacting with our shadow archetype. Discovering our dark sides through intentional actions is a lifelong practice known as "shadow work." Through it, we deal with our shadow selves, including our sexual impulses, animalistic cravings, instincts, traumatic experiences, and even some of the positive character traits we keep to ourselves out of fear of humiliation.

Journaling our feelings and dreams to identify the triggers of our shadow archetype is a familiar shadow work strategy. Our feelings of guilt and anxiety are also replaced with self-acceptance.

### 2. Seeking Professional Help

Although confronting your dark side can be frightening, the result is satisfying. However, the shadow has a problematic character. Because of this, shadow work may be followed by a series of extended hours of assimilation or psychotherapy and contemplation, frequently under the supervision of a licensed practitioner.

Here, the therapist assists clients in reassessing and recalibrating their actions and attitudes. In the end, customers maintain discipline in challenging themselves with life-related concerns. How often do you consider the nature of your world, for instance?

### 3. Dealing with Social Conditioning against Shadow Archetypes

While shadow work still occurs individually, society has a significant impact on how successful the practice is. The globe ought to be a forum for discussion and ongoing exploration. The shadow archetype transforms from a moral issue to a welcomed aspect of our existence. If you find such concepts regrettable, it may be a sign that you have some unresolved issues in your life.

## 13 SHADOW ARCHETYPES

Following are my thirteen categories, which I developed after examining both my findings and those of others:

- The Egotistical Shadow

This person is defined by arrogance, egocentrism, egotism, insensitivity, self-indulgence, narcissism, and extreme pride.

- The Neurotic Shadow

Paranoia, obsessiveness, suspicion, and picky/demanding/compulsive conduct characterize them.

- The Skeptical Shadow

Characterized by the following traits: secrecy, impulsivity, frivolity, irresponsibility, dishonesty, and unreliability.

- The Unstable Emotional Shadow

Characterized by the following traits: changeable, moody, dramatic, weepy, too emotional, and reckless.

- The Controlling Shadow

Defined by the following traits: suspicion, resentment, possessiveness, bossiness, and obsession.

- The Cynical Shadow

Defined as unfavorable, excessively critical, condescending, resentful, and fussy.

- The Furious Shadow

Defined as being vicious, vindictive, nasty, quick-tempered, and quarrelsome.

- The Intolerant Shadow

Uptight, rigid, racist, sexist, ableist, homophobic, transphobic, obstinate, unyielding, inflexible, and narrow-minded characteristics characterize them.

- The Glib Shadow

Defined by flimsiness, cunning, inconsistency, trickery, and craftiness.

- The Cold Shadow

Defined by the following traits: emotional detachment, distance, indifference, lack of care, and un excitement.

- The Perverted Shadow

Defined as being masochistic, wicked, cruel, vulgar, and libidinous.

- The Cowardly Shadow

Defined as being docile, apprehensive, timid, weak-willed, and unreliable.

- The Immature Shadow

Defined by the following traits: infantile, shallow, irrational, ignorant, and vapid.

Remember that the list of Shadow Archetypes above is by no means complete. There are undoubtedly a lot more out there that I have overlooked. However, you are welcome to use this analysis to guide your shadow exploration.

Additionally, you are free to contribute to this list or develop your own Shadow Archetypes, which I strongly advise. You might, for instance, have a judgmental and dogmatic Shadow you refer to as "The Nun" or a sexually perverse Shadow you refer to as "The Deviant." Try with different names and labels to determine which best describes your Shadows.

## CONCLUSION

One must be willing to embrace their shadow archetype if they wish to have complete control over their lives. It centers on accepting all facets of our lives, including our fears and desires. Here, we confront, examine, and internalize the darkness and our worries. Otherwise, rejecting the presence of your dark side will increase your ability to detect it in others.

The same is true of our society, which consists of individuals whose actions continuously conflict with your intentions. We should therefore work to identify the moral requirements that could reduce our suffering. And should regard everything beyond that with mistrust.

# CHAPTER 07
# WHAT IS GOLDEN SHADOW?

## WHAT IS THE SHADOW?

We must first comprehend the Shadow itself to understand the Golden Shadow. The portion of us that we adamantly deny is what Jungian theory refers to as "the Shadow." Our personalities' unconscious traits are what unintentionally occasionally emerge from hiding. These elements are viewed as undesirable personality qualities that, with time, are consigned to our unconscious. As humans typically do not wish to identify with their most immoral, greedy, and self-destructive tendencies, this is a form of self-preservation mechanism.

According to Jung, unless the shadow was brought into consciousness, it would still manifest in our lives as "fate." These negative characteristics, which appear to control our actions and later lives, would determine this fate. When they quarrel with others, some people will exhibit their shadow. Our worst shadow characteristics may be things we cannot stand about other people.

## THE GOLDEN SHADOW

It turns out that not all of the shadow consists of negative characteristics. In actuality, there are also a few essential gold nuggets there. These are your hidden talents, your beauty, your creative genius, and you're cunning—in other words, your gold. We also keep this hidden from other people. If we make these gifts known, we can appear too provocative or too bright. Once more, we might detect elements of our Golden Shadow in other people. When someone displays your Golden Shadow, you may adore them for their confidence or attractiveness.

"The shadow is ninety percent pure gold," claimed Jung once. This suggests that if we take the time to look, our Shadow side has many lovely things to give us. For instance, because we were taught to reject it as children, a large portion of our creative potential is hidden within our darkness. There are some bright spots in our Shadow.

The Shadow contains some of our most potent abilities, including those related to creativity, sexuality, rivalry, ingenuity, and even intuition. Additionally, the "Golden Shadow" offers us the chance for enormous psychological and spiritual development. We discover through Shadow Work that every emotion and pain within us has a gift to offer.

Even the most annoying, embarrassing, or "ugly" aspects of ourselves offer a way to return to Oneness. It is a harrowing trip but ultimately leads to spiritual enlightenment or illumination. Such is the power of the Shadow.

### Your Most Radiant Self

You might assume that your shadow consists of the less good sides of yourself that you have rejected. You may not realize that you disavow your brightest light as well. Why do so few of us live lives that are empowered?

We have a "Golden Shadow" that holds the solution. Consider that you are needed in your most bright and creative form by Creation. A Larger Life desires to express something special and potent through you that will contribute to the overall healing of your family, friends, community, and the planet.

Your hidden creative potential is what Carl Jung, a psychiatrist, called the "Golden Shadow." In your genuine adoration of others, you can find your bright shadow. The shining attributes you appreciate in others stand for the untapped portions of your potential.

Your brilliance is veiled behind the Golden Shadow. The Golden Shadow conceals your hidden talents. Your abilities are waiting for you to get over your emotional scars. Your special uniqueness is hidden beyond the gate of your emotional suffering.

### Strong or Weak Choices?

In a nutshell, we attempt to dampen down or destroy another's aliveness in the same way that we dampened down or destroyed our own because we perceive it to be a threat. Do unto others as you would have them do unto you.

Stephen Wolinsky

Throughout human history, specific individuals have triumphed against horrifically painful and neglected upbringings to become significant innovators, contributors, and healers. Others, who may have endured less severe types of neglect as children, go on to make decisions that negatively impact everyone they care about.

A unique set of disowned strengths required to overcome your life obstacles make up your Golden Shadow. You will learn the specifics of when you previously turned off your light as your self-awareness grows. And as you realize how you've reduced your light, you'll realize how you've unintentionally chosen to experience difficulties, despair, anxiety, sicknesses, addictions, and failures.

You can, however, decide in each instant whether to travel the path of strength or weakness, love or fear, inspiration or melancholy. Additionally, you can increase your power by making wise decisions at any stage of life, regardless of what has happened to you. Each decision to cultivate self-assurance, attractiveness, love, creativity, or thankfulness creates a powerful momentum towards the next positive choice.

## Your Exceptional Gifts

"There is anything you can give headdress the issue if you have one. T? ere were soul-level gifts we could have provided to stop trauma every time it occurred. Trauma was a poor decision that took us down the ego's road.

The gift that could have been provided was so great that most people feared it. The gift was sizable enough to alter family dynamics or assist a relative, but it felt too generous. They couldn't have hidden because it was so magnificent and would have made them stand out too much. They believed people would look to them to lead or do other notable feats."Chuck Spezzano

It's crucial to understand that you might or might not receive praise or admiration from others for your outstanding qualities. It could seem more straightforward to reflect the darkness around you than to show the light within you if you rely on the exterior mirror of everyday ego consensus.

Reclaiming your light may make you anxious and afraid of not being accepted by the mainstream dimness group. Before discovering a means to acknowledge, claim, and communicate your magnitude for your benefit, you must. You will need to revisit the points in your life where you made decisions to shrink yourself and make new decisions in or over your light.

## WHY WAS THE GOLD HIDDEN?

Now I know why we keep our dark side a secret from ourselves and others. We keep our immorality, greedy thoughts, and nasty little secrets from consciousness. But why would we conceal our gold? The cause is succinctly stated in Marianne Williamson's poem, Our Deepest Fear:

*Our deepest fear is not that we are inadequate,*

*Our deepest fear is that we are powerful beyond measure.*

*It's not our darkness; it's our light.*

*That scares us the most.*

*We ponder this*

*Who am I to be intelligent, attractive, talented, and fabulous?*

*Who are you not to be? You are God's child.*

So, the Golden Shadow is the most feared, but that is where your strength lives. Since the holy lurks within this Golden Shadow! What if everything you wished for yourself already came true? You wouldn't have anything to wish

for or despise about yourself because you'd be creative, affluent, attractive, intelligent, influential, talented, and desired.

Wow! No drama or whining here! What a terrible thought! We undermine our grandeur because we are inward masochists who want to continue living in a world of deprivation and discontentment. Recognizing our Shadow, bringing the darkness to our conscious mind, and attempting to sort out some of that muck are our best bets. At the same time, acknowledge our brilliance and picture ourselves having all the beautiful qualities we aspire to in life. We probably already have those qualities within us.

*All of us are here to shine.*

*Like a youngster.*

*We were born to bring into being.*

*The divine splendor that resides inside us.*

Williamson, Marianne

## IS EMBRACING YOUR GOLDEN SHADOW THE SECRET TO LEADING A MORE CONTENTED AND MEANINGFUL LIFE?

Do you ever feel that an additional "you" exists inside? A YOU who is at ease in any situation and self-assured, competent, gifted, and aligned? You are real; it isn't just a figment of your imagination! They are contained inside something referred to as the "golden shadow" and are present just below the surface of your consciousness. Continue reading, and I'll explain in detail how to locate the source of the golden shadow.

## BUT ISN'T THE SHADOW SCARY AND DARK?

Most people don't picture the golden shadow when they think of shadow. What does shadow mean to YOU? Is it anything banned, humiliating, hazardous, or dark? Something that you need to conceal since it's so *negative*. That's only partially true. We have mainly been taught to hide our shadows during this journey called human life.

However, if you remove the outermost layers, you'll find something golden—the golden shadow. And this is the part of you that has all kinds of outstanding, unusual, strong, and powerful qualities—qualities that still have room to grow.

You'll discover what's there when you look into shadow work, the "darker" side of your psyche, and even the long-lost piece of your soul. You'll also comprehend HOW your own shadow came into being. And when it comes to self-knowledge, the WHY can be incredibly helpful (which is what this work is ALL about). Don't skip beyond this section, then.

## QUICK SHADOW RECAP:

The shadow usually manifests when a particular trait you express is rejected by your culture, society, and even (especially) your own family. Therefore, we conceal and deny those qualities to keep ourselves secure and supported by our caretakers as children. This is entirely typical. It is known as conditioning.

## WHY DOES THE GOLDEN SHADOW APPEAR?

There's a good chance that some of the things in you that were criticized—those parts of yourself that you learned to repress and disown—were very rare. Exceptional characteristics that would have grown into most extraordinary test abilities and talents if you hadn't been prompted to reject them

Isn't that a most extraordinary

And what's even more unfortunate is that often, a person's creative potential isn't acknowledged or accepted, and as a result, that ends up in the darkness.

The golden shadow was first identified as the location of our creative potential by the Swiss psychologist Carl Jung.

So why does creativity end up in the golden shadow?
Because it's frequently untamed, unpredictable, expressive, loud, and free, and precisely these are the attributes that the general public does not tend to value. Consider that to be untrue. Where do governments always start cutting back on funding?

Do you think Instagram is brimming with "creatives"? How creative can you be with only a three-inch digital square as your canvas? Most creative endeavors don't involve unrestrained human expansion. It distorts creative expression.

It seems evident to me that creativity has lost sight of its actual essence as a result of spending too much time hiding in the background. Because, in actuality, true creativity is a danger to the status quo.

## What additional extraordinary properties does the golden shadow possess?
Other unique attributes and characteristics also contribute to the golden shadow. The list goes on and on. But the majority share a trait in common: They were formerly viewed as a threat to others in some way. Others may want to dim your light if it is shining too brightly so as not to step on your toes as you climb,

We are often afraid of our potential. The well-known Marianne Williamson quotation: "Our deepest fear is not that we are inadequate, but rather that we hold incomprehensible power." Our light, not our darkness, is what terrifies us the most. Debates occur regarding the golden shadow, so

# THREE QUICK METHODS TO EMBRACE, ACCEPT AND RELEASE YOUR GOLDEN SHADOW
Seeking your golden shadow starts with a practice of self-awareness, just like ALL shadow work.

Here are three methods.

## Method 1: identify the situations that cause you to criticize or pass judgment on others.
Do folks who exude happiness, enthusiasm, and self-assurance set you off? Or perhaps you find it challenging to be around driven people who have lofty ambitions or constantly bring up money?

Try to catch yourself criticizing or finding fault the next time this happens (even if you don't say it out loud, you are still making it about what they are doing incorrectly). Make careful note of their characteristics that most easily set you off. You can use this path to discover your golden shadow.

## Method 2: Determine the circumstances that cause you to criticize and judge yourself.
As previously, start noticing the people or circumstances that make you doubt or criticize yourself.

Exist any individuals who make you doubt your abilities?

- Who makes you feel inferior?
- Who causes you to question your babies?

Once more, pay close attention to the characteristics that set you off the most. This is an additional route you might take to discover your golden shadow.

## Method 3 – Explore Your Positive Projections.
Your relationship with a mentor, advisor, spiritual teacher, or guru can be a mirror for your golden shadow since it frequently takes the form of a teacher/student relationship.

Your optimistic expectations may be clear, but if not, consider.

- Who do you look up to?
- Who do you have envy for?
- Who do you look up to?

Once you've chosen someone, list the traits that particularly jump out to you about them.

- What about this person appeals to you?
- What do you particularly admire, want, or idolize?
- What is it about them that makes you feel something?

Try to focus on particular details and record them.

When you do this, the stronger the emotion you experience in your body, the more likely it is that those characteristics are stored inside your golden shadow.

Yes, it is correct. You already possess those qualities you desperately desire, so look no further! Only now that you're accustomed to denying yours are things different. However, that's about to alter!

## RECLAIMING AND INTEGRATING YOUR GOLDEN SHADOW

Shadow integration happens gradually. You must be careful since shadow pieces that have been in the unconscious environment for a long time become deformed. And you need to make sure that you align them before integrating. This typically takes place over time.

Before calling that precious fragment back up the scale from being disowned to being accepted, embraced, appreciated, and finally cherished and nurtured, it takes a lot of honesty and self-awareness. It ceases to be a shadow when you can FULLY SEE the portion of your shadow. It starts to become aware.

This is what emotional healing entails, and it's how we develop as people and discover our full potential.

## CONCLUSION

Your hidden creative potential is what Carl Jung, a psychiatrist, called the "Golden Shadow." In your genuine adoration of others, you can find your bright shadow. The shining attributes you appreciate in others stand for the untapped portions of your potential. Your brilliance is veiled behind the Golden Shadow. Some of our most potent traits, such as those connected to creativity, sexuality, rivalry, cleverness, and even intuition, are found in the Shadow. The "Golden Shadow" also gives tremendous spiritual and psychological growth opportunities. Through shadow work, we learn that each emotion and struggle we experience has something positive to contribute.

# CHAPTER 08
# THE SHADOW WORK JOURNEY: HOW TO HEAL YOUR INNER CHILD:
# THE SPACE BETWEEN HURT & HEALED

This chapter teaches how your inner child (and subconscious mind) might use shadow work to recover from emotional trauma or pain. Learn how to use empowering activities to move past the past so you can live a more fulfilling life and learn about the space between hurt and healing.

## WHAT IS A SHADOW INJURY?
A shadow injury occurs when we go through an experience that causes pain and suffering to either ourselves or others. This could refer to anything, from a seemingly unimportant event (such as a cruel remark made by a student at school) to more severe trauma (like abuse).

Typically, our shadow injuries develop when we are younger and less aware of what is happening. Any adverse event we go through in life, no matter how significant, can affect our mental health and emotional wellbeing. We must perform shadow labor to live our best (and happiest) lives.

## WHERE DOES SHADOW WORK COME INTO PLAY?
Shadow work can be a helpful approach to processing your ideas, feelings, and emotions while you're going through a challenging time, particularly when it comes to incidents from the past that negatively impacted you. It is analogous to crying or sharing what happened with someone in your mind (like a therapist). However, you can perform shadow work independently rather than paying someone.

## HOW DOES SHADOW WORK HELP IN THE HEALING OF THE MIND?
Allowing for catharsis or the release of repressed emotions is one of the real benefits of shadow work. This enables people to deal with their emotional suffering and trauma, which may enhance other aspects of their lives, such as their relationships and professions.

## WHAT IS THE SENSATION OF THE SHADOW WORK PROCEDURE?
In my experience, shadow work increases your ability to manifest your life goals and makes you feel lighter, more accessible, and more joyous. But I'll be honest; it's not so simple to go through the process.

1. Allow Old Memories To Surface

Allow your thoughts to return to earlier times when unpleasant memories were buried deep inside your subconscious while meditating. Painful emotions surface as you mentally replay those trying times or negative stories. Be ready for a few cathartic sobbing sessions; it's normal and a terrific method to let your body release buried feelings.

Do self-care exercises that make you feel fantastic after that. It serves as a sort of emotional reward for all the effort. When you confront your shadows head-on (and essentially "throw a light" on them), they lose their influence over you. You no longer feel limited or like a victim; you feel more empowered than ever.

2. Reframe Mental Stories

You can then reinterpret any internal narratives about that experience or story at that stage in the shadow work process. Start to perceive events or situations from a higher or more enlightened perspective.

For example, if you experienced feelings of abandonment as a child as a result of your parent's extensive work schedule, you may still be dealing with the same difficulties today. You may develop codependent adult relationships or become concerned when your significant other works additional hours. The good news is that you can change your perspective now that you're an adult and stop letting these emotions affect you.

Telling yourself that your parent worked hard so they may be taken care of is an effective method to reframe your mental story and help your inner child heal. Consider what it might have been like for your parents to be concerned about not having enough money to support your family. Or perhaps they were brought up by a workaholic who instilled in them the idea that this is how responsible parents behave.

### 3. Choose a Positive Attitude Regarding Negative Experiences

Can you view any former experience in a different light? It permits you to have a powerful mindset by doing this. It helps you move past adverse events by assisting you in choosing an optimistic viewpoint in its place. It's like the sunshine peeking out from beyond the thick clouds. As many people who have survived catastrophic events would attest, those dark times taught them important lessons that gave them courage.

Awareness of mental narratives is essential to healing since thought patterns affect our emotions, beliefs, and behaviors. Your shadow self requires assistance if any aspects of your life right now aren't working.

Never forget that your voice is the only one you ever hear. So, be mindful of your perspective.

## WHY DOES SHADOW WORK FEEL GOOD AFTERWARD?

Even if the shadow work procedure is complex, the good news is that you'll feel fantastic after it's over! You can overcome your emotional baggage from the past and your inner pain. If that makes sense, you need to concentrate on the healing rather than the pain for it to be possible.

Think of yourself like a hot air balloon tethered by enormous sandbags yet ready to rise. Even though you'd like to be able to fly in the air, something is keeping you on the ground. On the one hand, you were made to fly, but you cannot travel because of your baggage.

Now that your inner suffering has been healed (by uniting your shadow self with your consciousness), all you have to do is let go of the sandbags and float upwards toward the clouds. When shadow labor is finished, it feels liberating just like that!

## YOU CAN ENGAGE IN SHADOW WORK

Self-reflection, journaling, or even just writing down the words you say aloud in a conversation with yourself can all be considered forms of shadow work. It could also include moving outside of your comfort zone and engaging in unfamiliar activities (like dancing). I also discover that rewriting mental narratives and having a loving, comforting conversation with my "inner child" is beneficial in healing shadow injuries.

## WHY IS SHADOW WORK SO HEALING?

Shadow work may be able to help you if you have emotional baggage that is keeping you from living your best life. Because of this, doing shadow work—which entails learning to accept aspects of yourself that have felt unloved and how to reframe negative, disempowering stories in your head—can be highly therapeutic and helpful.

## THE SPACE BETWEEN HURT AND HEALED

A thin line separates hurt and healing. Sometimes going through a horrific, life-changing, or soul-crushing experience can take us to extremely dark places. Fear has the power to dominate. We might experience various emotions, like loneliness, pitting, emptiness, darkness, and melancholy. One moment we may be happy and at peace, and the next, we may be absolutely heartbroken and completely unsettled. torn apart. Tonight suffers flashbacks to painful memories from the past and moments when those memories play out like a scene from a movie about our lives. We fail to understand that if we let the darkness educate us, these moments of soul-crushing darkness lead us to the most beautiful and incredible soul growth.

The soul work, the challenging shadow work, and how we navigate this space are what takes us to the most breathtaking locations and spur significant progress. As the caterpillar in the chrysalis, think of the area between. The reborn child. A break.

Darkness, tightness, and discomfort are all present. It's a rebirth and a giving up on the unknown. Because recovering from a trauma of any kind is a rebirth. We are never the same for long. With a better appreciation and understanding of who we are and the world around us, we change and become someone new.

## TO LIVE WITH LIGHT TRULY, WE MUST EXPERIENCE DARKNESS

We foolish beings are afraid of discomfort in any form. We are seekers of happiness. We fail to understand that experiencing some darkness is necessary to comply with the whole present and discover a deeper purpose in our human life.

The light and the dark, or the ying and the yang, The tad bit of darkness? When it's there, we often cringe. We can completely give in to that darkness and let it instruct us in the lessons the experience offers. The mending takes place in this area between; all right gradually returns as we emerge from it restored with a new lightness and love.

*"To be alive, fully human, and fully aware is to be tossed out of the nest repeatedly."* - Pema Chödrön.

We can quickly become trapped in darkness and create deeply ingrained fear when we try to fill the void with fleeing behaviors and addictions (not just drugs and alcohol, but many other addictions). So many of us now battle melancholy and anxiety due to deep traumas dating back to our early years. We may enjoy brief highs and repeatedly seek them out through escape activities.

Instead of healing, we move on to more hurt, addictions, escape, more profound suffering, and anxiety. We frequently experience the same individuals coming into our lives while donning several masks. This is because we do not give our shadows enough room, and as a result, we keep receiving the same teachings.

The only way to genuinely heal is to stop running, "get there," put our energy where it's dark, scary, uncomfortable, and unfamiliar, and submit. This can be painful and disgusting, but it is the only way. Most people aren't willing to do this, but the key is to succumb to the suffering, the darkness, and the unsettling void between injury and recovery.

We don't mean the glamorous variety frequently promoted on social media when discussing shadow work. Exploring areas or behaviors that have been taboo or banned for various reasons is neither Shadow labor nor Shadow.

All the unconscious aspects of who we are that we are utterly ignorant of and passionately deny exist are included in our shadow selves. Everybody has a shadow. The "isms" that disgust us in others are those we also harbor inside ourselves but are unaware of. Every one of us is susceptible to shadows.

## A HURT SOUL BRINGS ABOUT HURT

Our shadow is that unpleasant emotion that appears when we recall when we were weak and s someone harmed us badly. Then, we inflict that same hurt on someone else while simultaneously denying that there is any part of ourselves capable of doing so. Without our conscious awareness, the shadow nonetheless continues to act according to its own free will. It's the aspects of ourselves that we've tried to ignore, but they still very much live in their lifeform.

The hurt soul causes more pain. Because guilt forced that aspect of her identity into the deepest recesses of her soul, the sexually abused youngster denies their true sexuality. A youngster witness his father verbally abusing his mother while witnessing her shrine accepts the abuse and shows no signs of resistance. The infant develops resentment toward the parts of himself that are timid and cower, much like his mother did.

To protect himself, he puts those aspects of himself away and denies having any fear. He adopts a stern demeanor and continuously drives any discomfort that dares to enter away. What private aspects of ourselves that we reject prevent us from becoming our authentic selves and reaching our highest potentialsWork Requires a Great Deal of Emotional Courage

What shadow work entails is finding and giving space to pieces of yourself that you have pushed outside of your conscious awareness. Engaging in this kind of personal work takes a lot of emotional courage. It's revealing the aspects of ourselves that we've neglected.

It's enabling these aspects to emerge, giving them recognition and room to exist, shedding new light on the situation, and fostering a more profound comprehension. It's a precarious line of employment. Acknowledging our fear, insecurity, humiliation, envy, rage, selfishness, prejudices, judgments, and hurt is not beautiful, sparkling, or enjoyable.

Working with shadows is quite humbling. At times, the pain in your knees is incredible. It involves core wound work. It's gut-wrenching and breathtakingly beautiful because it causes enormous soul growth. A transformation.

Even if the only options in life are suffering or running away, we always have options when facing challenges. We can cast even more shadows by driving the pain into our being.

Alternately, we can let all the uncomfortable things be a part of us and allow ourselves to feel everything that surfaces in the interval between injury and healing. Because our shadows and inner traumas emerge during these times, we have the opportunity to confront them, making tough times in our lives the perfect moment to complete this process.

You will view yourself and other people differently as you come to terms with all the aspects of yourself that you have suppressed.

When you stop rejecting certain aspects of yourself, you also stop transferring these traits to other people and stop rejecting other people. Relationships become more meaningful, deeper, and more accessible. New and diverse people can enter your life due to raising your spiritual level. Shadow work will always exist, so don't be afraid of it; give in.

*"No shadow exists without light, and no spiritual wholeness exists without flaw."- Jung.*

# CHAPTER 09
# WHAT ARE `SHADOW VALUES'? AND CAN WE DO ABOUT THEM?

Shadow values are the hidden ideals that support your company. They could be favorable or unfavorable. In either case, it is beneficial to make them public.

Shadow values, positive or wrong, are the values that an organization harbors underneath the surface.

Positive: These are the beautiful qualities of your workplace that your employer brand does not highlight. Positive shadow values prevent you from fully understanding your culture, developing your employer brand, and maximizing its potential.

Negative: Negative shadow values and unethical behavior are frequently linked.

Positivity in your shadow values prevents you from fully comprehending your culture.

## NEGATIVE SHADOW VALUES

So, as an example, you may recall that Sony Music announced the departure of their veteran CEO in 2021. They are listed as follows on the Sony Music website:

- Dream and interest
- Diversity
- Integrity
- Sincerity
- Sustainability.

However, media sources, including a Four Corners investigation, claim that the CEO's behavior was tolerated for years without any consequences. As a result, as an employee, I begin to question whether or not those corporate ideals are faithful when I consider those beliefs and the actions of my CEO.

If you missed the media frenzy last year, it was alleged that this CEO had dominated with intimidation and fear for many years and that many individuals were too afraid to speak up. Then, when they did discuss it, they claimed to have felt manipulated, abused, and even targeted.

If the Four Corners study was accurate, returning to the claimed values, would I feel free to "dream and be curious" if I worked there? That "diversity, integrity, and sincerity" were values held by the organization? Most likely not. Therefore, it is only reasonable to presume that significant shadow values were present during that time.

Volkswagen is another current example. According to reports, they purposefully programmed more than 500,000 diesel-powered cars to display erroneous emissions test results. Volkswagen now stands for the following:

- Excellence
- Professionalism
- Commitment to integrity.

Despite these declared values, unethical behavior is still occurring within the organization.

## POSITIVE SHADOW VALUES

While working with clients, especially when we do focus groups with employees, I have observed positive shadow ideals rarely mentioned in the media. Or when we conduct satisfaction and engagement surveys. We ask:

- Why do you work here?
- What does it entail to work for this company?

- What best describes the culture?

And that may surprise some business owners about why people choose to work with them. The good news is that surprises are gold nuggets since they represent your organization's culture and its positive shadow ideals. They may not be your proclaimed values, but they need to be.

## HOW TO UNCOVER POSITIVE SHADOW VALUES
How can we tell if our shadow values are constructive? The only real option is to communicate with your team members.

- Ask them to share instances when they were most proud to represent the company.
- Please give them a list of values and ask them to check the ones that, in their opinion, best describe the company.
- Ask questions about ethics and behavior in anonymous staff surveys.
- Examine psychological safety and consider ways to incorporate it into your organization.

Ask stories of times they were most proud to represent the company in their tales. The Google Rework website has many tools team members can use to raise issues, difficulties, and blunders. Naturally, all of this takes time.

As we work through those processes, how can we promote talks about values and behaviors in the interim? To tackle this, use the "demonstrate by doing" method. Words are far less effective than behavior. Although you should discuss the excellent ideals and address any problems, you must get the business's leadership to commit to changing behaviors.

## DEALING WITH NEGATIVE SHADOW VALUES
In larger organizations, you might launch an internal campaign, whereas, in smaller ones, the founder or CEO might address the entire staff during a team meeting.

In each case, the intent is to clarify why the behavior in question is unacceptable. We've taken this measure to clarify that we're no longer operating in that manner.

And this is how you proceed with whistleblowing, which is something we cherish. No one will believe it, though, if the leadership teams and management of the organization don't exhibit the behaviors they're promoting in those communications.

### Leadership
The way you behave is essential. And it's essential to enlist the support of your entire management team and leadership group to exhibit such behavior.

### Language
People need to be encouraged to speak up, and we need to listen when they do. But what did you do that for? A manager once asked an employee, which I overheard. When you use judgemental language like that, it puts the other person on the defensive.

Saying, "Can you tell me a little more about that?" is preferable. I was unaware that was happening. It's very distinctive. Sometimes, it comes down to being conscious of our language and finding ways to inspire others to speak up.

### Action
It's critical not to ignore inappropriate behavior. We take action if we notice something that doesn't align with our company values. The person who has been complained against is frequently entirely taken by surprise during workplace behavior investigations, such as those involving bullying. This frequently occurs as a result of the behavior being uncontrolled. People will only respond by saying, "Oh, it's only so and so; it's just how they are.

## DEALING WITH POSITIVE SHADOW VALUES
We must shout out the good aspects of our shadow ideals when they are present. If you conduct a focus group, let's assume that participants comment, "the one thing that is so distinct about working here is that we all genuinely care about each other." And if that isn't expressed in one of your values, now is a great time to include it in your job postings and start bringing it up in meetings.

# TAKE A SECOND LOOK
*It would help if you did something about whether your shadow values are favorable or unfavorable.*

I encourage you to revisit your company's core principles. And recall the moment you made your decision. When did you assemble them? What changes has your company undergone since then? Since values do alter with time.

Perhaps it's time to reexamine them if it's been a while or if there have been organizational changes. Do some anonymous surveys or hold focus groups with your staff. Start by examining how well we uphold these principles. Do people behave as we would expect them to?

This is also a chance to develop organizational ideals if you don't already have any. One of the resources on Brene Brown's website that we enjoy using. It is pretty straightforward and just a list of values. Please print it out and instruct individuals to begin marking the principles they observe being upheld by the organization with a checkmark. Following that, you hold meetings and workshops to narrow the list. A list of three to five items is ideal; aim for that.

## SHADOW VALUES: WHAT LIES BENEATH?
Respect, honesty, openness, and greatness. They are noble business values you would be happy to make official and display on the wall. Unfortunately, Enron shared the same values. Enron won praise for its 64-page Code of Ethics just 12 months before filing for bankruptcy in 2001, the largest in US history.

Fortune magazine recognized it as "America's Most Innovative Company" and won multiple prizes for its environmental and corporate social responsibility initiatives. The failures of Enron have received extensive coverage as the definitive case study of what may occur when an organization separates its official values, beliefs, and purpose - what we refer to as an Ethics Framework - from its day-to-day actions.

It's a consistent problem for all organizations. It is not simple to ensure that practices, procedures, policies, and systems align with that ethical framework. If a company's managers continually state one thing while doing completely else, it develops disillusionment and cynicism throughout the workforce. It gradually becomes clear to customers and other stakeholders as well.

### Hidden from view
The second set of ideals lurks beneath the surface of many organizations. The term "shadow values" refers to these unofficial values, which are no less potent than the official ones. Exposing shadow values might reveal the more profound aspects of an organization's actual working culture. An organization is better positioned to detect any early deviation in the alignment of its culture from its values and principles if it proactively identifies and monitors its shadow values.

Think about Volkswagen engineers' dishonest actions, which included programming 500,000 diesel-powered cars to generate false readings during emissions testing. Despite the business's stated commitment to excellence, professionalism, and honesty, it was evident from the testimony of both employees and investigators that several unofficial shadow principles were dictating the organization's culture.

### Volkswagen's official and shadow values
The alter ego is used frequently in psychology to express the shadow part of human nature. While Freud spoke of the Id, Jung referred to it as the shadow, which is the collective of all the negative traits we would rather keep hidden. The shadow gets strength by being routinely suppressed. Additionally, it manifests as a variety of symptoms and mental health problems.

Similar to this, a company's shadow ideals have strength since they are kept secret. At their worst, when they are harmful mutations of the official ideals, they pose an existential threat to the integrity of an organization's ethical culture.

Volkswagen's implicit leadership model was generally acknowledged as one that prioritized "autocracy" and achieving "success" at any costs, despite the company's stated ideals of "teamwork" and "respect for individuals." an accent on fear.

To meet sales goals, frequently used intimidation in a culture of "fear." Fear was a barrier to preventing dissenting voices from being raised to contest rulings. A culture that valued "internal rivalry" and "secrecy" silenced these voices.

In addition, shadow values might indicate slight differences in how official organizational values are perceived and used daily. Later discovered that Volkswagen's declared value of "excellence" was a particular value called "technical excellence." The organization has valued technical quality throughout its history.

Like it did in the 1970s when it was found guilty of using similar manipulative techniques to get around pollution restrictions, Volks wagon turned to it in that 2015 incident. The change in VW's aim is where these shadow ideals first emerged. Volkswagen established a goal for itself in 2007 after Martin Winterkorn was named CEO: "To become the largest automaker by 2018."

# CHAPTER 10
# 7 SHADOW WORK EXERCISES TO EMBRACE YOUR SHADOW & HEAL YOUR SOUL

Exercises in shadow work can help you confront your inner shadow, bring to light the negative aspects of your personality, and finally find peace with them.

## SHADOW WORK EXERCISES:

Our shadows are, by definition, hidden and difficult to access because they reside in our unconscious. Given that we are oblivious to these qualities of ourselves, it is understandable why we would reject them.

*"With the help of these activities, we can become more conscious of and at peace with our shadow tendencies."*

Keep in mind that we deliberately avoid certain traits since they are unpleasant. We naturally disavow and detach from them because they exist in our unconscious, where they are hidden from view. They exist below the awareness level.

Unfortunately, they consistently impose their presence. Shadow projection is ubiquitous, and we can frequently identify our shadows by observing the characteristics that irritate us in other people. It can be a skewed perception of a negative trait we have inside of us. However, there are many ways to recognize our shadow selves, including the methods listed below.

## WHAT ARE SHADOW WORK EXERCISES?

Exercises in shadow work are methods for identifying your inner shadow characteristics. According to the hypothesis, doing this will make those traits more conscious, diminish their influence on your behavior, and prevent their attempts to self-sabotage you.

*"It's your reaction when you don't use logic and reason to guide your feelings."*

With the help of these activities, we can become more conscious of and at peace with our shadow tendencies.

## 7 SHADOW WORK EXERCISES TO EMBRACE YOUR SHADOW & HELP YOU FACE:

Here are seven techniques for collaborating with your shadow:

- Journaling
- Observing emotional responses
- Engaging in inner dialogue
- Posing a threat to conscious goodness
- Meditation using shadow work
- The 3-2-1 Shadow Process
- Shadow work affirmations

Depending on what feels most comfortable, you can use one of these shadow work exercises or any combination.

### 1. Journaling

Journaling is my preferred method of self-improvement and personal development since it is adaptable and robust.

Journaling is my preferred method, whether we're discussing exercises in cultivating gratitude, positive affirmations, inner child work, or shadow work. And it appears I'm not the only one because many others are using my list of questions for the shadow jobs for this purpose.

### 2. Observing emotional responses

What does an emotional response mean?

It's your reaction when you don't use logic and reason to guide your feelings. It's an instinct. It's also significant because, if you pay attention, it will give you critical information. You may learn much about your shadow if you have the guts to look closely at your emotional responses.

This exercise starts by learning to recognize when powerful emotions and strong sentiments arise. To start identifying triggers, you're looking for trends.

> *"You must be impartial and detached for this portion of the activity. So that you know, it's challenging."*

Try asking the following queries yourself:

- What particular remarks, deeds, circumstances, or someone set off your response?
- What was your response? Think about the feelings that underlie the physical manifestation and the physical manifestation itself. How were you feeling?
- Why? What inspired those emotions?

You could proceed to the following phase if you already are aware of your triggers or once you can claim with certainty that you have identified them if you weren't before. You must be impartial and detached for this portion of the activity. So that you know, it's challenging. It is difficult to be logical when something or someone has made you uncomfortable and caused you to feel worried or afraid. But you must be present for it.

> *"Although this is quite typical, it is not beneficial. It doesn't benefit the individuals you are responding to, and it doesn't benefit you either."*

If required, put your ideas and emotions in writing. Then, return once you've calmed down. (This is why keeping a journal is great!)

Reconsider your triggers and your emotional responses to them when you are prepared. Think about where they came from. The challenging phase is now.

Validate your feelings by acknowledging that they are reasonable in the situation in which they arise, and then calmly, logically, and reasonably consider whether they remain reasonable in the context that sparked them.

There's a reasonable probability that if you can remain objective, you'll realize that the solid and overwhelming emotions you're going through are unreasonable. Although this is quite typical, it is not beneficial. It doesn't benefit the individuals to whom y you are responding, nor does it benefit you. The exercise reveals areas of appropriate aviators blatantly; inner child healing techniques may be helpful.

3. Engaging in inner dialogue

You can also communicate with your shadow self if you notice any shadow sides of yourself that don't necessarily stem from childhood trauma.

*"But it's your shadow, so it's a part of you."*

Please be patient with me if this sounds a little strange. Do you ever say or do anything and then immediately regret it? In these circumstances, there is frequently a component of shame present, presumably because the behavior has a negative edge to I might have been cruel or even malicious.

You never have to tell anyone about this, but for the p exercise, be honest with yourself. This is something that even the best among us experience. Although I know it is painful, no one has ever claimed that shadow work exercises are simple (because they are not).

If this resonates with you, please don't blame me for doing it; I'm sure we have all done it—where did that come from? It's not the version of you that you portray to the world most of the time or your purest day.

But it's your shadow, so it's a part of you.

These "inner voices," which are components of our shadow selves, have power and influence over our lives if we choose to ignore them. They do this by influencing the way we act.

We must pay attention to our shadow to its influence, stop it from controlling our behavior, and keep it from destroying our relationships.

Instead of silencing them, we can achieve this by conversing with them in our minds. Once more, journaling and this practice are a fantastic fit.

### 4. Posing a Threat to Conscious Goodness

The majority of people think they are inherently "good." I am erasure I do, and you are also.

According to the principle of shadow work, for every positive quality we consciously assign to ourselves, there is an opposite, opposing quality that we also have but suppress.

For example, you can be very proud of your organizational skills. There's nothing wrong with it, but there's also nothing wrong with occasionally acting a little scatty. Can you honestly say that you occasionally fall short of the standard of perfection you set for yourself if this example does indeed apply to you?

You successfully ignore the messy version of yourself when you define yourself as organized and in your shadow. By denying portions of who you are, you give shadowy elements strength. When they n, they undermine your more admirable qualities and will keep trying to destabilize and influence your behavior.

Unless you confront and accept them.

This practice aims to recognize, accept, and make peace with your shadow selves. Imperfect is acceptable.

### 5. Meditation Using Shadow Work

Sometimes, meditation can help us understand our emotions and where they come from, and other times, it can help us embrace who we are. You can meditate in various ways, either by trying to clear your mind or following a written plan, idea, or visualization.

It's possible that practicing meditation causes healing to occur spontaneously or in layers or phases. Whatever meditation technique you use, the only thing that matters is that you experience some growth, no matter how slight.

*Practicing meditation regularly is healing; if you're lucky, you might even feel this after just one session.*

### 6. The 3-2-1 Shadow Process

The philosopher Ken Wilber created and refined this method in Integral Life Practice, which can be used as a journaling or meditation technique.

The idea behind this practice is to approach it head-on, communicate with it, and then embody it. The goal is to acquire perspective and be reasoned and sensible in your thoughts and feelings by objectively looking at a bad scenario with another individual.

The idea is that by going through these phases, you'll acquire an understanding of yourself and the person you're having trouble with, and you'll hopefully be better able to go forward from a place of compassion and understanding.

## How to Do 3-2-1 Shadow Work?

Try Ken Wilber's 3-2-1 Shadow Process from Integral Life Practice for a step-by-step approach to working with your shadow. Wilber is an integral philosopher.

The basic steps are as follows:

*Step 1:*
- First, decide what or who "it" will be for the sake of this exercise. Remember that working with a friend, coworker, spouse, or family member with whom you have a terrible relationship is ideal for this particular strategy.
- Simply being around this person may make you uncomfortable or frighten them. Alternately, you can be smitten with or envious of them. The goal is to select someone with whom you have a solid emotional resonance and intense bond, regardless of your motivations, positive or negative.

*Step 2: Face It*

Visualize the individual you selected in your head. Concentrate on the emotions that are brought up in you after you imagine how they may seem.

Next, you can either continue journaling like you always have or do it verbally.

Describe the characteristics and features that annoy, interest, or attract you the most using the third person pronouns (s/he, they). You don't need to censor yourself because this is no one will criticize you, so feel what you're saying or writing, and don't overthink it.

*Step 3: Talk To It*

Now, talk to the person as though they were right in before. Utilizing the second person this time (you). Once more, use whichever communication method you make sortable.

Tell this individual what you need to say and how you feel about them. Ask inquiries like:

- Do you realize how this makes me feel?
- Why do you treat me in that manner?
- What are you expecting from me?
- What is it that you want me to comprehend?

Now, think of their responses to these queries and either speak them aloud or write them down in your journal. If you feel you have more to say in response, start a "discussion."

*Step 4: Be It*

"*It's not surprising if you feel uneasy because the notion goes that these are the precise qualities you've been suppressing or ignoring in yourself.*"

This step may feel awkward. Become the individual with whom you have been speaking. Take on the persona. Adopt as your own the characteristics you previously discovered and articulated; this time, utilize the first person (I, me), and make "I am" statements:

- I am hurt.
- I am angry.
- I am jealous.
- I am terrified.
- I am arrogant

It's not surprising if you feel uneasy because the notion goes that these are the precise specificities you've been suppressing or ignoring in yourself.

*Step 5: Growing From the 321 Shadow Work*

"*The benefit of using approach is that you should be able to harmonize and find serenity by bringing your unconscious shadow and aware self together.*"

Accepting that you already have these qualities inside of you and actively starting to see them is the last step in this process.

Refuse to feel guilty or ashamed; that is not what this exercise is about. Please acknowledge that you have these qualities and accept them as a part of who you are. Try to show the same compassion to the individual you were concentrating on.

Remember that both your and everyone else's decisions are subject to chance. The benefit of using this approach is that you should be able to achieve harmony and peace by fusing your unconscious shadow with your conscious self.

(If it also helps the person you were working with becoming more human and forgiving, it's not terrible!).

7. Shadow work affirmations

You might have noted that we utilized a few negative affirmations during the previous exercise. Well, as part of your shadow work, you might also decide to utilize more encouraging ones. Because of the nature of shadow work, not all affirmations will be 'positive' and upbeat; some are more firmly rooted.

But when combined, they can be a powerful method for illuminating the shadow self and helping you find the inner serenity you're looking for.

## CONCLUSION

You can lessen projection when you interact with people by engaging in shadow work exercises. Other people's personality traits and eccentricities are less likely to set you off. This can therefore make you more sympathetic to other people. Finding your shadow, or the hidden and repressed parts of oneself is the goal of shadow work. You work with the more sinister, secret aspects of oneself through the discipline of introspection. Shadow work aims to eliminate the baggage you brought into the relationship so you can present your best self and keep improving. It makes the hidden or disowned aspects of our personalities that we try to consciously avoid, ignore, or conceal.

# CHAPTER 11
# JUNGIAN SHADOW WORK: BENEFITS OF JUNGIAN SHADOW WORK

## THE JUNGIAN SHADOW: A FORMAL INTRODUCTION
*"The shadow is a moral issue that tests the entire ego-personality since nobody can become aware of the shadow without making a significant moral effort. It requires accepting the harmful components of one's personality as real and present to become mindful of them. The prerequisite for any self-knowledge is this action".*

—Carl Jung, Aion (1951)

The term "shadow" was initially used by Swiss psychiatrist Carl Jung to refer to those facets of our personalities that we actively choose to suppress and reject. We all have aspects of ourselves that we don't like for various reasons or believe society won't like, so we push those aspects down into our unconscious psyches.

Jung referred to this group of suppressed facets of our personality as our shadow self. You could be unsure if this applies to you if you're one of those people who generally love who you are. You can be saying to yourself, "I accept myself. I adore every aspect of myself.

The issue is that you might not even be aware of the aspects of your personality that you find objectionable. According to Jung's hypothesis, we psychologically separate ourselves from the actions, feelings, and ideas that we deem hazardous. Our mind makes it appear like something doesn't exist rather than dealing with it.

A few examples of shadow aspects are aggressive impulses, taboo mental pictures, shameful experiences, immoral drives, anxieties, irrational wishes, and inappropriate sexual desires. These are things people possess but do not acknowledge to themselves.

## FIVE BENEFITS OF JUNGIAN SHADOW WORK
The shadow doesn't have a lot of fans. Who likes to own their shortcomings, weaknesses, selfishness, nasty tendencies, hatred, etc.? It is more pleasurable and affirming to concentrate on our strengths. However, exploring our shadow side offers us many chances for improvement.

Here are five advantages of doing Jungian shadow work:

### 1. Improved Relationships
You have a clearer understanding of yourself when you embrace your darker side and come to terms with it. You develop into a more solid, complete person.

It is simpler to tolerate the shadow in people when you can accept your darker sides. As a result, you won't be as easily triggered by other people's actions. You'll also find it simpler to interact with other people. Your interactions with your spouse, family, friends and business partners may all be love.

### 2. Clearer Perception
You'll have a more transparent lens through which to perceive the world if you accept everyone as they are, including yourself. You're becoming closer to your actual self as you integrate your shadow self, which helps you make a more accurate judgment of who you are. Consider yourself as being exaggeratedly large or little (deflated). You can more effectively gauge your environment when you are self-aware. You'll have a more transparent, kinder, and nuanced perspective on people and events.

### 3. Enhanced Energy and Physical Health
It is exhausting to drag this unseen bag of things behind us. Repressing and suppressing all the aspects of ourselves that we don't want to confront as adults are arduous efforts. The unstudied life can be plagued with fatigue and sluggishness. Physical discomfort and disease can also result from cognitive suppression. By assisting them in

acknowledging the repressed wrath in their unconscious, Dr. John Sarno has helped thousands of patients suffering from chronic back pain find relief.

With Jungian shadow work, you can unknowingly release a vast reserve of energy used to defend yourself. Your physical, mental, and emotional well-being can all be enhanced by this. You can become more balanced and develop inner strength through shadow work, which will prepare you for life's obstacles.

### 4. Integration and maturity in psychology

A sense of wholeness and harmony is elusive as long as we suppress certain aspects of ourselves and deny our shadow selves. With a divided mind, how can we have a sense of wholeness and balance? You get one step closer to obtaining a sense of wholeness by integrating the shadow. It's an essential step in becoming a responsible adult.

### 5. Greater Creativity

Jungian shadow work enhances your creative potential, one of its significant advantages. According to psychologists like Abraham Maslow and Carl Rogers, creativity occurs spontaneously in those who are psychologically well (integrated).

## FIVE TIPS FOR PERFORMING JUNGIAN SHADOW WORK

The following five factors will make approaching your shadow simpler:

### 1. Center Yourself

Perhaps the most crucial action before beginning a shadow job is this. Yet, working with the shadow is seldom ever acknowledged in the literature. You won't get good results if you try to understand your shadow self while you're not grounded in yourself.

The shadow is a collection of numerous elements concealed within your psyche. You can only learn about these areas by starting from your Center. One of these components will "mix" with you and take control of the process. You'll be judgmental, harsh, or perplexed. This will hamper your capacity to integrate your shadow. Be a peaceful, clear, and neutral area before you start working with your shadow. You want to be in your Center, in other words.

### 2. Cultivate Self-Compassion

It is beneficial to develop a total sense of friendship with oneself before getting to know your shadow. Its name in Buddhism is Maitri. Examining our darker aspects requires friendship and self-compassion, which can be challenging. It is challenging to face your shadow if you are harsh on yourself when you err. If you frequently experience guilt or shame, you must learn to transform these feelings into friendliness, self-acceptance, and self-compassion.

Begin by acknowledging your humanity. Remember that we are all shadows in each other's soup, as Jung used to say. Connecting with my heart is beneficial, so focus on your heart. Inhale deeply and become aware of your heart. Exhale and say "Thank you" to your heart. Thich Nhat Hanh recommends this straightforward Buddhist practice.

### 3. Cultivate Self-Awareness

A self-reflective mindset—the capacity to consider and pay attention to our actions, ideas, and emotions—is necessary to see the shadow. The capacity to maintain present-moment awareness without engaging the inner critic or other forms of judgment is aided by mindfulness meditation.

Shadow work is preceded by self-awareness and self-reflection because they enable us to monitor and assess our moods and emotional responses objectively.

### 4. Be Courageously Honest

Shadow labor requires integrity and self-honesty. It's simple to give lip service to these virtues, but real self-honesty requires being open to recognizing our negative traits in our actions and personalities. The ego spends a lot of energy suppressing your disowned portions since it is frequently uncomfortable to do so. Acknowledging and embracing your despotic bad aspects and insecure selfishness can be difficult. It takes bravery to examine your attitudes, behaviors, troubling ideas, and negative feelings.

These direct encounters with your shadow help heal the rifts in your mind, so the benefits outweigh the suffering. This brave deed releases more of your creative potential and creates new avenues for your psychological growth.

## 5. Keep Track of Your Findings

The desire of some of our disowned portions to remain hidden from view fascinates me. Our disowned portions can elude us like a dream might vanish from memory right after waking up. A cure is to keep a writing notebook where you can chronicle your self-discoveries. It is easier to encode the discovery into your awareness when you write down your insights and review them afterward.

## Conclusion

Your shadow is not a shortcoming or an error; instead, it is an inherent aspect of who you are. The main goal of shadow work is to increase self-awareness, which leads to self-acceptance and compassion. You can perceive the various aspects of yourself through shadow work, which is frequently both therapy and more spiritual. The sex and survival drives make up the shadow, an archetypal. The suppressed thoughts, flaws, desires, impulses, and deficiencies that make up the shadow are a part of the unconscious mind.

# **CONCLUSION**

A shadow work journal is a written journal that can help you get ready to reflect on your flaws, energy blocks, and other potential "shadows" that might not be readily apparent to bring them to a high-level high rebelliousness so you can best work through them. You will find all you need in this Shadow Work Journal to confront your shadows. Keep this journal close at hand as a tool for exploring and healing your subconscious. You can become aware of unconsciously self-destructive tendencies by engaging in shadow work. One of the most widely used shadow work strategies is journaling. You can access your subconscious by recording your thoughts and feelings and employing prompts. These inquiries are meant to push you intellectually and shed light on your mind's most hidden corners. This shadow work diary offers simple-to-use sheets that provide tasks, exercises, prompts for journaling, and more.

Most importantly, it helps you stay consistent and accountable on your path to the health you deserve. Personal Commitment Contract, Interactive Shadow Work Exercises, and Over 30 Profound Journaling Prompts are all included in the shadow work journal. To confront your shadows when they arise, use the guided pages under "Get to the root of your darkness." Open area for writing, doodling, or taking notes. It also includes The Benefits of Shadow Work: Better interpersonal connections, Recovering from generational trauma, Establishing personal limits, Develop empathy for others and yourself. Get "un-stuck," greater awareness and clarity of your surroundings. The sex and survival drives make up the shadow, an archetypal. The suppressed thoughts, flaws, desires, impulses, and deficiencies that make up the shadow are a part of the unconscious mind. Our attempts to conform to cultural expectations and norms lead to the formation of the shadow. We can regain our wholeness through the practice of shadow work. To experience healing fully, you must be 100% ON your Shadow instead of avoiding or repressing it. Every individual must complete this problematic and frequently terrifying task.

Printed in Great Britain
by Amazon